The Pandora Principle

This book was inspired by the 1st BNITM Alumni Symposium hosted in Hamburg by the Bernard-Nocht Institute for Tropical Medicine in summer 2018 and was supported by the Alexander von Humboldt Foundation. My thanks go to Hagen Frickmann for his critical review of the manuscript and the fruitful discussions we had. This book reflects the opinions and views of the author and is not mandatorily in line with official points of view of the Bernard-Nocht Institute for Tropical Medicine.

Norbert Georg Schwarz

The Pandora Principle

The destructive power of creation

Copyright: Norbert Schwarz 2019, Hamburg, Germany
E-Mail: schwarz@bnitm.de
Translation Bernice Frey, Besigheim Germany

Printed and published by: BoD – Books on Demand, Norderstedt.
ISBN: 9783749470501

German National Library Cataloguing-in-Publication Data:
A catalogue record for this book (in the original German language) is available from the German National Library; detailed bibliographic data are available in the internet at http://dnb.dnb.de.

Contents

Contents

List of figures

Prologue: Intelligence of a species and survival

In a discussion with the astrophysicist Carl Sagan, the biologist Ernst Mayr described intelligence as a form of lethal mutation. Indeed, those species that have long existed on this planet and have spread over large areas do mutate fast and otherwise do not have any mentionable complexity, such as bacteria. Mayr's line of contention was designed to curb Carl Sagan's optimism regarding the existence of intelligent life on other planets. Sagan had argued that such life must exist in the universe, because of the sheer inconceivable huge number of planets that offer good conditions for intelligent life [1]. Mayr's reasoning countered that of Sagan: his line of contention is that there is little chance that intelligent beings exist that are able to make contact with us, since this would precondition a technology and level of civilization that in itself would necessarily have led to self-destruction, be it through environmental destruction, resource consumption or weapons of mass destruction.

It might well be the case that the complexity of an intelligent species restricts its chances of long-term survival. If intelligence were the condition for the capacity for self-destruction (for example, though nuclear war), there would indeed be a direct causal relationship between intelligence and a possible shorter existence of a species. Of course these statements are over-simplified. In a thought experiment, we could compare the long-term prospects of survival of intelligent to non-intelligent bacteria. Both would be prolific with a great capacity for mutation, and the only difference would be in their intelligence.

However, intelligence not only has the undeniable potential for self-destruction, but also the capacity to solve problems. If potentially life-threatening problems are solved with intelligence, the survival of the species *Homo sapiens* could be extended and its demise delayed. For an individual *Homo sapiens*, intelligence seems to be an advantage. As a species, too, *Homo sapiens* has come a very long way in the approximately 300,000 years of its direct existence on earth and in the competition with other species for food and resources. Without intelligence and the potential for adaptation that goes with it, our forefathers are likely to have been wiped off the face of our planet by other species or by adverse conditions.

1 Non-existential and existential threats

When considering safeguarding the future existence of all humanity, it is necessary to make a distinction between a threat that is existential, that is, one that could mean the end to humanity, and one that is not. Existential threats can lead to the extinction of mankind. Most threats are not existential, yet they could take on catastrophic dimensions. Just think of the devastating plague epidemics in the Middle Ages. Such mass human mortality does not automatically mean an existential threat to mankind. Nevertheless, such scenarios should be prevented.

The distinction between existential and non-existential threats will not be maintained consistently in this book, because it not possible to identify a threat as clearly existential or non-existential. This ultimately depends on the final outcome of this threat to mankind: what might be perceived as a non-existential threat today could become existential in the future. And if a threat were to prove existential, there would be no longer be humans to conclusively classify the threat as such.

The necessity to deal with threats – be they perceived as existential or not – can never be an absolutely comprehensive task. We cannot know in advance whether a perceived threat is existential for humankind. This is a known unknown.

On the uncertainty of safety expertise

The former US defense secretary, Donald Rumsfeld, is not only known for preparing wars of aggression on Afghanistan and Iraq that contravene human rights laws, but also for his statements at a press conference on 12 December 2002 that led to an epistemological debate.

Rumsfeld was confronted with the fact that there were no indications that the former US ally and subsequently hostile Iraqi president Saddam Hussein had weapons of mass destruction. In his response, Rumsfeld avoided answering the question. This seems to clearly justify the accusation that his confusing response was consciously designed to avoid stating that the reasons for the war of aggression were specious. Nonetheless, his statement has come to be regarded as a tightly compacted philosophical debate [2]. Rumsfeld's phrased his statement as follows:

– *"[…] there are known knowns; there are things we know we know. We also know there are known unknowns; that is to say we know there are some things we do not know. But there are also unknown unknowns – the ones we don't know we don't know." (Donald Rumsfeld)*

There are three dimensions in Rumsfeld's statement:

known knowns: **known knowledge**

known unknowns: **known questions with unknown answers**

unknown unknowns; **unknown questions, or, no knowledge of the existence of these questions.**

Another dimension of the *known-unknown* constellation was added by the Slovenian philosopher Slavoj Žižek [3, 4]. Žižek *broadcast his statement on the* internet platform Youtube:

"I think he [Rumsfeld] should have gone on. Making the next step to the fourth category, which is missing, which is not the known unknowns but the **unknown knowns.** *Things we don't know we know them. We know them they are part of your identity, they determine our activity, but we don't know that we know them [...] The tragedy of today's American politics is that they are not aware of theses unknown knowns, which is why [...] Americans don't even control themselves." (Slavoj Žižek)*

According to this statement, there is a fourth constellation of the unknown knowns (unknown knowledge), that is, those things that we do not know, or want to know that we know. In other words, those matters that are actually known, but not admitted. Žižek refers explicitly to the concept of the subconscious in a psychoanalytical context.

The four dimensions of knowledge can be tabulated as follows (Table 1).

Table 1:   Known vs. unknown of known vs. unknown

		Knowledge	
		knowledge (knowns)	non-knowledge (un-knowns)
Metaknowledge	*Known*	*known* knowns	*known* unknowns
	Unknown	*unknown* knowns	*unknown* unknowns

It is precisely those events that are not predicted that often influence the course of events and impact global history, as Nassim Taleb described in great detail in his book 'Black Swan. The impact of the highly improbable'[5].

An oxymoron holds a contradiction within itself, irrespective of how the observer interprets it, whereas contradictions may depend on the interpretation of the observer. Such 'pseudo oxymorons' are often used in the news media with propagandistic effect. Examples can be observed in such phrases as "humanitarian war" or "friendly fire". Contradictions in the mind's eye of the observer are a veritable invitation for humorously ironic exaggerations implicit in pseudo oxymorons such as "military intelligence", or "creative destruction". Or even "sustainable growth" and "homo sapiens" (wise man). Pseudo oxymorons, whose absurdity will be illustrated in this book.

2   The non-sustainability of sustainable growth

Al Bartlett was a physicist at Colorado University in Boulder. He died on 7 September 2013 at the age of 90. He is best known for a one-hour lecture that he held a total of 1742 times, from 1969 to his death: "Arithmetic, Population and Energy". He began each of his lectures with the following sentence: "The greatest short-coming of the human race is our inability to understand the exponential function" [6].

Bartlett always started his lecture by establishing that stable growth, or sustainable growth, is something that sounds good and unproblematic at first glance. He then went on to give an impressive, but easily comprehensible explanation of what this actually means. In order to illustrate what stable growth of, say, 5 % means, he gave his listeners a simple rule of the thumb to calculate the doubling time of this fraction:

Doubling time = 70 : growth in percent per unit time

In this example, growth is assumed to be 5 % per year, so the doubling time is calculated as 70/ 5 = 14 years. (70 is the natural logarithm of two x 100).

Let us imagine a small town with a population of 60,000 – that was the size of Boulder in Colorado in 1969, when Bartlett held his lecture on how difficult it is for the human race to understand the exponential function. The town Boulder had a stable population growth of 5% per year. Using the mathematical equation reveals doubling time of 14 years. If the annual growth rate of Boulder had been a stable 5 % during Bartlett's lifetime, the population would have doubled to 120,000 in 1983, and, another 14 years later, in 1997, it would have quadrupled to 240,000. And finally, another 14 years later, in 2011, it would have multiplied by eight, to 480,00. This simple example clearly uncovers the fact that "stable population growth" is not linear at all, but exponential. (In reality, Boulder's population was only 100,000 in 2011.)

The world population figure was 5 billion people in 1986 with a growth rate globally of 1.7 % (doubling time 70/: 1.7 = 41 years). The figure for 1999 was 6 billion, the growth rate being 1.3% (doubling time 70/ 1.3 = 53 years), and in 2017, it was 7.5 billion, with a growth rate of 1.1% (doubling time: 70 : 1.1 = 64 years). So we see that the growth rate of the world population has been decreasing since its highest point in 1970, while the global population has continued to increase (illustration 1).

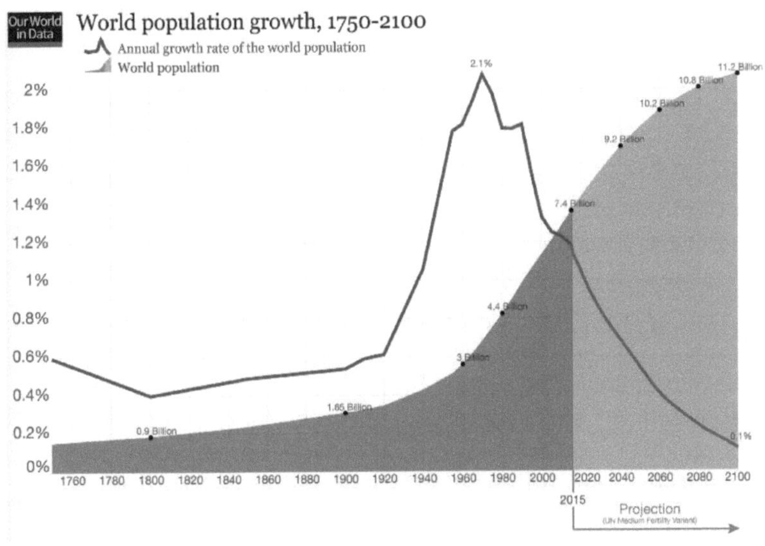

Figure 1: World population and population growth between 1750 and 2015, world population projection to 2100 in billions [7] Source: Roser & Ortiz-Ospina (CC BY-SA 3.0 AU), Our World in Data

The earth has a land surface of 150 million km^2. The surface currently used for farming worldwide is estimated at slightly less than approximately 50 million km^2 [8]. So this corresponds to a third of the land surface worldwide. With a world population of currently 7.5 billion people, one square kilometre of agricultural land needs to be shared by 150 persons on average. In figures, this means that in order to feed each individual person, the available area per person is an average of 6666 m^2 that is, a square measuring 80 m x 80 m. If the world population were to grow at a stable rate of 1.1 %, in another 64 years, the world population in 2080 would count 15 billion people, which corresponds to 100 persons per km^2 (1,000m x 1,000) of land surface. The available land remaining for each individual person would be a square of 100 m x 100 m - de facto even less, since not all land area is habitable, i.e. can be used for the production of foodstuff.

A global economic system based on growth provides the future leaders with incentives to propagate growing population figures. A larger population is often associated with a growing gross domestic product, and a country with a larger population is considered to have more power on the international stage.

Measures to reduce the population

The development of the population in any one region of the earth is influenced by the birth and death rates (natural population development), and also by emigration and immigration, while the size of the world population is only influenced by birth and death rates. In his famous lecture, Al Bartlett drew up a list of measures to increase the population and those to decrease the population figures. This list is absolutely neutral, and is soberly brutal, without any ethical evaluation. (Table 2).

Table 2:   Al Bartlett's tabular comparison of measures to increase and decrease the population

Increase population	Decrease population
Procreation	Abstention
Motherhood	Contraception / abortion
Large families	Small families
Immigration	Stopping immigration
Medicine	Disease
Public health	
Sanitation	
Peace	War
Law and order	Murder / violence
Scientific agriculture	Famine
Accident prevention	Accidents
Clean air	Pollution
Ignorance of the growth problem	

Some of these "measures", such as war or disease are certainly not desirable and it would be ethically and morally reprehensible to implement them. Yet, we should not ignore them. Some of the measures to reduce the population could come about naturally as a result of a scarcity of resources, e.g. famine, or by a war for resources - and against competing persons or powers. Also, the active implementation of murderous population reduction measures by brutal totalitarian systems such as the national socialist regimes of the 20th century is thinkable. In rather dystopic scenarios one could imagine elites (genetically optimised humans, for example) that consider themselves so superior to the masses that they feel entitled to decide over life and death of inferior members of society (very similarly to the way we slaughter entire animal populations when we consider this to be necessary, e.g. to contain animal epidemics).

Many of the "measures" used to favour population growth are regarded as positive. Hygiene, medicine and peace are measures which I myself as a medical doctor and epidemiologist feel committed to and of which I am convinced that they improve human life on earth.

In most parts of the world, population growth is a very recent phenomenon, which was only perceived as a problem with the onset of the industrialisation in the 19th century. Prior to this time, population growth was a sign of prosperity and wealth, and basically, it was also perceived as such in the emerging economies of the industrialisation era. However, the perception of a normal human being that competes with other normal people for resources, living space and work will tend to be less optimistic.

Real reduction in population growth in some countries

The global population is increasing. However, this growth is by no means spread evenly – it is not balanced. Whereas the natural population growth in Africa of 4.7 children per woman is very high, in Europe and Japan, this figure is distinctly below the 2.1 children per woman required to maintain the population (not including immigration and emigration) [9]. This leads to new challenges for these countries, namely, to an increasingly aged population with the corresponding burdens on social systems and generational balance. Another possible concern employers may have are rising labour costs in the long run, with the working population decreasing in numbers. Interestingly enough, the number of children is decreasing in the middle classes in particular, where the parents are particularly involved in working life, while poor and rich families continue to have more children than average [10, 11]. Due to the lack of young, creative people, it is feared that less innovation coupled with a decrease in the economic growth of the society will result.

Since sustainable growth becomes de facto exponential, permanent global growth does not seem desirable (this also applying for the economy). The problem is that, due to global competition, the size of the national economy is a significant element of power. This in turn creates incentives for growth (at least for the elite members of a society).

Let us contemplate the results in those countries whose natural population growth has fallen to 2.1 children per female or lower. These are Eurasian countries between Lisbon and Vladivostok und Japan (including China, thanks to its one-child policy, which was in force until recently). Expressed in very basic terms, it can be said that material prosperity and wealth appear to go hand in hand with a decline of the natural population growth. Other factors associated with declining natural population growth are higher education levels, particularly among women, and gender equality.

Disintegration of society as a painful aspect of mild, gradual population reduction

However, those countries with declining population growth have also experienced a change in their moral values. The value of families, for instance, has declined considerably. Whereas in former generations, a family with children was considered to be central to defining the meaning of life, this is no longer the case in our modern times. This is particularly true for women: in former times, women regarded the family as the expression of their self-actualisation, and their central focus was on their role as a mother. In the past fifty years, young girls have increasingly been brought up to regard professional life as their focal point, and not the family. This means that the labour market has a greater potential workforce, a factor that has certainly reduced labour costs and led to significant economic growth. The original act of emancipation by gaining access to paid labour has meanwhile changed from a possible way to reach individual fulfilment into an economic necessity.

True, the fact that explosive population growth has been curtailed in many countries can only be welcomed on the whole. For the individual, however, this development can mean loneliness as a result of the increasing disintegration of traditional family structures and social alienation.

The industrial revolution led to a separation of the working place and the domestic environment. Farmers, craftsmen and small business owners once normally went about their work within the family environment. Even if it was predominantly men who carried out those tasks that today are regarded as a profession, all the family members were involved in supporting the family as far as possible. For unmarried women or for those who had lost their husbands, it was very difficult to be able to maintain their livelihood. Children born out of wedlock were a catastrophe for women, since this meant that the mothers not only had another mouth to feed, but were also ostracised from society. The chances of survival of children born out of wedlock were correspondingly restricted.

During the period of industrialisation, home and the working place became physically increasingly removed from each other. At the same time, the increase in material prosperity was associated with enormous population growth. The individual person experienced a gradual dissolution of the direct connection between labour and maintaining a livelihood for the family such as previously existed in a subsistence farming economy. In the industrial society characterised by division of labour, wages were paid in the form of money, i.e. in an abstract form, which was needed to buy goods and foodstuff.

With the advent of the feminist movement, not only gender equality, but increasingly, capitalist-oriented narratives appeared among the demands of women's liberation movements. Meanwhile, gender equality in the working world has become the central issue of feminism. This cannot be regarded as self-evident, since the discrimination against women has taken many other forms. For instance, instead of an upward revaluation of women's contribution to society by creating financial incentives for the work women do within the family, or by making better social security available to single women, the traditional role and daily life of women within the family was demolished.

This may well be a logical consequence of a capitalist economy: financial remuneration (i.e. wages) for family work only results in costs for which there is no means of direct reciprocal financing, since the task of caring for the family cannot be sold and monetised. As a result of the implementation of the demand for women's participation in professional life, the size of the labour force has increased, which in turn has reduced the price (i.e. the wage) of each individual member of the workforce. This, in turn, has led to higher corporate profits. In capitalist competition among the nations, the mobilization of a female workforce in commerce, i.e. employment remunerated in terms of money, (wage-dependent work) has thus become a competitive advantage.

In view of the explosion of the world population, the resulting lower birth rate appears to be a positive development. However, this has also led to the previously mentioned disintegration of society. Despite our material security, we may find it difficult to find happiness in our modern western societies if we have to cope with social isolation.

Throughout Europe, natural population growth has fallen below 2.1 children per woman. Nevertheless, with a view to finite resources, it seems easier to cope with the resulting problems (ageing of society, isolation and social alienation) than to cope with the problems resulting from a rapidly growing population.

The prognosis for the African continent is that the population will double from the figure of 1.2 billion in 2015 to 2.5 billion people in 2050 (calculated at a doubling time of 35 years and a population growth of 2% per year).

Growth: locally desired, globally catastrophic

Permanent stable global growth, whether it be of the population or the economy, ultimately leads to impaired quality of life, due to resource consumption or to rivalry and conflicts over resources. At the same time, at most organisational levels lower than the organisational level humankind (e.g. at state, regional, urban or corporate level), growth is regarded as positive and is rewarded.

Let us recall Al Bartlett's simple rule-of-the-thumb formula for calculating doubling time:

Doubling time = 70/ growth in percent.

Economic growth of 2% leads to a doubling of the economic performance in 35 years. This is the stuff of success stories!

If the there is an increase in the population of one of the sub-global units (such as at state or urban community level), this growth comes along with an increase in political and economic prowess. State leaders of large and populous states claim more power – just as do state leaders of flourishing economies. Economic growth leads to prosperity and a good life. Prosperity increases in proportion to the easier access to cheaper energy. States that do not sell or use cheap natural resources for their own benefit, but instead forego them in consideration of their scarcity, are perceived as giving up the competitive advantage they could have over other states [12].

Viewed in global terms, however, the living space available to humankind is limited. How should humankind survive on earth if all the reward systems favour growth processes that inevitably lead to overconsumption of resources and to exceeding the proverbial limits of growth? On the other hand, does going beyond the limits of growth necessarily mean an existential threat for the survival of *Homo sapiens* as a species, or can it be assumed that, despite mass mortality and the collapse of civilization, a sufficiently high number of humans will survive to secure the continued existence of humans? This will probably depend on the extent to which the limit of growth is exceeded, and how much this coincides with a destruction of the planet's biosphere. It will also depend on whether the resulting wars for resources are fought with weapons of mass destruction, which have the potential of wiping humans off the face of the earth.

When do we perceive the limits of growth?

At what point in time do we as human beings perceive the approaching limits of growth? Probably only shortly before they are exceeded.

In his legendary lecture on stable growth, Al Bartlett draws a comparison with a bacterial culture. He asks his audience to imagine a bacterial culture that doubles every minute. The bottle with the cell culture containing the bacteria represents limited living space. If the bottle is full exactly at midnight, at what point in time was the bottle half full? The answer: one minute before midnight, since the last doubling time from half-full to full requires only one single minute!

When would a bacterium realise that the bottle is running out of space? Let us take a look at the culture bottle in the last five minutes before midnight. One minute before midnight, it is half full, two minutes before midnight, a quarter full, three minutes before midnight, an eighth full, four minutes before midnight a sixteenth, and five minutes before midnight, a thirty-second full. So, five minutes before midnight, only 3 % of the total available space is taken up with bacteria. As a single bacterium, I thus still have plenty of space for development at five minutes to midnight, so I have no reason at all to think that this will change in just a few minutes. (In this thought experiment, the fact is ignored that bacteria become stationary when they have attained a certain density, i.e. they suspend growth.)

Now let us imagine an island state with its population spread evenly throughout the island and a population growth of 3.5 % (the doubling time is thus 70 divided by 3.5 = 20 years). Twenty years is also a realistic generation gap in a country with high fertility. Assuming a stable population growth rate of 3.5 %, if fifteen-sixteenths (94 %) of the island was unpopulated 60 years ago, then seven-eighths (88 %) of the island remained unpopulated by the subsequent generation 40 years ago. Twenty years ago, a much as three-quarters (75 %) of the island remained unpopulated. Meanwhile, the degree of urban sprawl is slowly becoming obvious, since only half of the island is still unpopulated. There has long since been insufficient land to feed the population and large quantities of food supplies must be imported. In the next 20 years there will be no vacant space. If this island is assumed to be our planet, there is no means of obtaining resources from an external source.

3 Oil

In the second part of his lecture, Bartlett placed his emphasis on the steadily increasing consumption of resources, with special emphasis on mineral oil.

Global dependence on oil is a comparatively recent phenomenon, being no older than about 250 years. Prior to this time, people used their own muscle power and that of animals. Pre-industrial systems such as mills were driven by hydro or wind energy. For thousands of years, wood had been the most important source of fuel. In the early industrial age, brown and black coal, but also charcoal, were the most-used fossil fuels. Mineral oil, too, had been known for thousands of years, but only became as significant as it is today in the mid-19th century.

Mineral oil is a fossil fuel, in the same way as natural gas, peat, brown and black coal are. All these substances containing high levels of carbon were formed aeons ago through decomposition of plants, animals and microorganisms. Coal formed from the plants that rotted at the bottom of moors under the exclusion of air. The decayed material sank into deeper layers of the earth and was covered by new layers of earth, which in turn resulted in increased compression and higher temperatures. This led to highly condensed high-carbon compounds. This energy can be released by combustion, and thanks to its compressed state, can be transferred into a restricted area (such as the tender of a steam locomotive, or the petrol tank of a motor car). Black coal has a very high level of density and is a pure substance, whereas brown coal has a lower density, is more impure and contains higher levels of sulphur, which is why its combustion process is the form of energy generation with the highest carbon-dioxide levels.

Most of the mineral oil that we extract today "lived" about 150 million years ago, when the dinosaurs dominated the earth. Both mineral oil and natural gas were formed from decayed algae, which is why the two are often found close to each other. By means of a process of new layers covering older ones and their sinking further into the earth, these carbon-rich algae were covered by ever more layers, where higher pressure and temperature resulted in a transformation into one or two physical states: a fluid substance (mineral oil) or a gaseous substance (natural gas). Natural gas has a high methane content. In a non-combusted state, methane is a potential green-house gas. Fortunately, natural gas burns very efficiently, with only a small volume of the green-house gas methane being released into the atmosphere. For this reason, it is cleaner than other fossil fuels.

Due to its low density, mineral oil reaches the surface of the earth on its own, if the rocks are sufficiently porous. It has long been used for ointments and lubricants and to produce tar masses (such as are used to seal ships). In regions where mineral oil was found, there was more to be found by digging or boring in the vicinity.

Today we associate the largest mineral oil reserves with Middle-Eastern countries, especially Saudi Arabia. However, the first oil nation was the USA. In the outermost north-eastern part of Pennsylvania lies a town called Oil City with about 10,000 inhabitants. Here, the Oil Creek River flows into the Allegheny River. A particular attraction is the Drake Well Museum named after Edwin L. Drake, who managed the drilling process in 1859. This marked the first extraction of mineral oil for industrial purposes and thus the start of the mineral oil age. The particular innovation in Drake's boring process was the use of drilling pipes to stabilise boreholes, thus allowing safe deep drilling. The men in Drake's team bored a hole 21 meters deep before they found oil.

Mineral oil was the ideal fuel – its reserves seemed to be unlimited, it was easy to transport (with pipelines) and was much better as a fuel for mobile machines (cars, ships, airplanes) than solid fuels: whereas the fuels for coal-driven steam engines had to be extracted from the coal fields with muscle power or by using cranes, oil could simply be pumped into a tank [13].

Oil as a fuel for industrial purposes came just at the right time. Since the end of the 1840s, lamp oil, which was used to light European streets, became ever more expensive. Greed for this kind of fuel based on whale oil (or 'train oil') as it is also known, had led to the sperm whale population being reduced drastically, as a result of which the market was hungry for alternative fuel sources.

Oil barons

One might assume that Drake became hugely rich as a result of his inventing a new means of oil drilling. This was not the case, however. Drake was very ill and was reduced to using a wheel-chair increasingly more often. His wife tried to earn some money by doing casual work, such as sewing. Ultimately, the financial situation of the family was so precarious that the citizens of Titusville petitioned the Pennsylvanian legislature to provide a pension for the family in 1873. This was granted as was an income for the family after Drake's death in 1880. Although the name Drake is associated with the wealth from oil in America, he himself was not an oil baron. Indeed, the first oil millionaire was Jonathan Watson, the owner of the land where Drake had drilled.

The company and stockholders for which Drake developed his well-drilling method was the Seneca Oil Company, named after the Mohawk tribe, the Seneca. The Senecans had used the mineral oil that seeped from the Oil Creek as a basis for medicinal cures long before the arrival of the European settlers. But the Senecans did not become rich from the oil that was extracted from their (former) land.

Other persons, such as John D. Rockefeller, H. L. Hunt and J. Paul Getty were the ones who became genuine oil barons. The Standard Oil Company emerged from the original company Rockefeller, Andrews & Flagler. Henry M. Flagler invested capital in the Standard Oil Company. He later played a significant role in the construction of the Florida East Coast railway. Samuel Andrews was a chemist: it was due to his improvement of mineral oil refining methods that the company was able to achieve its success. During the 36 years after 1870, the Standard Oil Company developed into an industrial imperium of hitherto unknown size and power – until the government under Theodore Roosevelt dissolved it into 34 corporations by passing the Sherman Antitrust Act. This was the first legislation in the USA that regulated competition. This law caused the share price of the company to plummet. Once again, J.D. Rockefeller benefited from this situation by buying up the all-time low-priced shares, making enormous profits when the share price rose again. (Roosevelt himself was the offspring of an American dynasty. Basically, the history of the USA can probably be told as the history of family disputes between the various dynastic families.)

With the emerging automobile industry, there was increasing dependence on oil. Today, the companies emerging from the Standard Oil Company form the very backbone of modern US oil companies, which are central components of the American military industrial complex.

Haroldson Lafayette (H. L.) Hunt accumulated enormous wealth from the East Texas Oil Field. However, the name Hunt is not as well-known as that of Rockefeller, possibly due to Rockefeller's philanthropic activities, such as the Rockefeller Foundation. Nevertheless, the Hunt clan have considerable influence and wealth in the USA. H.L. Hunt is suspected of having played a role in the plot to murder the Democrat president John F. Kennedy in 1963. He certainly had a motive: Kennedy was planning to reduce the tax privileges for oil companies, which would have reduced the income of the Texan oil baron by several hundred million US dollars per year (but which would not have ruined him) [14, 15]. Hunt must have been a colourful personality. He was the inspiration for the fictional character J.R. Ewing, the central figure for the soap opera *Dallas*, which gained international success, running from the late 1970s to the early 1990s.

Through his images agency Getty Images, Mark Getty has secured himself a firm position in the 21st-century media landscape. The wealth of the Getty dynasty is also based on oil: from the patriarch of the family, Jean Paul Getty, the founder of the Getty Oil Company, to Paul Getty II and then Mark Getty, the wealth accrued by this family has been passed on from generation to generation. Similar to Rockefeller, J. Paul Getty found great satisfaction in using his considerable wealth to foster the arts and culture, being an avid collector, establishing foundations and museums.

The Bush clan, which to date has brought forth two American presidents (George H.W. Bush, 1989-1993 und George W. Bush, 2001-2009), is an industrial and oil dynasty. Prescott Bush, father of President George H.W. Bush ("Bush senior") and grandfather of George W. Bush ("Bush junior") increased the fortune of the Yankee steel- industrialist family in Ohio by managing German steel industrialists' property in the USA, having no qualms about having a shareholding in industrial companies using forced labour during the Nazi era. Prescott's son, later president of the United States, George H.W. Bush ("Bush senior"), moved to Texas after completing his studies at Yale in 1948, and , facilitated by the network of the Bush clan with the world of high finance, became an oil mogul. His political career involved posts as a UN ambassador, CIA director, director of the 'Council on Foreign Relations', and vice-president, and ultimately, the 41st president of the USA in the White House. The Bush family was involved in the five key areas of American power: i) US investment banking, ii) the weapons industry, iii) the CIA, iv) the control of the international oil reserves, and v) the close cooperation with the former imperial power, Britain [16], (to be precise there is a sixth key area of American power in which he was involved, namely think tanks, such as the Council on Foreign Relations).

George W. Bush's ("Bush junior") road to the White House was also paved by the Bush clan's involvement in the global structures of power. George W. Bush founded the oil company Arbusto Energy in Texas with "clan money". However, the oil reserves in the USA that could be mined conventionally were already diminishing (see next chapter) and the oil drilling in Texas was not successful. His father, "Bush senior", stepped in to offer support by intensifying the contacts between the Bush clan and the Saud Family, who own the country with the largest oil reserves (Saudi Arabia). George W. Bush's company Arbusto transitioned into "Spectrum", this company being bought up by Harken Energy in 1986. According to George Soros, one of the major Harken Energy shareholders, this transaction was made to benefit the good contacts of the Bush clan in the Gulf region and the Saud clan, rather than the company itself. Not surprisingly, Harken Energy became unusually attractive for Saudi investors, who were granted exclusive drilling rights on the coast of the island kingdom Bahrain. George W. Bush was elected 43rd president of the USA in 1989. The financial transactions of Harken Energy Deals were handled by the Luxemburg Bank BCCI, which was foreclosed in 1991 by the Bank of England, 20 billion US dollars disappearing without a trace during the process. The collapse of the BCCI is the greatest scandal in financial history to date [17].

Apart from the good relations with the Saud family, the Bush family maintains close business connections with the Saudi building construction industrialist family Bin Laden (whose probably most famous son is Osama Bin Laden) [18, 19]. The relationship between the Saud family and the American oligarch clan remains as close as ever. Saudi Arabia has pledged the current American president Donald Trump the purchase of weapons worth several hundred billion dollars [20] and Trump's son-in-law Jared Kushner's personal debts make him directly dependent on the Saud family. [17]. Blood is thicker than water, but oil is thicker than blood.

"Peak Oil"

Rockefeller, Hunt and Getty – these names alone clearly reveal the strong impact that the oil industry of the globally imperialist superpower USA has had on the history of the country. Bush and Trump – these names in themselves convey the great influence of the Saudi-American oil industry on the present-day globally imperialist superpower USA.

Ever since the nineteen-seventies, when the quantity of oil mined in the US has been on the decline, the eyes of the oil-hungry industrial nations have turned to other regions of the world, particularly to the Middle East. But what has become of the American oilfields?

Well, as far as more or less easily accessible oil is concerned, i.e. oil that does not need to be extracted by fracking or from hundreds or even thousands of meters under the earth, the answer is: it has simply been used up. In 1956, Marion King Hubbert, chief geologist at Shell Laboratories in Houston/Texas, made a disturbing announcement in connection with the volume of oil and gas available for extraction: he forecast that the maximum level of oil extraction, the "peak oil" period, would be reached by about 1970; after this time, the quantity of oil mined annually would decrease every year. And precisely this has turned out to be the case: since 1970, the amount of oil mined by conventional methods has decreased decade by decade (figures 2 and 3).

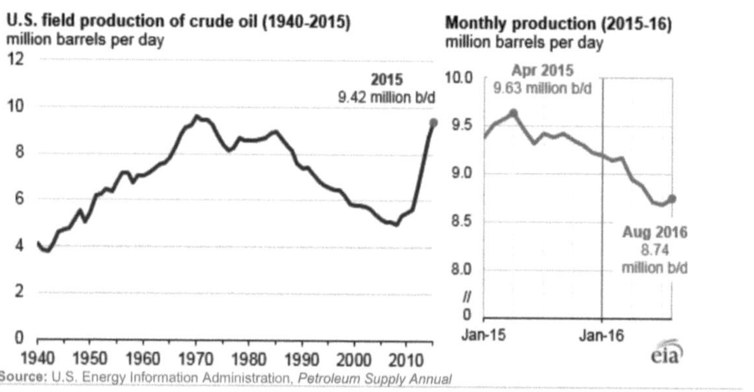

Figure 2: US field production of crude oil between 1940 and 2015 in millions of barrels per day [21] Source: U.S. Energy Information Administration, Public Domain.

Only when fracking technology started to change the trend in the USA in 2008 was it possible to again mine the same quantities in the country that had been drilled in the 1970s. While writing these lines (in February 2018), the daily oil production figures are 10.27 million barrels per day and therefore slightly above the peak-oil level of 1970. When I was in the process of completing this book in December 2018, a new peak-oil level of 11.6 barrels per day was recorded.

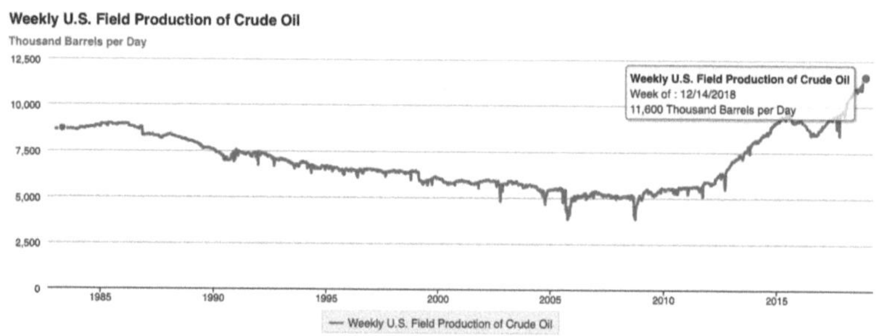

Figure 3: Weekly US field production of crude oil between 1983 and July 2018 in thousands of barrels per day including the current field production in July 2018 [22] Source: U.S. Energy Information Administration, Public Domain

In 1956, Hubbert also forecast that the global oil production would peak in about half a century, thus in about 2006. Since that time, annual oil production has even increased and, due to fracking technology, the USA is again one of the most important oil producing nations worldwide, competing with Saudi Arabia for the leading position in annual oil production. So at present, there is no sign at all of a lack of oil. Rather, the oil price is so low that the oil producing states have huge problems concerning oil revenue, and Venezuela, the country with the largest oil reserves on the American continent (or perhaps even worldwide), is having to cope with economic collapse.

How did plummeting oil prices come about? The oil price is not only governed by the laws of the market, but also determined by political interests. The OPEC countries dominate the scene, but so does the USA, whose currency, the 'petrodollar', is linked to all crude oil transactions. (It seems quite plausible that the intention of Iraq under Saddam Hussein and Libya under Gaddafi to sell crude oil in other currencies, rather than the dollar, was an important reason for the attack of western military powers on Iraq and Libya.) The United States, the most powerful military force in the world, thus benefits from the privilege of the most important natural resource in the world (namely, crude oil) being traded exclusively in dollars, which also happens to be the global key currency and the main reserve currency.

At the same time, since 2008, fracking technology has once again made the USA the largest crude oil producing country in the world. However, oil extraction using fracking technology is considerably more expensive, which is why some competing countries, such as Saudi Arabia, assumed that the American oil producing companies would not survive such a low oil price. But the USA drills more crude oil at present than any other nation, including Saudi Arabia. I, too, cannot see that the geostrategy of the USA will allow the extraction of oil by fracking to be discontinued, even if the companies involved require state subsidising. From the point of view of the USA, the certainly intentional side effect is that rival oil-producing countries, whose economies are strongly dependent on the oil price (e.g. Russia, but especially Venezuela), have to bear the loss.

Let us now turn to a parameter that paradoxically has little to do with the oil price, namely demand, i.e. global consumption. In 2008, the consumption figure for oil was calculated at about 86 million barrels per day. After nine years of steadily rising consumption, the figure in 2017 was 97 barrels per day [23]. Annual consumption growth is thus approximately 1,22 %.

Using Al Bartlett's rule-of-thumb formula, which was introduced at the beginning of this book, the doubling time can easily be calculated:

Doubling time = 70/growth in percent = 70/1.22 = 57.4 years

Accordingly, assuming the same consumption growth, global oil consumption will double by about 2065. During this period, the global population of 6.8 billion in 2008 will have increased from over 7.6. billion in 2017, and to about 10.4 billion in 2065. This figure of 10.4 billion corresponds to the median UN population projection for 2065, the lowest figure being 8.6 billion and the highest, 12.4 billion inhabitants. [24]. All of these projections (i.e. the highest as well), assume decreasing population growth. However, if the population continues to grow at a rate of 1,19%, as it did in 2015, the population of the earth can be expected to have reached 13.3 billion by 2065.

Thus, the low oil price is deceptive. Those people who believe that the fear of running out of oil is only panic-mongering should know that demand for oil is moving in only one direction at present: upwards! [23]. Of course it is essential for industrialised countries to curb oil consumption by means of new and cheaper technologies or alternative forms of energy. While consumption per person in almost all African countries south of the Sahara is lower than one barrel per year, some even below one-third barrels per year, German consumption per person averages 12 barrels per year, the figure for Americans being as high as 25 barrels per year [25].

At the same time, China and India, both former developing countries, and now emerging market countries with the highest populations in the world, are undergoing a process of industrialisation. The two countries, both of which have a population of about 1.3 billion, have a comparatively low annual crude oil consumption: China's is 2.14 barrels per year, that of India 0.94. These figures will increase in the years to come [25].

Africa is the continent with the highest population growth, but also the highest level of underdevelopment. In 2015, Africa had a population of 1.2 billion inhabitants. According to the UN projected median population figures, the population on the African continent is expected to reach the level of 2.5 billion by 2050. This means that the population on this continent will double in 35 years! According to the same projection there will be 3.2 billion people living on the African continent in 2065 [24].

Average oil consumption of most Africans has been low up to now. But often, outdated technologies are used in Africa (for example, second-hand cars from Europe), which usually are fuelled with fossil fuels. Added to this, outdated technologies are used that do not fulfil the high European environmental standards set to achieve the so-called "energy revolution". If oil consumption increases on the African continent, it will soon no longer be possible to satisfy the demand in Africa, since it must be assumed that those countries that have the greatest military, economic and political power will secure the oil reserves for themselves.

Oil colonialism

The post-second-world-war years saw the era of colonial imperialism coming to an end. The lost Algerian War in 1962 is regarded as the end of direct French colonialism, even if France still has départements and colonies overseas. In direct colonialism, a colony belongs to the mother country, which exercises political and military power directly within the country. Direct colonialism cannot be sustained in the long run: maintaining administrative structures and military presence within the colony is expensive. Added to that, the domestic population could question the legitimacy of the colonial power at any time.

From an ethical and moral point of view, foreign control by a colonial power can only be justified by the alleged genetic superiority of the colonial power (racism), or by a metaphysical and/or religious line of contention (missionary work to save the souls of the indigenous population). While both lines of contention were very successful in the past, they can hardly be upheld in view of modern enlightened viewpoints. This leads to the following question: How can a country continue to benefit from the wealth of natural resources available in other countries without having to carry the high costs for maintaining the expensive administration and military apparatus within the country? The answer: through the commodity-markets businesses owned and run by the local elite population together with powerful global players in the country!

During the course of the last century, the French crude oil industry has gone through various transitional phases. After the first world war, France exploited the Iraqi oilfields in particular, which had been ceded to France by the defeated German-Ottoman Alliance in the first world war. However, the promise of oil discovery in the French colonies in north and west Africa long remained unfulfilled. It was only after the second world war that rich crude oil sources were discovered in Africa. The post-colonial model of private companies exploiting oil fields in foreign countries proved to be very successful. The resulting development of the French oil industry culminated in the founding of international companies such as Elf Aquitaine and Total, which are active globally to this day.

What is even more revealing about the immense power of the post-colonial international corporations and their enormous capacity to exploit natural resources is the 20th-century history of Iran [26]. Iran was never a British colony. Nevertheless, oil production and refining was dominated by the Anglo-Iranian Oil Company (AIOC), which was formed in 1935 from the Anglo Persian Oil Company, founded in 1908. In the mid-1950s, Iran was a country with a history going back over thousands of years and a significant cultural heritage, which, however, was lagging behind on the international political stage. Nevertheless, the country underwent steady development in the first half of the 20th century: its legal, economic and financial systems were modernized, the education system improved, and with German aid, the trans-Iranian railway was constructed. Despite these developments, most Iranians were living in poverty after the second world war, during which they maintained neutrality at first, but ended up shoulder to shoulder with the victorious allied powers. Nevertheless, civil society continued to take a sane view of the situation. In 1950, the Iranians were well aware of the fact that the Arabian-American Oil Company had pledged the Saudi-Arabians a 50 % share in the oil production.

It is clear that the majority of the profits from oil drilling in Saudi-Arabia found its way into the coffers of the Saud dynasty. The rulers used the oil revenues to silence their population by ensuring a rich lifestyle of every Saudi citizen, thus concealing the repressive and totalitarian nature of the regime. At the same time, the Saud family promised the Americans that their thirst for oil would be quenched when required (and in return for petrodollars). At first glance, it might appear that ceding 50 % of the share to the Saudis must have constituted an enormous loss for the Americans. However, in retrospect, it must be admitted that it was an extremely clever political move, since even at that time, it was certainly obvious how great the Americans' dependence on oil was. In consideration of the fact that this move guaranteed a readily available supply of oil for America, halving the already very generous profits was an entirely viable concession for the American oil companies.

The agreement with the Saud family established the groundwork for the petrodollar system, a central cornerstone of American global imperial power. Added to this, having loyal, well-paid rulers in Saudi Arabia came at a considerably lower price than deploying American military troops, whose presence would also have had the disadvantage of triggering the resistance of the people to alien dominance.

This state of affairs worked for 40 years. Nevertheless, for the American geo-strategists it was only a matter of time until American military presence would be established in the Gulf region. In 1990, Saddam Hussein invaded the oil emirate Kuwait in 1990, providing the pretext to deploy American troops in the strategically significant Gulf region with its vital oil supply. The troops are still stationed there today.

The Britons did not show the same geo-strategic skill in Iran that can be said for that demonstrated by the Americans in 1950. The Iranian demands made towards the AIOC for a fair division of its oil profits was ignored or brusquely rejected by the British owners. The Iranian elites did not relent, and in the early 1950s, there were loud calls for the state to take ownership of the Iranian oilfields and their infrastructure from the AIOC.

In 1951, parliament in Iran voted for nationalisation of the AIOC shortly after which the Iranian people elected Mohammed Mossadegh Prime Minister in a free democratic election. Mossadegh was willing to implement the parliamentary decision to take over state ownership of the AIOC. He was quite prepared to make compromises, for instance nationalisation with the involvement of an international American-British oil drilling company. While the Americans had long supported such a solution, the Britons became ever more confrontational, planning to overthrow Mossadegh. Finally, in 1953, the Britons succeeded in involving the American secret service in a plot to oust the prime minister. Although the British had initiated this plot, it was mainly carried out by the American CIA in 'Operation Ajax', since the British no longer maintained diplomatic representation in Iran and thus had to rely on the American embassy. There was large-scale bribery of politicians, policemen and the press, but also street protesters to take part in the coup. The Shah of Persia, Mohammad Reza Pahlavi, took over government after Mossadegh was overthrown. The coup stood in complete contradiction to all democratic principles and served to prevent the nationalisation of Iranian oilfields [27].

Although after the coup, the nationalised AIOC was administered pro forma by an international consortium, the American oil company Standard Oil, the Dutch Shell Company, and the British AIOC (later British Petrol, BP) really held the reins, while operative business was carried out by two Iranian puppet companies registered in Holland [26, 28].

The Carter Doctrine: Right to oil, no matter where

The western imperial power USA claimed the worldwide right to have access to natural fossil resources. This claim was expressed openly – the document is readily available to the general public - in the Carter Doctrine of 1980. In this document, the USA clearly announced its claim to access of the fossil resources in the Persian Gulf, clearly emphasising that this claim can also be enforced militarily.

The Carter Doctrine was occasioned by the invasion of Soviet Union into Afghanistan, and the overthrow of the US-loyal Shah Mohammad Reza Pahlavi in Iran in the Islamic Revolution in 1979. Up to that point, the USA had relied on the US-friendly dictator Reza Pahlavi to secure the oil exports from the Gulf region for the United States. The government implemented after the Islamic Revolution under Ruhollah Khomeini subsequently declared the United States an enemy state. The declining oil production resulting from this geopolitical event led to the USA unequivocally making its claim to the crude oil in the region.

An important mastermind of the Carter Doctrine is probably the then National Security Advisor in the Carter administration, the recently deceased geo-strategist Zbigniew Brzezinski, (1928 – 2017). Similar to the Republican rival Henry Kissinger, it was important for Brzezinski to subordinate everything else to the unilateral interests of the USA. In his book published in 1997, *The Grand Chessboard*, Brzezinski explained his geostrategic views for the early 21st century. He pointed out that he regarded Eurasia as a key region in a global economy, not least because of the significant oil and natural gas reserves in the region [29]. Interestingly, the formerly US-hostile Khomeini government actively reported the election of Carter's Republican competitor Ronald Reagan in the 1980 campaign. In agreement with the future Reagan administration, Khomeini ensured that the 52 American citizens who were held hostage in the American embassy in Tehran by a group of Iranian students were not set free before the American elections took place, since their release would have been considered a success for the Carter's Democratic party.

Oil wars

Apart from the sabotage of the Eurasian economic region, the claim of the USA to free access to the oil and gas reserves throughout the world plays a decisive role for the underlying causes of current and past wars and conflicts, including the present power struggles in the Eurasia Basin (e.g. Ukraine crisis) [30] and in the Middle East (e.g. Syrian war), but also in the Gulf wars since the 1980s. The first Gulf War was the Iraq-Iran War of 1980, the second, the Kuwait War a decade later, in 1990, and the third the occupation of Iraq by the USA and other western vassal states and Arab oil rivals ("Coalition of the Willing") in 2003. Mention must also be made of the war of occupation in Afghanistan since 2001.

The Iraqi attack on Iran in 1980 (first Gulf War) was carried out with the support of western powers under the leadership of the then President Saddam Hussein. It targeted the Khuzestan province in the extreme southwest region of Iran at the Persian Gulf, which is rich in natural resources. The ideological justification for this attack was propagandistically underpinned by the antithesis between the culture of Arab and Persian ethnic groups, since the majority of inhabitants of the Khuzestan province is of Arab origin. Through this ideological construct, the Bath Party, in principle governed by secular principles with a tendency towards Sunnite views, was able to cover up the fact that both countries (Iran and Iraq) have a Shiite majority.

On the Iranian side, the precursor of this war was the Islamic Revolution of 1979, which brought Ayatollah Khomeini to power, leading to the formation of an Islamic theocratic republican government. On the international level, post-revolutionary Iran was isolated. The Iranian army also showed signs of decline after the revolution, whereas Iraq enjoyed considerable military and economic support from the Arab states, France, the USA and the Soviet Union. After an attack by militant Shiites in early 1980, when eleven students were killed, and the Iraqi vice prime minister, Tariq Aziz, nearly lost his life, Saddam Hussein no longer made any secret of his anti-Persian sentiments: in a highly-acclaimed speech on 2 April 1980, he drew parallels with the Battle of Kadesh in 638, in which the defeat of the Sassanid Persians was regarded as a decisive step towards Arab-Islamic expansion. (Persia under the Sassanids was not yet Islamic, but had various religions, Zoroastrianism being the dominant one). Six days later, Khomeini responded with a call to overthrow the "non-Islamic" Iraqi government.

Due to the decline of the Iranian army after the revolution as a result of the execution of officers who were accused of being "hostile to revolution", and also due to flight and desertion, Iraq saw itself in a position of strength. After numerous minor skirmishes in the region bordering the two countries, Iraq initiated a major invasion on 22 September 1980. The following eight years saw complicated trench warfare similar to that of the first world war, the only difference being that in this instance, the stronger force of air raids had a far greater impact on the civil population [26].

When the war came to an end in 1988, both sides had casualties running into the hundreds of thousands, while producers of armaments throughout the world were able to funnel the Iranian and Iraqi national wealth into their own coffers.

Apart from the negative impact on human life, the war was a financial fiasco for both countries. For the Iraqi government, the intention behind initiating the war was to capture the oil-rich Khuzestan province, so that the oil reserves seized there would pay the war costs. A significant proportion of the war debts were those owing to Kuwait. At the same time, Iraq accused Kuwait of overstepping its oil production quota at the expense of Iraq, and made Kuwait responsible for the low oil price, which made it more difficult for the Iraqis to repay their war debts. Geopolitically, by conquering Kuwait, Iraq would have greatly improved its access to the Persian Gulf and control of the mineral oil and natural gas resources.

The Iraqi president Saddam Hussein was certainly aware that, in terms of international law, this was no justification for declaring war. It was thus important for him to secure the assurance from the USA, which had supported Iraq up to that point, that he need not fear military intervention in Iraq in case of an attack on Kuwait. Saddam Hussein consulted US Ambassador to Iraq, April Glaspie, who had told him "… but we have no opinion on the Arab-Arab conflict". In addition, a statement by the US

State Department expressed that the USA had " no special defense or security commitments to Kuwait" [31]. Saddam Hussein wrongly concluded that the USA would not intervene should Iraq attack Kuwait.

When Iraq then invaded Kuwait on 2 August 1990, thus contravening international law, the USA used the opportunity to establish US military presence in the geostrategic key region of the Persian Gulf. There had been no previous large-scale military deployment on the part of the USA and no permanent presence in the region. Saddam Hussein's attack on Kuwait thus gave the USA the opportunity to implement the Carter Doctrine militarily: the perfect excuse to enter the region with hundreds of thousands of soldiers and to establish permanent military bases there.

As the country under attack, Kuwait officially called on the international coalition under the leadership of the USA for assistance, and since the assault was also covered by a resolution by the UN Security Council, the deployment of US troops in the Persian Gulf was in keeping with international law. The Iraqi army stood absolutely no chance against the dominant international supremacy of the US and the participation of numerous Arab states. There are no records of the precise number of Iraqi fatalities; the figures vary between several ten thousand and several hundred thousand deaths, while on the side of the US-led international coalition, there were slightly more than 300 fatalities, many as the result of accidents or "other causes". The Iraqi president Saddam Hussein remained in power after the defeat.

However, the Iraqi people had to bear terrible years of economic and societal decline. Shortly after Iraq attacked Kuwait, the UN Security Council imposed almost full financial and trade sanctions, which remained in force until 2003. The controversy over figures on the child mortality in Iraq as a result of the embargoes continues right to the present day: while older publications suggest a mortality rate of several hundred thousand [32, 33], a London School of Economics publication from 2017 contradicts such reports vehemently, and accuses Saddam Hussein's government of having manipulated older UNICEF studies, among others [34] and of having used them for propaganda purposes [35]. This article, too was vigorously contradicted, the accusation being raised that the authors had allowed themselves to be used for western imperialistic propaganda interests [36].

As an outsider, I find it difficult to form an opinion about the matter. True, children who are war victims do tend to be exploited for propaganda. At the same time, the sanctions ruined a more or less functioning economy and society and has driven the development of Iraq from an economically stable secular dictatorship with opportunities in education and development for both men and women to a failed state, in which religious fanatics fight for power [26].

The third Gulf War in 2003 was a war of aggression fought by the USA and Britain, in violation of international law. The attack led to the overthrow and killing of the Iraqi president Saddam Hussein and sparked the decay of the Iraqi state [37]. In the USA, the high war costs led to a potentially ruinous burden for state and society, which is likely to have exacerbated the social divide in the USA [38].

In the second Gulf War (Kuwait was recaptured in 1990), the USA had the support of the UN Security Council and had been called upon for assistance by the cornered Kuwait government. Thus, this war was fought within the bounds of international law. At the same time, it was possible for the USA to realise its dream of a long-term legitimised military presence in the Gulf region. The motives of the USA to wage a war in Kuwait might have been somewhat cynical, even Machiavellian, but they are rationally comprehensible and, viewed geo-strategically, are well conceived.

How the war on Iraq in 2003 was beneficial for the USA is a source of puzzlement for me, however. The main motive might have been securing the petrodollar privilege, i.e. the conventional custom of trading oil and gas exclusively in US dollars. Saddam Hussein wanted to trade Iraqi oil in euros [39, 40]. This might have been his downfall.

The destruction of Libya

In this context, I would like to turn my attention briefly to the military destruction of Libya by a NATO alliance in 2011 led by France and the USA. In this case, too, the intention of the government in Libya to no longer trade in petrodollars might have been an important motive for war, at least for the USA [41]. The economic war motives of the USA were revealed after information in email correspondence of Hillary Clinton became public. Clinton was the US foreign secretary at the time. According to the information, the Libyan government had accumulated gold reserves designated as backing for a currency for an African currency, the 'gold dinar'. This was a challenge for both the US in its role as world-currency hegemon and the currency interests of France. The post-colonial central- and west-African currency CFA (Franc de la Communauté Financière d'Afrique) was tied to the French currency, the franc, and later to the euro. France alone makes decisions regarding the CFS-franc, without requiring consent from the central banks of the respective African countries or the European Central Bank. Viewed from a purely power-political point of view, both France and the United States had great interest in overthrowing the Libyan government and preventing the introduction of the African gold dinar. The leaked Clinton emails confirm this motive for war on the part of both France and the USA [42].

The so-called Arab Spring in early 2011, in which armed opposition groups were formed and the demonstrations soon became very violent, offered the opportunity to bring about the fall of Muammar al-Gaddafi. The resulting civil war was portrayed by the western propaganda apparatus in very one-sided reports, with clearly assigned good-bad roles. In this narrative, the government side clearly represented the "baddies", who brutally massacred the rebels fighting for a noble cause and the civil population. By arguing that the air-force of the political ruler Gaddafi was bombing civil targets, NATO succeeded in gaining the consent of the UN Security Council to install a no-flight zone over Libya (Resolution 1973). Incited by the Americans and led by the French, NATO then brought down the rulers in the Libyan government and destroyed the Libyan state apparatus. This "regime change" was not covered by Resolution 1973, which annoyed the permanent members of the Security Council China and Russia, without whose consent the resolution could never have been passed.

Similar to Iraq before the state was dismantled, Libya was an economically stable secular dictatorship with opportunities in education and development for men and women alike, and which even had social-state-like structures. After the NATO "intervention", the country descended into civil war and also became a failed state, in which, in part, Islamic extremist groups fight for power [37].

Allow me to mention in passing that in March 2018, the former French president, Nicolas Sarkozy, who was responsible for the war in Libya, was placed under formal investigation. The French courts were not concerned about Sarkozy's contravention of international law, but took up investigation on his unlawfully having accepted party funds. Sarkozy is accused of having accepted a single donation from a foreign country that was considerably higher than the permitted amount of 4,500 euros. [43]. The donation of over 50 million euros is said to have come from one single person: Muammar al-Gaddafi [44].

If we look at a map of the Arab peninsula, we see that Saudi Arabia's coastline stretches to the Persian Gulf and to the Red Sea. In order for Saudi oil tanks to reach the open sea, they have to leave the oil harbour Ra's Tanura in the Persian Gulf and pass through the Straits of Hormuz, which is controlled by Iran. The alternative is to load the oil in Yanbu and transport it through the 27-kilometer-wide strait Bab al-Mandab from the Red Sea to the Gulf of Aden in order to reach the Indian Ocean. The Bab al-Mandab lies between Yemen and the Horn of Africa. This means that the passageway from the Persian Gulf is controlled by Iran and that from the Red Sea by Yemen. Saudi, supported by all the states bordering on the Red Sea and the oil states of the Arabian peninsula and not least France, the USA and above all, Britain, has been fighting a bloody war against Yemen since 2015. Apart from ruthless bombardments, the blockade of Yemen by "starvation" is the cause of the high death rate in Yemen. This blockade is upheld by the UN Security Council's Resolution 2216 (with the abstention of Russia). This resolution is by no means a legitimization of the war of aggression on Yemen. It is war that is not legal according to international law. Rather, this resolution must be regarded as a complete and utter failure of the designated role of the United Nations. Germany has already delivered 15 patrol vessels to Saudi Arabia. These contribute to starving the people of Yemen. It has now been determined to refrain from delivering the last four boats to Saudi Arabia. However, a frigate is to be delivered to Egypt, which is also involved in the war on Yemen.

Subsequent to his presidency, Jimmy Carter established a foundation, which has performed great service in the fight against poverty and sickness. It is also thanks to this foundation that the parasitic medina worm found in the tropics and which also inflicts humans has virtually been exterminated. Jimmy Carter appears to be a benevolent person who has the well-being of people at heart. He spoke very critically of the state of the USA in 2015, describing the US as an "oligarchy with unlimited political corruption" [45].

Apart from expressing the claim of the USA to the Gulf oil, the Carter Doctrine would perhaps have been an opportunity to initiate a reconsideration of energy resources. The time would have been appropriate, since there was an increased awareness worldwide of the finite natural resources in the 1960s and 1970s.

The Club of Rome, which shares a common concern for a sustainable future of humanity, was founded in 1968 and strong environmental movements formed throughout the world. It would also have been in the geopolitical interest of the Americans to work towards conditions fostering dignified human life on the planet, since this is the very basis of human existence, in the USA too.

But it seems that the entanglement of military and industrial power referred to as "military industrial complex" by Eisenhower in his farewell address as president of the USA in 1961 does in fact form the guideline for American politics. Prior to this speech, in his book *The Power Elite* the sociologist C. Wright Mills had analysed the symbiotic entanglement between highly capitalistic industries and government and described how this had turned the economy of the USA into one dependent on war. This analysis appears to have been the inspiration for Eisenhower, when he warned of a "military-industrial complex" taking control of the United States. The wealthiest players in this military-industrial complex in America are oil and armament companies [46].

Mills' extensive analysis of the relations between government and major corporations in the American power apparatus was summarised by the musician Frank Zappa in easily understood words: "Government is the Entertainment division of the military industrial complex". The next US president after Jimmy Carter was film actor Ronald Reagan.

"Peak gas"

The natural gas reserves are also finite. Now already, huge volumes of natural gas are used to generate power. Hubbert postulated three 'maximums' for natural gas: at first, the frequency of natural gas discovery will reach a maximum, then there will be a maximum in volume of known gas reserves, and finally, there will be a maximum in gas production. As far as the number of new gas fields is concerned, the maximum was already exceeded in the early 1970s [47]. The hitherto largest known gas field, South Pars, lies below the Persian Gulf. Neighbouring countries are Qatar and Iran, which share the gas field. South Pars is not only the largest gas field in the world, but also has another significicant magnitude: it is about five times the size of the second-largest gas field, the Russian Urengoy gas field [48].

Although the number of newly discovered gas fields has decreased year by year, the volume of known gas reserves and also the quantity of gas extraction has risen steadily in recent years. This suggests that the increase in extractable natural gas volumes must result primarily from the discovery of further gas reserves within the already known gas fields.

So, when can the natural gas extraction maximum be expected? The prognosis before fracking, the technology used for the extraction of shale gas reserves, is that the "peak gas" period will be reached at around 2020 [49]. Even if more natural gas can be extracted with new technologies, we have merely gained time to expand alternative sources of energy. But the gas reserves are also finite.

Geostrategic motives for exploiting the largest existing natural gas field South Pars could be the true reason for the Syrian war. The uprising during the Arab Spring of 2011 was only used as a ready occasion to attempt to overthrow the Syrian president, and the claim that the intention was to install democracy in Syria only the excuse for deploying war to enforce natural-resources interests [50]. Just as in Libya and Iraq, Syria was also a dictatorship, but one that was economically solid and secular, with education and development opportunities for both men and women. People from different religions and tribes coexisted more or less peacefully and perceived themselves as a nation [51]. Unfortunately, such diversity in religion and tribes can be instrumentalised to destabilise a country.

Thus seen, the Syrian war is probably really a bloody means of staging a pipeline dispute. Facilitating transport of the natural gas is decisive for exploiting South Pars. Interests in Qatar and Iran are in direct conflict with each other. In 2000, Qatar had announced a plan to construct a pipeline to Turkey through Saudi Arabia, Jordan and Syria. The western powers in Europe and the USA supported this project. The gas pipeline would avoid having to first liquify the Syrian gas and then ship it to Europe; as in Russia, gas could simply be supplied via pipelines to the bulk consumers in Europe. This competition did not please Russia, this being a further motive for the USA to support the project.

Russia supported the alternative plan of the Iranians, who were planning a gas pipeline to Lebanon via Iraq and Syria. This plan was rejected by Qatar, Saudi Arabia, Turkey, the EU and the USA. Since Syria was the country through which both pipelines would be laid, the decision had to be made by the Syrian government to determine which project would be granted authorisation for the pipeline through the country. Syria announced in 2009 that it would support the Iran-Lebanese pipeline, which led to those states supporting the failed Qatari-Turkey plan setting out to overthrow Assad. Freedom and human rights apparently play a subordinate role in the Syrian war [50]. In the meanwhile, it seems that the Russian-Iranian- Syrian alliance to sustain the Assad government has won the Syrian war. Turkey changed sides in time, or, better said, has concentrated on its own game and occupied Kurdish territory in North Syria, probably with the long-term goal to displace the Kurdish Syrians and replace them with Arab Syrians.

At present, American soldiers are still protecting the allied Kurds. At the moment of writing, in late 2018, it appears that the troops will be withdrawn [52, 53]. Fritz Edlinger, editor of the journal "International" pointed out in an interview with Ken Jebsen that huge gas fields have been discovered under the Eastern Mediterranean Sea. Countries with claims to these gas fields are Egypt, Palestine, Israel, Syria, Lebanon and Cyprus (which is split between Greece and Turkey). These gas fields could fuel future wars in the region. There are also oil and gas reserves on the Syrian Golan Heights, and the American company Genie Oil has already been granted the rights to extract these oil and gas reserves. The board of directors consists of prominent and powerful Americans such as the former US vice president Dick Cheney, the US media Mogul Murdoch, the former head of the CIA Woolsey and Jakob Rothschild. Although, according to international law, the Golan Heights belong to Syria, Genie Oil granted drilling concessions for exploitation by the Israeli oil company Afek Oil.

Fossil fuels are finite

The wars over oil and gas give us some idea of how much our society depends on fossil fuels. When at some future time, the distribution of the last reserves are at stake, we can assume that this will not be carried out according to the principle of fairness, but according to the political, economic and military strength of the countries involved and their access to the reserves.

As for natural gas production, it seems that the time has been extended during which gas is available to us humans, since shale gas fields can be developed with new technologies (one example of this is the Marcellus shale gas field in the USA).

Nevertheless, the time of easily available fossil fuels seems to have come to an end. Poor countries without great geopolitical and military power should avoid making their development dependent on fossil fuels, since they will not have the power to enforce their claims to the ever scarcer fossil resources. The only chance for African countries to become industrialised is the consistent use of alternative energies. In other words: they must leapfrog the period of industrialisation dependent on fossil energy sources and instead concentrate on alternative energy sources.

The earth is approximately 4.5 billion years old. Humans, or human primates have existed for about 4 million years, the modern *Homo sapiens* for about 300,000 years – and the industrial use of mineral oil for about 160 years. In the debate about whether mineral oil reserves will hold out for another few years or decades (or even centuries) more, this may be long enough for me as an individual. But once we consider the lives of our children, the issue becomes really disturbing. Measured by the short time during which modern man has existed, the mineral oil age is extremely short.

By the way, the above-mentioned 30,000 years of the existence of *Homo sapiens* is a very recently estimated span of time, having been reckoned by finding skeletal remains in 1968 in Morocco, which has made a new measure possible. Prior to this, it was estimated that *Homo sapiens* had been in existence for about 200,000 years. Due to the fact that the evolutionary development of our species takes tens of thousands of years, the question if *Homos sapiens* have existed for 200,000 or 300,000 years plays only a negligible role.

If we assume that *Homo sapiens* has existed as a species for about 240,000 years, and imagine that a day has 24 hours, then one hour corresponds to about 10,000 years. At about an hour before midnight, the first humans became settled and began to till fields, and about one minute before the end of the day marked the beginning of large-scale industrial utilisation of mineral oil. On discussing the expansion of exploitable oil reserves, we are talking about mere seconds of our fictional day.

How can each individual human adapt to the challenges of the waning era of fossil fuels?

We have all learnt meanwhile that as individuals, we have to save energy and recycle waste. We do so wherever it fits into our lives – and use resources whenever this is not the case. For myself, I can say with some measure of pride that I have no car and always use my bicycle or public transport to get to wherever I need to be. If I want to feel good about this, I have to stop here and not mention that I live in a part of town that has good facilities, is well developed, attractive and bustling with life, that I work close by and for this reason, need no car. Can I allow myself to feel morally superior to people commuting from a distance, who live in the countryside or who, because of high rents, are forced to live on the urban fringe, where the infrastructure does not make it easy to get to work, which means that they need a car? I fly to far-off countries a few times a year as part of my job. Should I have a guilty conscience about this and do penance?

When I speak about my "eco behaviour", one could gain the impression that it results from planning my life in accordance with consumption of natural resources. This would mean that I have never had a car in order to save resources. But the reality is that I have only constructed an ecological balance sheet from my behaviour that itself only results from adapting to my living conditions, my needs, wishes and desires.

If our intention as humankind is to conserve resources and to protect our planet, it does not suffice to simply preach pseudo-religiously about moral eco-standards. This might even be counter-productive, since we humans tend to take on a defensive stance when being confronted with patronising rhetoric. Making a religion of the climate issue is what a few saints and a few heretics do. Most people live their lives somewhere in between the two poles, and every now and again, align themselves to the prevailing moral ecological standards, placing their emphasis on the accepted norms of behaviour, so that they can bask in the feeling of their own ethical and moral superiority.

But this attitude will not solve the problem of the rising consumption of resources and the burden on our atmosphere of increasing CO_2 levels resulting from the steadily growing global population and ever greater industrialisation in emerging countries. The European population constituted about 7 percent of global population in 2010 – and is on the decline. Hence, global problems, such as air and marine pollution, are increasingly originating from other continents.

In order to improve the climate balance of each individual, the living conditions of each individual must be so arranged that contributing to the conservation of our resources demands as little sacrifice as possible from each individual person.

Throughout the world, a growing number of people live urban areas. The challenges that face European cities cannot be compared to those in rapidly growing cities in countries with an inordinately high level of population growth. If urban areas are designed to allow each individual not to permanently rely on using a car, then air pollution and the burden of noise and stress can be reduced. To achieve this, it is necessary to avoid division between the various areas of life (such as living space, leisure, shopping, gastronomy, work and the economy). If I have everything I need within walking distance and can also get to my place of work without using a car, my ecological footprint is reduced without my having to experience any personal disadvantages.

Can such habitats develop if the market laws are simply given free rein? Perhaps. But probably societal organisation rather requires a combination of rationally conceived planning and active public involvement with market mechanisms: markets that are not only defined by the power of money, but that facilitate the balance of true-life interests. Basically, what seems to be the answer is to dare to live more democracy.

GM suburbia: the march of victory of individual transportation

In some cities in the USA, the strict division of the individual areas of life has led to what is typically termed 'suburbia', suburbs that appear to be lifeless, and where it is practically impossible to live without a car. Such restrictive urban planning has caused the cities to work to the advantage of powerful business lobby groups and to the disadvantage of the inhabitants.

In the 1930s, many American cities had a well-functioning public commuter system with streetcar networks. In the early 20th century, the automobile corporation, General Motors (GM) was one of the largest and most powerful companies ever. In order to increase its turnover, the company used its own market monopoly and economic prowess and formed an alliance with oil companies (such as Standard Oil) to demolish the streetcar systems and replace them with motor cars, trucks and buses from its own production. GM bought up streetcar operating companies via subcontractors, dismantled the streetcars and replaced them with buses that the corporation itself had produced. The overland 'Greyhound' bus line was established and equipped using GM buses. GM also used its political influence make cities dependent on the automobile. The increasing individual mobility meant that city life was divided into residential space, leisure activities, shopping, gastronomy, work and business. The natural result was that people who moved into these areas also needed a car. This led to increasing traffic. The road networks were expanded, using up the space that was previously used for other purposes [54].

In both Germany and France, the automobile industries and their lobbies are very potent, and here, too, the infrastructure has been adapted to the automobile. Nevertheless, these countries have been successful in creating more or less well functioning local and national public transport systems, with the necessary maintenance and development. The two countries have a tradition of regulated market economies that include steering and planning mechanisms of communal interests, such as urban development.

Russia, too, the largest country of the former Soviet Union, long governed by socialist, planned-economy principles, has a well-functioning local transport infrastructure (the subways in Moscow and St. Petersburg are not only functional, but highly pleasing to the eye). In view of the virtually infinite distances of the huge country, Russia also has a railway network that fulfils its function fully and is convenient.

It would be one-sided and a complete over-simplification to maintain that a planned economy is a wondrous system. Market mechanisms are an essential ingredient of human trade relations without which fair cohabitation and trade would not be possible. However, without regulation and planning, all-powerful monopolists rise, and influence societal decisions so strongly that political decisions reflect the profit-greed of these monopolists rather than the interests of the society. The consequence is that public welfare, which cannot simply be expressed in terms of monetary value, is ignored. The costs that are incurred in a society must often be borne by that society and not by those who make a profit from incurring the costs. Such expenses, namely, those that are burdened on the society, are termed externalised costs.

Alternatives to fossil energies

Measures to save energy are important. In view of the fact that fossil fuels are finite and in view of the increasing demand for energy from the growing world population, cutting energy consumption can at most delay the depletion of fossil fuels. Of course we have gained time by fracking – a few decades perhaps, at most, a few centuries. However, the human civilization will only be able to survive if alternative sources of energy can be found and harnessed.

The most important source of energy on earth, the energy that generated the development of life, does not need to be found – we already know what it is: the sun. What (only) needs to be done is to make solar energy exploitable and usable. Basically, we already do so by the combustion of fossil fuels whose energy stems from solar energy absorbed millions of years ago and is stored for just as long until we release them (together with enormous volumes of CO_2). Since fossil fuels are finite and CO_2 causes the greenhouse effect, we need to find way to utilise solar energy directly.

As a layperson, what immediately occurs to me are solar cells: they certainly make it possible to utilize solar energy to cover the requirements of our civilisation (for mobility, heating, cooling, production processes, water desalination). Let me try to explain for laypeople, such as I myself am, how solar cells function. From my physics lessons, I vaguely recall that electricity, voltage and resistance are somehow connected. In a few words: without voltage, no current – meaning no electric **energy**.

Solar cells

Silicon is used in solar cells. Silicon irradiated with sunlight releases electrons. So far, so good. But to really generate voltage and produce electricity, something more is required. We recall that voltage sources always have a plus and a minus pole, the minus pole being the result of a surplus of negative charged electrons (negative charge), which the plus pole does not have (positive charge).

If a layer of silicon is spiked with phosphorous, a surplus of electrons is generated. The underlying silicon layer is spiked with boron, which in this case results in a deficit of electrons. In order to balance this deficit, the surplus free electrons move from the upper layer downwards, where they become bound electrons. The irradiation of the sun again releases the electrons, forcing them to return to the positive layer above. This manipulation of the electrons can be diverted via an electrode lying at the margin of the upper positive layer, which is attached to an electrode at the lower margin of the bottom negative layer. This generates a closed electrical circuit, which can be switched on for energy consumption of, say, a light bulb.

This sounds really simple. So why has this technology not been utilised more widely? Is the rival fossil fuel more energy-efficient?

When solar energy was still in its infancy, a point of criticism could in actual fact have been that the solar cells transform only a small proportion of the actually irradiated solar energy into usable energy. Conventional solar cells achieve an efficiency level of 15%. But the technology is advancing rapidly. In the meantime, there are solar-cell systems that collect the sunlight in various wavelengths and achieve an energy efficiency of 46 % by distributing it to sub cells. Even so, half of the energy from sunlight is still lost. That is not necessarily bad performance, if we draw a comparison: in coal power stations, water is heated to steam, which then drives turbines. Energy utilization in such power plants lies between about 33% minimum to 45 % maximum. As far as energy exploitation is concerned, modern solar cells are thus even now more efficient than fossil-driven power plants! [55]

But is the energy efficiency of solar cells really the most important criterium for determining the degree of their utilization? The only thing that less efficient solar cells require is more space, they do not emit CO_2 (except for the CO_2 used to produce them). At present, a practical problem is the daily fluctuating sunshine levels: on sunny days, solar cells can produce much more energy than can be consumed, and at night, the sun does not shine. The decisive factor is thus technologies that store energy. Such energy storage technology is also important for wind energy, which can also only be generated irregularly.

A further problem is the high cost of solar cells, which means that solar energy cannot compete with fossil fuels. But there is reason for optimism: the more widespread solar energy becomes and the more normal it becomes, the less expensive solar cells become and the greater the competitiveness of solar technology. Germany has provided huge subsidies to create incentives for further development of solar technology. This provoked loud complaints from neo-liberal economists, but it did help the technology and its implementation to get off the ground. [56]. However, the subsidies also benefited foreign suppliers. This led to the innovative, but also expensive German solar energy sector being unable to compete with suppliers from other countries, China being a case in point [57]. This is an unfavourable development from the German point of view. But for humankind, it is to be welcomed, if the distribution of solar energy worldwide can be accelerated, and the dependence on fossil fuels reduced correspondingly.

Energy storage technologies

Energy is needed at all times, not only when the sun shines. We therefore need batteries – chargeable batteries with enormous storage capacity. And here the same applies: batteries are still too expensive to compete with fossil fuels. The basic principle of batteries is that they store chemical energy, which reacts to transform it into electric energy. A redox reaction occurs when an electron flows from one reactant (oxidation) and docks onto another reactant (reduction). This releases energy. The redox reaction flows in only one direction in disposable batteries. The electron gradient is reduced steadily until the battery is empty. Chargeable batteries can be recharged (for instance by using solar energy). This induces the redox reaction to flow back in the other direction and the electrons are "pumped back" into the electron transmitter. The electron gradient resulting from the charging process can then be retrieved.

To date, chargeable batteries have lower energy density (energy per volume, measured in watt-hours per litre) than disposable batteries have. Modern lithium-ion-batteries achieve an energy density of about 300 watt-hours per litre at most. Petrol has an energy density of 9000 watt-hours per litre – thus, thirty times higher. The battery thus has to be correspondingly larger than the petrol tank to be able to deliver the same energy that a full petrol tank delivers [58]. This is a decisive disadvantage for mobility energy (the motor car). For stationary usage, the lower energy density of chargeable energy storage is a minor problem, however: the energy storage system of a house can be charged repeatedly during the day using solar cells. The oil tank in the cellar is usually filled once a year.

One argument that is frequently cited is the relatively high energy input required for producing solar panels. The concept of energy payback time, or energy amortization time, has been developed to factor this in. This is the operating time that is required for the energy required for production to be generated. In older solar technologies, this period was as much as three years; thanks to new developments in production processes, it has been reduced to less than a year and a half. [59]. For those who find this period too long, it is worth considering that fossil energies cannot be amortized at all, since their operation permanently requires new resources.

Do we need to fear scarcity of resources for the production of solar cells?

Basically, no. Silicon, the most important resource, is one of the main ingredients of the earth's crust (i.e. the uppermost layer of our planet). A requirement for resources to produce solar cells being available in unlimited quantities is that photovoltaic modules based on silicon can maintain their market leadership. Should this leadership be endangered at some stage by less sustainable solar technologies that rely on rare and finite resources (indium or selenium for example), measures to counter the market forces should be initiated by political leaders.

Attention is now shifting to the global supply of lithium, since lithium is needed to produce lithium-ion batteries. There is no absolute certainty of the availability of large lithium sources in the long run. This will depend on how many lithium resources are discovered when this resource gains in significance and how well recycling systems for lithium can be established [60]. At present it is not to be feared that the supply of lithium will run dry [61].

As an informed layperson, I ask myself why solar technology is not more widespread today. Or to be more precise:

Why can solar cells not replace all fossil fuels short-term?

Well, you can probably guess the answer: the cost is the reason – and the power that comes in association with oil wealth. Oil money plays a significant role in the military-industrial complex of the USA, and forms geostrategic and economic policies, as I have already shown in examples in the section on oil wars. As for Germany, the automobile industry is of such significance that Germany regularly undermines EU-level initiatives to reduce fuel consumption and pollutant emissions of cars. Consequently the German car industry makes practically no effort to produce small and thus economical cars [62].

At the same time, established and stable existing structures hinder the implementation of newer technologies. Whoever buys a car would like to drive it for a few years or even decades. Heating is also not installed in a house for short-term use; is expected to be available for a lifetime. But this also means that a decision to change an energy source only becomes operative after a latent period of years or decades. Also, the survival instinct of organisations is not to be underestimated. An organisation whose services are found to be harmful or are no longer required does not mean that it just dissolves into mid-air. People who devote themselves to a task, such as energy production in an oil company, for example, and to whom we owe warm heating, filled petrol tanks and a flourishing economy, will continue their lifework by training future generations to similarly devote their life and engineering skills to wealth creation by using easily available fossil energy. The financial survival instinct of fossil energy companies is fostered by a society that works on the basis of profit and which provides benefits for society, but also ensures that competitive advantage is maintained. Why should such a business be closed down as long as it is running so well?

4   The infinitely finite nature of water and sand

From the moon, our earth looks like a blue-green-brown marble with white streaks. What appears as white streaks are the clouds and ice from the pole caps. The greenish-brown parts are the land surfaces. But it is the water masses that make the earth appear to be a blue planet. A little over two thirds of the earth's surface is made up of water. This water is composed of 97.5% salt water, which is neither drinkable nor can be for used agricultural purposes. Of the remaining 2.5 % fresh water, four-fifths are frozen in the two polar circles of the North and South Poles. This leaves de facto only 0.5 % of the water worldwide for use as drinking water and for irrigation.

Water scarcity

In January 2019 the body of a 2-year-old boy who had fallen into an illegally drilled waterhole in Spain was found at a depth of 71 meters. The hole was 107 meters deep, but did not touch any ground water. Apparently, such illegally drilled waterholes have become more and more common in Spain, where water is scarce.

South America and Southeast Asia have large amounts of water. However, this does not mean that water scarcity does not play a role here. The water supply of the Brazilian Mega city Sao Paolo is very critical and nearly collapsed in 2014. Australia is an absolutely water-scarce continent, but has only 24 million inhabitants. The water scarcity in North Africa and the Middle East is much more dramatic. North Africa (Egypt, Algeria, the Sudan, Morocco, Tunisia, Libya and Western Sahara) has a population of 237 million. The population density is 31 inhabitants per km^2; however, in contrast to Europe with its denser population, large areas of North Africa are covered by deserts [63]. The current population growth rate is 1.8.%, making the doubling time 70/1.8

= 39 years (assuming stable growth). The data platform www.worldometers.info lists the Middle East region under "Western Asia". These include Turkey, Iraq, Saudi Arabia, Yemen, Syria, Azerbaijan, Jordan, United Arab Emirates, Israel, Lebanon, Palestine, Oman, Kuwait, Georgia, Armenia, Qatar and Bahrain (Iran is regarded as belonging to South Asia). This region has a population of 271 million people. Assuming stable population growth of currently 1,8% (as in North Africa), the doubling time is also about 39 years.

Can I save a significant quantity of water if I wash myself less frequently and drink less? Locally, yes – perhaps, especially in areas where water is scarce, water-saving does play a role. Viewed globally, however, one person's direct water consumption (washing, drinking, cleaning) has a negligible effect when compared with water consumption in agriculture and industrial production. An estimated 70% of water consumption worldwide is for agricultural purposes (irrigation, cattle rearing) and approximately 20% is used for industrial purposes. A mere 10% of all water is consumed in private households or in the public sphere.

The individual consumer has only little direct influence on the water consumption in the industrial and agricultural sectors. Individual indirect water consumption can be reduced by a vegetarian or vegan diet with seasonal – and regional – products. However, this is truly the proverbial 'drop in the ocean'. In order to reduce water consumption worldwide or in a society, far-reaching changes are necessary. In view of the increasing population growth and the fact that emerging countries are adopting a water-intensive lifestyle, the water consumption is much more likely to increase than to decrease worldwide.

In contrast to oil, water is not traded over wide areas in large tankers or via pipelines. Water supply is usually a local, communal matter, which seems logical. Nevertheless, there is a lobby-driven movement to privatise water supply. The director of the global food company Nestlé is quoted as having stated that water is not a human right, but a foodstuff and should have a market value. This statement caused outrage worldwide and led to protest against the commercialisation of water [64].

The basic idea – that water should have a price – has already been realised, namely in the form of the water bill. Since the amount of water consumed is determined by the industrial sector and still more by agriculture and cattle rearing, a low water price plays a major role when agricultural companies decide about their location. As in many other profit-oriented production forms, competitive underbidding means that the major consumers, i.e. the industrial corporations, not only do not pay the real price for a product, in this case water, but are not held responsible for the costs to the environment of a lower ground water levels and water scarcity. These costs are externalised, that means, they are not borne in a cost-by-cause principle, but by society.

The phenomenon of externalisation is not only restricted to private-capitalist economic forms. During the era of the Soviet Union, there was large-scale water extraction for agricultural usage, and particularly for cotton cultivation, from the Aral Sea and its two tributary rivers: the Aral Sea lies in Kazakhstan and Uzbekistan. The (formerly) huge round inland lake used to be the fourth-largest sea in the world, and covered an area of 68,000 km^2 in 1960. It dwindled to a thin sickle-shaped water expanse with satellite lakes to the north, covering an area of 13,500 km^2 in 2009 [65]. Just how dramatic this development is can be seen even more clearly when the decline in water volume is considered. This volume was estimated at 1093 km^3 in 1960 and at 105 km^3 in 2009, only 9.5% of its original volume. With the decreasing volume of water, the salt content i.e. the salinity, which was always high for an inland lake, rose from 0.9% in 1960 to 10.2% in 2009 [65]. (Fresh water usually has a salinity of below 0.1%; water that has a salinity volume of 1% is defined as salt water. Water that has a salt content lying between these two values is defined as brackish water. Oceans have an average salinity volume of 3.5%)

The Kazakh dam project, the Kokaral Dam, is an attempt since the 1990s to salvage the northern part of the Aral Sea. This has indeed brought about an expansion in the size of the remaining northern Sea areas and has improved the quality of the water. However, this improvement has come at a cost for the southern parts of the remaining Sea, which lies completely in Uzbekistan. This has resulted in tension between Kazakhstan and Uzbekistan. Kazakhstan argues that the southern-lying Aral Sea cannot be saved because of Uzbekistan's continuing large quantities of water extraction from the Amu Darya River, which meanwhile no longer flows into the Aral Sea but peters out in the desert. Despite the controversy, the two countries are making an effort to manage the region's water supply in mutual agreement. The Syr Darya River access, which flows into the northern Aral Sea, is strongly regulated by dam barrages on the Kazakh side. Since the river is a confluence of two Kyrgyz mountain rivers, there is a high degree of fluctuation in the water volumes. A water expanse, the Ay Dar Sea, has been formed from the seasonal excess water flowing into (unplanned) overflow gutters, this Sea lying on the Uzbek side. This makes it crucial for Kazakhstan and Uzbekistan to coordinate their water management.

The area surrounding the former Aral Sea has meanwhile become one of the most hostile regions on earth. Former fishing villages now lie in a salt desert. Those people remaining in the area are constantly exposed to toxic aerosols, pollutants used as herbicides or pesticides. The former Vozrozdeniya Island, where free-range biological-weapon experiments were carried out until 1990 has meanwhile merged with the mainland, leading to the concern that residue from the biological weapons, such as traces of anthrax spores or bubonic plague bacteria could spread [66].

Karachi lies in Pakistan in the estuary delta of the Indus River and has a population of about 21 million, as GOOGLE informs me when I enter "Karachi inhabitants". Wikipedia tells me that the (disputed) 2017 census recorded a population of 14.9, while the estimated population is 18 million (early 2019). An article in the Swiss daily *Neue Zürcher Zeitung* puts the population at about 25 million inhabitants and its annual population growth rate at 6% [67]. Perhaps all three population figures are correct. With a population growth of 6% and a population of 16 million in 2010, a population of 21 million in 2015 and of 21 million in 2018 is a feasible figure. According to Al Bartlett's equation, and assuming consistent growth of 6% (70/6), the doubling time is a mere 12 years.

Apart from the high demand for water due to the water-intensive textile industry and the high population figure, high volumes of water are lost because of the bad state of the water-pipe systems. Much of the loss of water is not coincidental, however, but is caused by the mafia-like networks that channel water off and then sell it for a high price. The illegal wells that are also bored by these criminal networks or simply by Karachi citizens result in the ground water in Karachi falling to ever-lower levels.

Wealthy inhabitants of the city have their water supplied to their homes through private pipelines, but most of the common population have to buy their water in canisters and carry the water home themselves. Those who can afford it have their own private (illegal) borehole or install a water tank in order to have a regular supply of water, especially in the hot summer months, but also so that that they have access to greater volumes of water, which makes it cheaper. The tank trucks that deliver the water are usually filled at (illegal) taps that are attached to the urban pipeline network. This is another reason why water pipelines run dry, and why those households that are affected have no option but to rely on their water supply from (the very same) tankers.

The Indus river is the main source of water supply in Pakistan. The water is not only taken directly from the river, but also refills reservoirs and aquifers. Pakistan sources its water supply from the Karakorum, Himalaya and Hindu Kush mountains, the largest volume of snow and ice water outside the pole caps. Nevertheless, ground water levels have been falling steadily over the past few years, resulting in the aquifers collapsing. The quality of the water is also declining. Approximately 50 million people in Pakistan are exposed to arsenic-contaminated ground water [68].

The source of the lifeline of Pakistan, the Indus river, lies in Tibet, which is Chinese territory. It flows through India on its course from Tibet to Pakistan. The course of the river thus has a geopolitical impact: in the two countries India and Pakistan, both armed with nuclear weapons, and which tend to have hostile relations, huge volumes of the water from Indus are used for agricultural purposes. India is planning the construction of dams and hydro-power stations. This will give the Indians more control over the water. The Pakistanis living downstream are observing the development of events with suspicion. The international legal basis for negotiations is the Indus Water Treaty, which is regarded as a solid piece of international diplomacy that has repeatedly facilitated compromises for the two hostile countries. Pakistan views the Indian measures to control the Indus water as an existential threat and has thus announced that a withdrawal from the treaty would be regarded as a reason for war, a casus belli [69].

The water shortage with collapsing aquifers also leads to the ground sinking, which raises the risk of widespread flooding and aggravates the impact of strong weather events (this also impacts Bangladesh). Widespread flooding in countries that lie on the Indian subcontinent occur annually during the monsoon period, but was particularly grave in 2010 and 2017.

Balancing the water supply throughout the world, for example in countries that share major rivers or main tributaries, can become a key issue in international relations. Ethiopia is about to complete the Grand Renaissance Dam, designed to dam the Blue Nile, of which 85% flows into the White Nile. The construction of the dam thus causes the two countries Sudan and Egypt to feel threatened. Ethiopia hopes that the dam will be the source of a reliable energy supply and that it will lead to improved agricultural conditions in the area. Sudan was pacified by being granted energy-supply concessions, but Egypt in particular fears that a reduction in the volume of water from the Nile will rob millions of farmers of their basis of existence [70]. It is particularly the speed at which the dam is to be filled that is a subject of debate, since the filling will lead to the greatest reduction in the volume of water flowing to Egypt. However, what the Egyptians fear most of all in the long term is that the dammed water in Ethiopia will result in a water-intensive industrial boom in that country that will sap the water supply.

The Egyptian population continues to grow at a steady 2% rate (doubling time: $70/2 = 35$ years) and will exceed the 100-million mark in 2020. At the same time, large areas of the country are desert land. Human habitation is limited to the few kilometres of the fertile strip on the banks of the Nile. Egypt regards long-term loss of arable reach as posing a threat to its national security. The fact that diplomats see their national security threatened not infrequently induces them to take drastic steps, including military action[71].

Sea-water desalination

As already mentioned, 97.5 % of all water on earth is salt water. So can sea-water desalination be a solution to possible water problems? Some countries already making large-scale use of de-salination systems, especially in the Middle East, where water is scarce. Obviously, with this method, fresh-water supply in water-scarce regions can be guaranteed.

What, then, are the disadvantages? One is that the process of desalination used at present requires a lot of energy. In the Middle East, oil and gas are (still) readily and cheaply available. In Saudi Arabia, water for drinking and industrial purposes is ex-clusively produced through desalination using mineral oil and natural gas as the energy source for this purpose. Large scale thermal processes, but also membrane filter processes, are used to produce condensed water, involving salt water being pressed though a salt-impermeable membrane to release the fresh water [72].

The oldest desalination method is flash evaporation (flash distillation). This technology heats salt water, which is then transported into a low-pressure chamber, where it vaporises and then condenses as water with a lower level of salination. This process is repeated for up to 40 times (multiple-effect distillation MED), producing desalinated water. In principle, this process follows the natural water cycle of evaporation and was already used centuries ago on ships crossing the oceans to secure a supply of drinking water in cases of emergency. In order to produce about 1 m^3 (about 100 litres) of water, about 290 MJ/m^3 (approx. 80 kWh) of thermal energy is required to heat the water and 3 to 5 kWh to operate the pumps and the complete system. It can thus be said that multiple-effect distillation requires about 85 kWh to produce 1000 litres of water [73]. To illustrate the energy requirement, let us consider the energy required for washing one load of laundry in a washing machine, which is about one kwH. By using multiple-effect distillation, the energy required for one load of washing can produce a mere 12 litres of water (1000/85 = 12).

In reverse osmosis (RO) technology, sea water that has gone through a process of rough pre-filtration is forced into a vacuum chamber under high pressure, overcoming osmotic pressure by means of a semi-permeable membrane. The membrane filter retains salts, bacteria, viruses and lime, also various toxic substances and heavy metals. The driving force is the hydraulic pressure, which must exceed the osmotic pressure. Reverse osmosis is more sophisticated and complex because of the heavy maintenance required for the system, the preliminary treatment of the sea water and the deposits of highly concentrated residue matter, but requires less energy than flash evaporation, since the thermic energy requirement is negligible and only the energy required for operating the pump and the system (approx. 3.5 kWh) must be taken into account [73].

In view of the considerably lower energy costs and potential process improvements resulting from developments in materials technology, reverse osmosis appears to be the way forward. However, many systems still work on the basis of flash evaporation, since these systems are often located in parts of the world (the Middle East), where fossil fuels are (still) readily available at a low cost. However, energy will always be needed for the process of water desalination.

Apart from oil and gas, there is a further important source of energy available in the dry Middle-East regions: the sun. Using the energy provided by the sun, advanced desalination systems can operate with low energy requirements. Desalination using photovoltaic energy could also be used to produce water in those countries that do not enjoy an abundance of rich fossil-fuel resources. Unfortunately, the sun only shines by day, but supplies of energy and water also need to be available when there is no sunshine. Advances made in energy-storage technologies (such as batteries) and good water reservoirs are thus important for securing water supply. Just as with energy supply, a few centralised industrially driven desalination plants could be replaced by numerous small decentralised plants.

Unfortunately however, there is no way to avoid burdening the environment to a certain degree. Both systems cause a hyperosmotic brine residue, which is mostly transported into the ocean, and can result in considerable damage to flora and fauna.

Icebergs as a source of fresh water

As previously mentioned, a mere 2.5 % of the water on earth is natural water suitable for human consumption, of which 80% is found in the ice of the polar regions. Hence it appears to make sense to use these polar water reserves. The idea to haul icebergs from the polar region to solve the problem of water scarcity is not a new one. At present, it is once again being debated to supply the 3.8 million inhabitants of Cape Town in South Africa with water [74, 75]. Situated on the southern tip of the African continent, Cape Town lies closer to the Antarctic than any other city in Africa (however, the African continent does not stretch as far south as South America does). Even so, the distance from Cape Town to the Antarctic is over 4000 km, thus greater than the distance between Iceland and Morocco, for instance.

Meanwhile, some experience has indeed been gained from controlled haulage of icebergs, which is a process used when icebergs are on collision course to oil-drilling platforms on the Canadian coast. The procedure entails a ship sailing around the iceberg and drawing a harness around it, similar to laying a fishing net to draw a school of fish. A small iceberg can be manoeuvred relatively easily this way. But clearly, the larger it is, the more difficult it is to do so.

In order to protect a drilling platform from an approaching iceberg, it must only be moved a few kilometres and can then be left to float. Also, the iceberg does not need to be moved to a certain location, but only moved away from its collision course. Harnessing an iceberg in the Antarctic and moving it 4000 kilometres to a specific target further north to the Cape Town bay is a rather more difficult undertaking. What is unavoidable is that the ice will partially melt during its journey. In order to minimise this, the surface of the ice can be covered with a sheet to deflect the direct sunrays.

Icebergs float, since their relative density is a little below that of water. In water with a high saline level and with numerous air pockets in the iceberg, the buoyancy of the iceberg is a little greater than for icebergs in natural water. The shape of the iceberg is also significant: a flat iceberg with a large, flat surface is more stable in the water than a cylindrical or wedge-shaped one that can topple more easily and then break apart.

About 90 % of an iceberg lies below the surface of the water. The higher the temperature of the water, the greater the loss in size at the bottom of the iceberg due to melting. This means that the water temperature needs to be considered when planning the undertaking. Once the iceberg has reached its destination, it needs to be stored in a salt-free basin in order to collect the melting fresh water.

Another part of the world that is considering supplementing the low water reserves with water from icebergs are the Canary Islands. The distance between the Canary Islands and the ice zone of Canada in Newfoundland is about 3,500 km. With an estimated average speed of 1.5 kilometres an hour, the journey would take 140 days. A mathematical simulation showed that about 4 million tons would remain of a 7-million-ton iceberg. A ton of water has a volume of about a cubic metre (1,000 litres.) Is it realistic to calculate that about four sevenths of an iceberg is likely to reach its destination, no matter the size of the iceberg? Unfortunately, no. The smaller the iceberg is, the greater the disadvantages of its surface to volume relation. The larger the original iceberg is, the smaller the relative loss through melting. A volume of 4 million tons of natural water could supply about 70,000 people with water for a year. However, the transport would also require about 4,000 tons of fuel, i.e. about a litre fuel per 1,000 litres of water [76].

Cape Town has a population of about 3.75 million inhabitants. If the Canary-Island simulation is taken as a point of departure, for a water supply of a year, about 53 icebergs would be required with an initial volume of 7 million tons each to ensure a residual volume of 4 million tons each (3,750,000 / 70,000= 53.6).

Good knowledge of the ocean currents can facilitate the task. In the Cape-Town project, the Antarctic Circumpolar Current moving clockwise around the Antarctic could largely have been utilised for an iceberg to take its natural course and the iceberg would simply have been hauled northwards in the Benguela

Current, which would have carried the iceberg to the Cape of Good Hope. Fortunately, with the persistent rainfalls in winter 2018, Cape Town was saved from drought this time, but it is to be hoped that the country will learn from the lessons of the drought period and continue to conserve water [77].

Sand scarcity

Oil and water scarcity are definitely problems that humankind needs to face. But sand? Sand is freely available – yes, like all the sand in the sea, - or in the desert. In fact, after water and air, sand is the most-used natural resource on earth. So, could the developing Sahel countries around the Sahara Desert solve their desertification problems simply by selling the sand? Unfortunately, no. Though sand is sought after as a raw material for building construction material, there is a great difference between the different kinds of sand. The sand required for producing building materials such as concrete must be exclusively rough-grained and irregular. Wind-borne Sahara sand grains are too smooth and fine to be used as a bond in building material. River sand is the best sand grain for building construction. Beach sand is in high demand, too. Desert sand and sand from the ocean floors are often less suitable. The population is usually most dense along rivers and the coastal areas, which is why the locally available sand in settled areas is often rapidly exhausted. There is less sand left in denatured rivers, namely, those changed as a result of water construction, than in rivers left in their natural state. Barrages and levelling lead to less sand being deposited in sandbanks or in river estuary deltas.

Not only are huge amounts of sand used in the building construction industry, but it is an important raw material for producing glass. Siliceous earth is used in electrotechnology for producing semi-conductors, but also for the extraction of natural gas and mineral oil in fracking technology. Sand is also used as backfill material for land reclamation. A spectacular example can be seen in the luxury residential artificial island constructions in Dubai with their characteristic palm design or world-map forms. Since the desert sand was unsuitable, sand had to be imported for the backfill [78].

What are the consequences of ruinous sand extraction? One is that there will be no more lovely beaches on the coasts, which will make them less attractive for tourists. Another is that there is no natural protection against flooding when sand extraction results in islands along the coast disappearing or no longer forming a protective sand rim. Coastal regions will be more prone to catastrophic flooding without sand to form a protective barrier. Apart from that, the lack of a protective barrier could result in the seawater seeping into the ground near the sea, causing salinization and making the land useless for agriculture. In 2012, a hurricane in the USA caused enormous flood damage in the densely populated and industrialised northern states, reviving the debate on the effects of climate change and the significance of coastal protection. Ironically, the name of the hurricane was "Sandy".

Dredging sand from the ocean floor leads to destruction of ecological systems in the seabed. This can have dire consequences for the entire marine ecological system, since the food chain is thrown into confusion. Fishers experience this in the declining fish population.

As already described, river sand is particularly suitable as construction material, which is why the ecosystems of rivers throughout the world are suffering as a result of the battle for sand. In India, there are news reports about the criminal scheming of the sand mafia. Gangs with mafia-like structures dig for sand illegally everywhere at rivers and on the coastlines, and then sell the sand by obscure means [79].

5 Climate change

Without a doubt, life on earth will change considerably when the reserves of fossil fuels are depleted. And very possibly, the period of adaptation to life without fossil fuels will not be a pleasant one. It is quite feasible that the collapse of energy supply will lead to a disintegration of the social order as we know it today and to mass mortality. However, should wars for resources not be fought with weapons of mass destruction, the continued existence of *Homo sapiens* as a species is unlikely to be endangered, since the biological properties of our organisms evolved in a civilisation are not dependent on fossil fuels. Until 200 years ago, all cultures existed largely without fossil fuels. However, during the short period of time starting from 1859 and reaching into the present, the continued existence not only of *Homo sapiens* as a species but also that of many other in species on our planet has come under threat – not due to the lack of fossil fuels, but through the potential effect of their combustion on the climate of our planet.

It appears that humans are capable of surviving within a wide range of temperatures. But this impression is misleading, since it is based on the fact that we focus our attention on the range of temperatures that make human existence possible.   However, there is only a very small range of temperatures that the human body can cope with comfortably without protection (clothes). We feel most comfortable living in temperatures of 25 to 27 degrees Celsius (75 to roughly 80 degrees Fahrenheit). Any temperature below this level is perceived as too cold, and above that, too hot [80].

Clothing and housing have provided humans with a certain degree of flexibility in allowing us to live at lower temperatures. Survival at temperatures below a certain living is more difficult, however, mainly because food production is lower in icy temperatures, rather than because of the direct threat of low temperatures to humans. Although humans can prevent the body from over-cooling with appropriate housing and clothing, survival in cold temperatures without easily available energy for heating is considerably more difficult.

Higher temperatures are even more critical to survival: from a temperature of 42 degrees Celsius (108°F), the protein in the blood clots. There are only limited means of compensating outdoor temperatures that lie above our body temperature. Building construction technology is practically our only means of adapting to heat and compensating temperatures above our body temperature. (Another possible way could be cooling clothing.) The body can readily survive for an indefinite period of time in temperatures that are far lower than our body temperature with suitable clothing and protective housing, be it hours, days or even years. Spending a few hours in a sauna at 95 degrees Celsius, i.e. just below boiling point, would be fatal for most people.

When we discuss human-made climate change at present, which mainly manifests as warming, our attention is (quite justifiably) mainly directed at the indirect effects, such as extreme weather conditions and droughts. But what if in ever more regions of the world the climate permanently exceeds temperatures that the human organisms can survive in? This seems unlikely in the short term, but the processes that govern the climate are so complex that we still seem a long way from truly understanding them. There are already scenarios for a self-perpetuating rise in temperature: the greenhouse effect could amplify itself in its own momentum, if, for example, millions of cubic metres of permafrost ground were to melt as a result of moderate increase in the temperature, releasing methane gas, while at the same time there would be less reflection of solar energy, due to the loss of ice at the pole caps [81].

Making a religion of the debate on climate change

The combustion emissions during the last two centuries have impacted the global climate, quite possibly leading to a rise of the average temperature due to the greenhouse effect. However, there is far too little objectivity in the debate on this matter, which, after all, concerns the future of human existence. An objective debate cannot be conducted in at atmosphere of almost religious zeal resulting in a division into "climate-change believers" and "climate-change deniers". Nor is demanding an all-inclusive political solution productive. It must be possible to question the theory of climate change without being silenced by the apostles of climate change. It must be just as possible to admit quite clearly that one considers human-made climate change a reality, without being silenced by climate-change sceptics.

There is no absolutely neutral authoritative view. The wealthiest organisations in the world, i.e. the oil and gas industries, have a strong interest in denying that there is any such thing as climate change, playing down its threat, or at least negating that it is caused by carbon emission resulting from the combustion of fossil fuels. Of course, these parties will also make a point of emphasising the potential advantages of climate warming. Among those who regard climate warming as a reality, some scientists might exaggerate a problem in the hope that they might have access to funding that could become available for them to deal with the problem. (However I sometimes wonder if scientists are not rather too conservative in their claims, not wanting to appear alarmist, which could lead to an overall underestimate of potential hardships humans may face).

In writing about this topic, I do so as an educated layperson. I am no expert on the topic. What I can say for myself is that I have little personal interest in either exaggerating the problem or negating it, since I do not benefit personally either way.

Mechanisms of human-made climate change

Let me start by briefly setting out the theory governing human-made climate change: climate change is based on a change in the balance of energy of the atmosphere, inducing a change in the thermic-radiative equilibrium of the earth, in turn causing more solar energy to be absorbed than is emitted. The atmosphere is heated, resulting in the so-called greenhouse effect.

The solar energy balance of the earth is influenced by three components:

- the Milanković cycles: these are extended-period fluctuations (over ten thousand to a hundred thousand years) of sun radiation caused by the inclination of the earth's axis and the earth's orbit;
- the part of the energy from the sunlight that the earth casts back into the atmosphere (*albedo* = lat. "white"). This is determined mainly by the surface of the oceans and the ice surfaces;
- greenhouse gases. The most significant natural greenhouse gas is water vapour, which develops naturally from evaporation. The main human-made greenhouse gases are carbon dioxide (CO_2) and methane gas (CH_4).

The most crucial relevant questions for estimating the threat of human-induced climate change are the following, to which I will respond briefly at first, and subsequently, in greater detail:

(1) Is the proportion of human-induced greenhouse emissions in the atmosphere increasing (and if so, how)?
Yes, their proportion in the atmosphere has been rising significantly since the late 19th century (mainly due to industrial activities involving combustion of fossil fuels).

(2) Do rising levels of greenhouse gases lead the earth's atmosphere to absorb more thermic-radiative solar energy than it gives off? Yes, that is the case.

(3) What are the consequences for living conditions on earth?
This question cannot be answered in a few words.

(1) Is the concentration of CO_2 in the atmosphere increasing?

If the volume of CO_2 emissions has increased so dramatically in the past 200 years, it should be possible to measure higher CO_2 levels than in former times. This is indeed the case! Certainly, it was not technically possible to measure CO_2 levels in earlier times. However, today we can measure atmospheric CO_2–content of earlier times by measuring air bubbles trapped in ice cores from ice drillings [82].

Figure 4 shows atmospheric CO_2-content in the period 1006 to 1978 A.D. Until 1750, the values lie below 290 ppm (parts per million). Towards the end of the 19th century, thus, during the time of industrialisation, the values increased to over this level of 290 ppm. Ever since, they show only one direction: upwards.

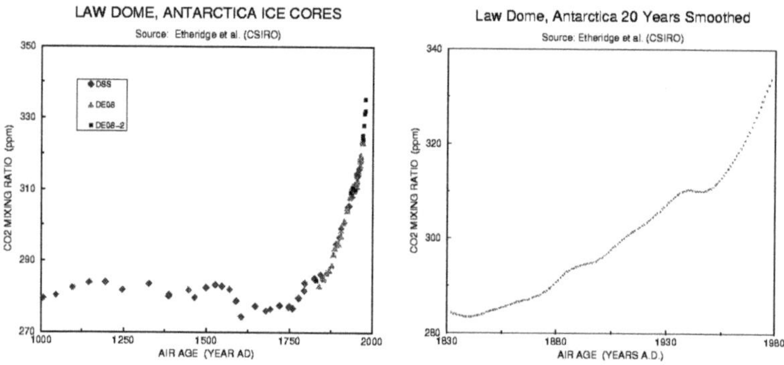

Figure 4:   Ice-core-based CO_2 measures corresponding to the period 1006-1978 [82, 83] Source: Etheridge et al. Scientific Journal of Geophysical Research 1996

In 2017, the average global CO_2 concentration was estimated at 403.3 ppm [84]. The last Antarctic reading in 1978 shown in the curve of the graph above is 333.7 ppm. If we divide the 2017 reading by that of 1978, we see an increase in the atmospheric CO_2 concentration of 21% in 40 years (403.3 / 333.7 = 1.21). That is the equivalent of about 0.5 % per year. The Al Bartlett formula allow us to calculate the doubling time:

$$CO_2 \text{ doubling time} = 70/0.5 = 140 \text{ years} \rightarrow \text{the year 2157}$$

The readings from the ice cores for the past millennium showed a constant level of about 280 ppm. If we take 280 ppm to be the normal atmospheric concentration, we see that the level induced by human activity has not yet doubled. Assuming a stable annual increase of 0.5 %, the twofold level of 560 ppm (2 x 280 ppm = 560ppm) will have been exceeded by 2083, thus in the lifetime of younger readers (reference value: 403.3 ppm in 2017, annual growth of 0.5%). In summer of 2018, the level of 410 ppm was exceeded, according to levels measured at the Mauna Observatory on Hawaii (https://www.co2.earth). So unfortunately, we have to conclude that an annual increase in atmospheric concentration of only 0.5 % tends to be optimistic, if anything, in view of levels measured in the past 10 years [85].

Just for the fun of it, let us take a short look at the direct effect on the human organism of CO_2 concentration in the air we breathe. (Since the information in books on physiology and working-place regulations is often given in percentages, this is also done for the CO_2 in table 3):

Table 3: Effect of various CO2 concentration levels in breathing air on the human organism

CO$_2$ in ppm (parts per million)	CO$_2$ in %		Year of approximate excess of level, calculated by a stable annual CO$_2$ increase of 0.5 %
280	0.028	Historical CO$_2$ concentration	
400	0.040	Current CO$_2$ concentration	2017
560	0.056	Double historical CO$_2$ concentration	2083
600	0.6	Beginning influence of CO2 level on wellbeing (desire to air a room)	2096
1.000	0.1	Limit of safe oxygen levels for human breathing, e.g. in classrooms	2199
1.500	0.15	Increased frequency of headaches, dizziness und tiredness among schoolchildren in classrooms	2280
5.000	0.5	Maximum concentration at working places	2520
15.000	1.5	Breathing time for necessary volume increases by 40 %	2740
40.000	4	CO$_2$ concentration in exhaled air	2940
50.000	5	Dizziness, headaches	2980
100.000	10	Respiratory distress, fainting, unconsciousness, death within 30 – 60 minutes	3120
200.000	20	Rapid unconsciousness, death within 5 – 10 minutes	3260

The right-hand column listing the year in which the level is exceeded, calculated by a stable CO$_2$ growth rate of 0.5 % is purely hypothetical, of course, since fossil fuels will no longer be available at some point in the future. The table is reassuring, because neither we ourselves nor our children will have to suffer direct physiological harm as a result of excess CO_2 concentration in the air. CO_2 levels in excess of 1500 ppm are regularly recorded in offices. But even levels of below 1000 ppm can impair performance or at least be perceived as uncomfortable ('Won't somebody open a window, please?) [86-88]. So, at the close of this millennium, in only in a few generations, direct health hazards can be expected.

The justified objection should be made at this point that percental growth is to be expected in biological growth processes, and that CO_2 molecules do not multiply in the same way as biological cells do. So, the increase in CO_2 levels would tend to accumulate linearly rather than exponentially.

Let us assume that the CO_2 level in the atmosphere has an incremental linear increase of 2 ppm per year (0,5 % of the 400 ppm level shown in the table above). The twofold historical CO_2 concentration of 2 x 280 ppm 560 ppm would be measured in 2097. The CO_2 concentration of 1500 ppm, resulting in an increase in headaches, dizziness and tiredness would be measured in 2807 (instead of in 2280 as shown in the 0,5 % growth model). The maximum concentration at the working place would only be reached in 4952. This means that *Homo sapiens* would have considerably more time in the evolutionary process to adapt to rising CO_2 concentrations than the purely percentual-growth model in Table 3 indicates.

The measured levels of CO_2 concentration easily lead to solid results, and this also applies to the past, when we look at the results of ice core studies. The question whether the CO_2 concentration has risen in the past 200 years can thus be answered with a definitive yes.

Ocean acidification

But perhaps not all living beings on the planet can live with such a large span of CO_2 concentration levels? Or perhaps some eco-systems react very sensitively to an increase in CO_2 concentrations? CO_2 dissolves in water: we can see this in the sparkling mineral water that is so popular in Germany. If you order water at a German restaurant, the usual question is whether it should be sparkling or not. When CO_2 dissolves in water, this results in a mild acid, carbonic acid. So, when more CO_2 dissolves in water due to increased levels of CO_2 concentration in the atmosphere, the pH level falls slightly.

Unfortunately, we have only a very vague idea of the damage that slight acidification of the oceans and seas causes to their eco-systems. Frequent mention is made of the damage done to the coral reefs resulting from a drop in pH levels, since less calcium carbonate can be formed when the acidity increases. (Corals craft their homes, the coral reefs, from calcium carbonate.) At present the pH level of the oceans is 8.1. This level is expected to decrease to 7.8 pH by the end of the century. At this level, the ocean is still slightly alkaline, but more acidic than before. (A pH level of 7 is neutral, one above that is acidic, below that, alkaline.)

Throughout history, there have been repeated changes in CO_2 concentrations, causing the corresponding changes in the oceanic pH levels. However, the current human-induced changes are taking place faster than ever before: the CO_2 concentration and the pH levels in the oceans are changing at extremely short inter-vals [89].

Apart from that, there appear to be disturbing feedback mech-anisms in the world climate involving an important autoregulato-ry role of the oceans, and which we only vaguely grasp. What is certain is that the oceans regularly absorb CO_2 (which was our point of departure regarding processes of acidification). The low-er the pH level of the water, (i.e. the more acidic it is), the more limited is the capacity to absorb CO_2. This could well lead to an increase of the CO_2 level in the atmosphere.

Possible changes in thermohaline circulation

Different saltwater density resulting from different temperatures and saline content, but also wind, weather and the Coriolis force generate the ocean currents. These thermohaline circulations consist of vertical and horizontal movements of the water masses in the seas. The system of currents forms a global oceanic circulation which links all the oceans to each other. What generates the major currents is the exchange of water between the warm equatorial regions and the cold polar regions. So it is logical that climate change cannot fail to have an effect on the circulation of the ocean currents. Another aspect that factors into this is the melting of the ice from the polar regions, which adds fresh water to the polar sea. This reduces the water density, a factor that has great influence on the vertical stratification of the water columns.

However, explanations of how the thermohaline circulation is influenced by climate change still remain speculative: we have only a rough idea about thermohaline circulation itself, and still less knowledge of which components play what role in the mechanism as a whole, or of how fragile or anti-fragile the system is.

In Europe, we have at least understood that the favourable weather conditions in northern European regions are largely a result of the Gulf Stream. The Gulf Stream is a thermohaline ocean current in which warm water from the Caribbean flows past the southern tip of Florida in a north-westerly direction, ultimately to Europe. If this water current were to become weaker, for whatever reason, or peter out, this would turn Europe into a cold region. [90]. The Gulf Stream makes Europe warmer than other places on the same geographic line of latitude: the 41° line of latitude passes through both Barcelona and New York, Frankfurt lies on the 50° latitude, and so does Newfoundland on the other side of the Atlantic. The 60° parallel north passes through the southern tip of Greenland, and, if you run your finger further to the west, you will find names such as the Labrador Sea and Hudson Bay that are associated with low temperatures and polar expeditions locked in ice in search of the Northwest Passage. In Europe, on the other hand, the 60° parallel north passes through the four capitals Oslo, Stockholm, Tallinn and Helsinki, and not least, St. Petersburg with its 5 million inhabitants and a centre of exceptional cultural and economic significance. A city as magnificent as St. Petersburg would not exist without the favourable climatic conditions resulting from Gulf Stream influence. In Canada, cities such as Yukon or Quebec with a population of a few ten-thousand inhabitants lie on the same line of latitude.

The slowing of jet streams and its effect on weather conditions

Wind is the result of different temperatures spread over large areas, which causes air to move from high-pressure to low-pressure zones until the pressures are equalised.

Jet streams are fast-flowing rivers of air in the higher troposphere caused by a combination of differences in temperature and the rotation of the earth. Cold air lies on the northern hemisphere and warm air further south in the middle regions down to the equator. The temperature gradient and differences in air pressure are compensated by air flows, which are the driving force behind the jet streams. The Coriolis Force, which results from the rotation of the earth, deflects the air movement heading to the pole to the right into the northern hemisphere and to the left into the southern hemisphere. The closer the distance to the polar regions, the stronger this deflection becomes. The jet streams generate ribbons of fast flowing air currents in the stratosphere meandering in undulating waves from north to south around the polar regions. With the warming of the earth in the Arctic in the northern hemisphere, the temperature gradients become lower and the jet stream becomes slower, resulting in an increase in the amplitudes of the wavelike air currents meandering in waves around the Pole. This moves cold air zones further south and warm air zones further north. In Europe, jet streams have a considerable influence on weather changes, resulting from the more or less rapid succession of high and low air pressure moving from the North Atlantic to Europe. Long-term stationary high-pressure zones could become more frequent as a result of jet streams slowing. In summer 2018, such a high-pressure zone remained stationary in northern Europe, resulting in uncharacteristically stable warm weather for months, even as far as into the far northern regions of Europe, causing problems for the European agricultural sector, because of the lack of rain [91]. Every year, there is a surplus of grain produced worldwide (this also goes for 2018), but there are signs of decreasing grain production worldwide in future.

(2) Does an increased CO_2 concentration result in warming of the earth's atmosphere?

The next question is whether increased CO_2 concentration will mean a warming of the earth's atmosphere. We are all familiar with the term 'greenhouse effect', a term used frequently in connection with the debate on climate change. But what exactly is it?

The most important source of energy for life on earth is the sun. The ultra-violet rays of the sun shine through the atmosphere onto the earth and warm the earth's surface and water. This supply of energy is the basis of life. Some of the heat radiation is reflected as infrared rays. This prevents the surface of the earth from overheating. Without the atmosphere and its greenhouse gases, nothing would obstruct these infrared rays from being reflected back into space. Without atmosphere, it would be considerably colder on earth. Life as we know it would be virtually impossible.

Greenhouse gases reflect some of the infrared rays back to the surface of the earth. The most significant greenhouse gases are water vapour (H_2O), carbon dioxide (CO_2), methane (CH_4), nitrous oxide (N_2O) and ozone (O_3). Furthermore, chlorofluorocarbons (CFCs) should be mentioned. Although there are only small concentrations of these gases in the atmosphere, they tend to remain in the atmosphere for a long time and some of them have a tremendously high greenhouse potential, apart from their commonly known destructive effect on the ozone layer. CFCs are also commonly termed 'Montreal gases', after the 1989 Montreal

Protocol banning their use worldwide in order to protect the ozone layer.

The concentration in the atmosphere of these greenhouse gases affect the energy and temperature levels on earth. There have always been such changes. In the chapter on mass extinction you will find several estimated levels of carbon dioxide and oxygen concentration at various points into time over one hundred million years ago. Whenever there was an increase in greenhouse gases, this was usually accompanied by a corresponding warming of the earth. This was the case in the Permian-Triassic Extinction, also known as the so-called 'Great Dying', when the most extensive mass extinction of complex life ever known took place. However, the transformation processes took place over an extremely long period. Even the geologists' estimate of a very rapid increase of CO_2 and methane gas of volcanic origin, which is thought to have been one main reason for the mass extinction in Permian-Triassic extinction, extended over a period of several hundreds of thousands of years. The CO_2 content in the atmosphere has risen from about 280 ppm in the pre-industrialisation age to over 400 ppm – an increase of 43 % in a mere two hundred years!

In 1988, the United Nations Intergovernmental Panel on Climate Change (IPCC) was founded. In 1990, this institution published a first-time comprehensive summary of the scientific findings on climate change. Further similar publications followed in 1995, 2001, 2007 and 2014. The next world-climate report has been announced for 2022. These reports also include summaries of the levels of concentration of greenhouse gases in the atmosphere, based on readings of the atmosphere and ice core drillings.

Table 4 below is based on figures taken from the world climate report of 2014. It provides an overview of the development of the levels of the four most significant greenhouse gases, namely CO_2, methane (CH_4), nitrous oxide (N_2O) and CFCs (chlorofluorocarbons), which together account for almost 99 % of the greenhouse effect quantified by RF (radiative forcing).

Table 4: Greenhouse potential of CO_2, methane (CH_4), nitrous oxide (N_2O) and CFC, their greenhouse concentration in 1750, 2005, and 2011, and their proportional significance in the greenhouse effect in percentage of RF (radiative forcing)

	Green-house poten-tial	Concentration in ppm ppb or ppt			RF in W/m²		Percentage of RF	
		pre-1750	2005	2011	2005	2011	2005	2011
CO_2 (ppm)	1	280	379	391	1.66	1.82	62.3 %	64.3 %
CH_4 (ppb)	28	730	1774	1803	0.47	0.48	17.8 %	17.0 %
N_2O (ppb)	298	270	319	324	0.16	0.17	6.1 %	6.0 %
CFC (ppt)*		0	1193.6	1196.4	0.331	0.330	12.5 %	11.6 %
Montreal*		0	1024.6	983.4	0.33	0.33		
Others								
Total					2.64	2.83		

ppm = parts per million, ppb = parts per billion, ppt = parts per trillion

*   Montreal gases. Sum of CFCs, HCFCs, CH3CCI3, CCI4 (English term in IPCC Report of 2014)

** Montreal gases excluding chlorofluoromethane (HCFC-22), i.e. gases affected by the Montreal Protocol

The greenhouse potential of a gas indicates its greenhouse effect in CO_2 equivalents per century. Methane, for example, has a greenhouse potential of 25. This indicates that 100 years after its release into the atmosphere, the contribution to the greenhouse effect of one kilogram of methane is 25 times that of a kilogram of CO_2. Sometimes, the greenhouse potential is given for 20 years. This figure is higher (for methane, 84), since the initial level emitted into the atmosphere after 20 years is higher than after 100 years.

When looking at the high level of other greenhouse gases, the question could arise why we want to reduce the CO_2 content, when the greenhouse effect of a litre of CO_2 is so small (compared to methane, for example). Well, the answer is that it is the overall volume that makes the difference. No other anthropogenic emission (i.e. related to or resulting from humans) of any other greenhouse gas is higher than that of CO_2. In 2017, more than 40 gigatons of this gas were emitted due to combustion of fossil fuels. On considering the table depicted above, one should not be deceived by the high absolute figures for methane: the CO_2 levels are given in ppm and the methane levels in ppb (which is a factor of 10^3 lower).

In order to understand the combined level of greenhouse gases emitted into the atmosphere and their greenhouse potential, the figure for radiative forcing (RF) must be considered. Carbon dioxide emission since 1750 contributed to about 64.3 % of the greenhouse effect in 2011, while the methane emission was much lower, a mere 17 %. Methane is also produced anthropogenically, especially by cattle farming and rice production. Since 1750, the level of methane emissions into the atmosphere has more than doubled. According to estimates given in the IPCC World Climate Report, almost half of the annual methane emissions are anthropogenic [89].

According to a climate-catastrophe scenario, it is feared that huge volumes of methane gas will be emitted from melting permafrost, which is a process that has already been observed in the far north in the past decade. An example of such a process with a particularly dramatic impact could be observed in 2017 in Siberia, when massive gas bubbles were formed on the earth's surface from the trapped methane gas [92]. If the percentage of methane of RF decreased slightly between 2005 and 2011, this simply means that the increase in CO2 concentration in the atmosphere was even greater than the methane increase. At the same time, the fact that there has been an increase in the concentration of both gases cannot be ignored.

Measures to reduce the greenhouse effect

What can be established is that only CFCs have decreased, a positive effect of the Montreal Protocol banning CFCs worldwide. The greenhouse potential of CFCs varies, but, depending on the particular gas type, can constitute several thousand CO_2 equivalents. For trichlorofluoromethane (CFC-11), which contributes the largest share of RF among CFCs, the greenhouse potential is approximately a 5000 CO_2 equivalent. Some still more potent greenhouse gases have a negligible greenhouse potential, since their volume is very small.

The Montreal Protocol, which was mainly agreed to protect the ozone layer, thus also has a positive impact on climate protection. The concentration of Montreal gases decreased measurably between 2004 and 2011, but only if the chlorodifluoromethane (HCFC-22) levels are ignored. While HCFC-22 is also harmful to the ozone layer, it is less so than CFC-11 (trichlorofluoromethane). HCFC-22 quickly became a widely used replacement refrigerant. Chlorofluoromethane is illegal in the EU and the USA, but its use as a refrigerant agent has risen significantly in developing and threshold countries [93]. The greenhouse potential of HCFC-11 (chlorofluoromethane) is 1810 CO_2 equivalents. That of CFC-11 (trichlorofluoromethane) is 4750 CO_2 equivalents. The report in 2018 of violations of the Montreal Protocol of one (or several) not yet identified institutions that illegally emitted CFC-11 should thus be taken very seriously [94, 95], since they contribute to the greenhouse effect on the one hand, and on the other hand damage the ozone layer (which is why this gas was forbidden in the Montreal Protocol).

But is it really enough to reduce our emissions? Even if we were to succeed in preventing the emission of all greenhouse gases, this would not stop the process of climate warming: we have to work under the assumption that the process of climate change will be continued by the greenhouse gases that are already in the atmosphere. Of course it is vital to reduce greenhouse gases. The Montreal Protocol led to measurable reductions of CFC emissions and thus is a prime example for the sense of global climate agreements and of their effectiveness. This is also a counter-argument to fatalistic voices that consider the political agreement on climate change to be senseless and superfluous.

Yet, what is if we are already beyond the point (without knowing it) at which a climate catastrophe can still be avoided by a reduction of emissions? In this case, we can only hope for innovations that make it possible to remove the greenhouse gases from the atmosphere. How this can be done is a mystery to me. And: Would we then really have the process under control, or simply be replacing one catastrophic development with another? What we should hope for in any case is that the global climate is really as resilient and anti-fragile as some climate-change sceptics proclaim. (For an explanation of the term 'antifragile' see [96].) Planting trees instead of chopping them down all over the world would be a good start and cause no harm.

Other processes driving the greenhouse effect

However, currently even a reduction of the greenhouse gas emissions is showing no success. And then there are mechanisms that may even accelerate the greenhouse effect. The threat posed by the emission of methane gas from the melting permafrost has already been mentioned.

As polar ice thaws, the dynamics of climate warming can increase in intensity. When the area covered by ice is reduced, potent reflectors for sunlight are lost, leading to more solar energy being stored in the sea and the atmosphere. We have to assume that we can hardly perceive most of the stored energy at the moment, since this occurs in the oceans. At present, we can only vaguely imagine the effects of warming and acidification of the oceans on the aquatic ecosystems. However, there is some fear that when and if marine phytoplankton becomes extinct, the basis of the food pyramid of the oceans will be destroyed, constituting a threat to the entire marine ecosystem, from plankton to whale [97, 98]. At the same time, all plants containing chlorophyll and phytoplankton are CO_2 absorbers, and they, too, will no longer exist. Optimistic voices point out that global warming and organic carbon input will result in an increase in phytoplankton, and that this will act as a regulator, possibly making the global climate system more resilient. It is certainly the case that phytoplankton plays a key role in the CO_2 content of the oceans and by extension of the atmosphere [99].

It is quite possible that the true extent of energy absorbed by the oceans is greater than we can perceive at present, since the process of melting the ice requires a lot of energy. If you heat a pot filled with ice and stir it all the time, the ice melts, but the temperature of the water does not rise above freezing point, as long as there is enough ice to transform the thermal energy into melt energy (or enthalpy of fusion, as it is termed). Only when there is only very little or no ice left does the water warm up, but then it does so very quickly. If this (admittedly very simplified) analogy of water in a pot is transferred to the oceans, we can expect that after the ice meltdown, there will be a great rise in temperature, possibly in a short span of time. Apart from that, excessive ocean warming, particularly in shallow continental shelf seas, could result in more frozen methane being released from the sea floor. A third effect of ice thaw is that this will result in rising sea levels. Fourthly, ice thaw could dissolve fresh-water reserves contained in the ice.

As already mentioned, plants containing chlorophyll can transform CO_2 in the process of photosynthesis and can thus extract carbon dioxide from the atmosphere. It cannot be said with any certainty that greening the planet will reverse the road that our atmosphere is taking. But at least it is no mistake to cover large areas of land with plants and at least to prevent vegetation on earth from being reduced. Unfortunately, the increase of the world population and the corresponding appetite for land of the *Homo sapiens* make it rather unlikely that we are heading for a greener planet. One of the most-used land clearance methods is that of slash-and-burn, which is not only used to clear land initially so that it can be cultivated, but is regularly used to burn the dry grass in dry savannas during the dry period, for example, also on areas that are not used for agricultural purposes. Slash-and- burn releases the CO_2 in the biomass, thus also contributing to climate warming.

Is the Arctic ice really melting?

I have already explained what effects ice thawing can have: the reduced white areas of reflection increase the greenhouse effect, since less thermo-energy from the sun is reflected back into the atmosphere. At the same time, the thawing fresh-water ice results in rising sea levels.

Images from satellites allow the extent of Arctic ice to be observed well. However, this data has only been available since 1979. Such short periods of observation do not allow historical comparisons. Contrary to ice drillings such as described above, where data can be collected on the composition of the atmosphere over long periods, estimating the extent of the Arctic ice in the past is speculative and based on old reports and sea charts. Attempting to estimate ice extent in pre-human times is even more difficult.

Seasonal fluctuations can be seen clearly on the satellite images, a maximum being reached in the Arctic winter und a minimum in the Arctic summer. Figure 5 shows the Arctic ice extent in the month of June between 1979 and 2018. The ice extent decreased from about 12.5 million kilometres to 10.7 million kilometres in this period (a decrease of 14.4%). The gradient of the regression line corresponds to a decline of 3.7 % per decade.

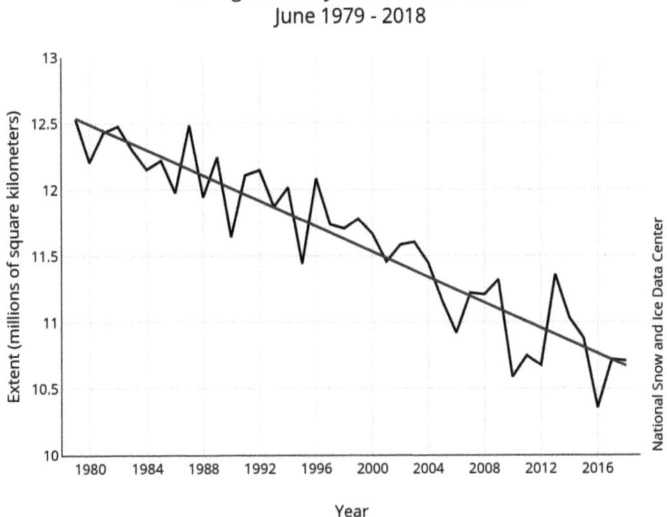

Figure 5:   **Average monthly Arctic Sea extent June 1979 – 2018. [100] Source: (US) National Snow and Ice Data Center (http://nsidc.org/), University of Colorado, Boulder**

It is not only the total area of the sea ice that is of significance, but also its quality. Young ice from the most recent winter season is thin, fragile and melts more easily. Thin ice allows the sun to penetrate it, warming the water below the ice. The more robust "old" ice, however, is decreasing every year. Beaufort Sea, located north of Canada and Alaska on the far edges of the Arctic Ocean, has large areas of robust old ice, i.e. ice that does not melt in summer. However, it is precisely this ice expanse that has decreased significantly in the past thirty years.

The Northwest Passage, the famed sea route from the Pacific Ocean to the Atlantic Ocean, motivating North Sea expeditions to find it in the 18th and 19th century, can meanwhile be crossed in the summer months. This has reduced the seaway from Europe to Japan (Rotterdam – Tokyo) from 21,000 km to 15,900 km. The

Northeast Passage has also been ice-free since summer 2007, opening the shortest route of 14,100 km between Rotterdam and Tokyo. The closer the shipping route is to the North Pole, the shorter the two North Passages. In August 2008 the two North passages were ice-free at the same time for several weeks, and in the years after, the North Passage was ice-free in late summer. In summer 2017, a liquid gas tanker was able to cross the Northeast Passage to South Korea without requiring an icebreaker [101].

This is without question a worrying development for the global climate. The reduced ice in the North Sea will lead to an economic zone of North-Sea countries being established, from which mainly Canada, the USA, Russia, Norway and Denmark will benefit. The extent of the looming conflict about who has the right to exploit which oil or gas field can only be imagined. But perhaps the participation of the USA in the North Sea Economic Zone will serve to mitigate the feeling of panic arising in the USA regarding a consolidation of the Eurasian economic zone. Or we will slide into the next conflict over natural resources, this time in the North Sea. A military conflict would certainly be a catastrophe for the ecosystem of the North Sea.

To return to our question, whether the Arctic ice is really thawing: Yes, this is the case at present. Is this bad news? Possibly.

Is the Antarctic ice melting?

Is the Antarctic the counterpart in the south to the northern Arctic, and the processes similar, only six months apart? No, it's not as easy as that. Let us start with the most obvious differences: there are polar bears in the Arctic (North Pole), and penguins in the Antarctic (South Pole). During the winter months of the northern hemisphere, it is summer in the southern hemisphere. The South Pole is situated in the middle of a continent with a land mass of its own, whereas the North Pole lies in a (still) frozen inland sea (whose ice surface is shrinking) and is surrounded by the northern limits of Eurasia and North America.

Ice swims in water, since it has a lower density than water. There is no change in the water level when swimming ice melts (otherwise a glass filled to the rim with ice cubes would overflow when the ice thaws). When we speak of the danger of sea levels rising, we are actually interested in the land ice. In the Antarctic, there are huge masses of water frozen as land ice. If this ice were to melt, this would indeed lead to rising sea levels.

The apparently trivial question whether the land ice masses in the Antarctic will increase or decrease in the long run is certainly important; however, it is not easy to answer. Because of the humid coastal climate at the Antarctic, there is a lot of snow. This can increase the volume of frozen water in the Antarctic. However, ice currents cause the Antarctic glacial ice to flow toward the sea, where floating ice sheets are carved out of the glaciers. At the same time, water masses that have previously evaporated fall as snow on the land mass of the Antarctic.

If the transfer of ice from the land to the sea via the ice currents were in balance with the ice transferred from the sea inland through snowfall, no change in the sea level could be expected from the Antarctic. While snowfall tends to be a continuous process, the formation of ice shelves can be very spectacular. With climate warming in the southern hemisphere, there is more water vaporization. This should lead to an increase in the snowfall on the Antarctic continent, but also increase the volume of ice sheets lost on its borders. The volume of ice water-turnover would thus be higher – but will this result in a net gain or loss of Antarctic ice?

The sea ice in the Antarctic can be observed well via satellite images. In winter it expands in all directions around the Antarctic landmass, but in summer it thaws almost completely right up to the periphery of the continental land mass. This means that the sea ice in the Antarctic is mainly young ice, not several years old. The seasonal fluctuations since the satellite images became available in 1979 are typical – and similar every year. An increase or decrease of the sea ice mass around the Antarctic between 1979 and 2018 is not as clearly visible as the decrease of sea ice at the North Pole.

In order to assess whether the land ice will increase or decrease, it is necessary to assess the volume, i.e. to assess how thick the ice is, since the ice surface is fixed by the Antarctic landmass. There are studies that have attempted to estimate this. But, due to the complex mechanisms of increase and decrease in the volume of Antarctic ice, it is difficult to measure. This is why, at first view, the results of the studies do not seem as clear for the Antarctic as they are for the Arctic. However, it does appear that there is a tendency towards ice shrinkage in the Antarctic which would result in an increased sea level (land ice melt!) [102]. Studies published in 2018 appear to not only confirm the hypothesis that the Antarctic is melting, but also that this process is accelerating and that the rate of shrinkage has tripled in the past decade. The annual ice reduction since 2012 is estimated to be 219 billion tons of ice per year. The ice melt in the first decade of this millennium was an estimated 73 billion tons of ice [103]. Not only in the West Antarctic are the glaciers thawing, but in the East Antarctic, too, large volumes of ice are thawing and ice sheets are breaking away from the glaciers [104].

Is the sea level rising?

It has been normal procedure for centuries to measure the levels of seas and rivers locally on their coasts and banks. Such measurements are valuable records of local processes and serve as a basis for corresponding local action. Since the sea levels fluctuate enormously in various regions at various times, (just think of the tides at some North Sea coasts that cause the level to fluctuate by several meters), average changes in ocean levels as a whole, which are mostly only a few millimetres measured over years, are difficult to assess. Nevertheless, the sea levels for the 20th century were estimated to have risen by about 17 cm in 100 years [105].

Only since the advent of satellite technology in the 1990s has it been possible to measure global sea levels. These statistics suggest that the rise in the sea levels globally was 3.2 mm/year (which would add up to 32 cm in 100 years) between 1993 and 2012, thus nearly twice the level of previous calculations of the water levels. This could be due to inter-decade fluctuations, or – somewhat more worrying – an indication of more rapidly rising levels.

The results show great annual fluctuations that vary considerably region by region, both with regard to sea levels and their increase or decrease: in some regions there was a considerable rise, while in others the level even fell. The areas with the strongest rise were found to be the western Pacific regions around Indonesia and particularly west of the Philippines [105-107]. The regional differences are the result of wind, currents, wave propagation and seabed profile, tectonic profile changes and the moon's gravity [108]. (The increasingly serious inundations in the Indonesian capital Jakarta are probably due to overuse and volume depletion of groundwater aquifers leading to a "sinking" city rather than to global sea level rise.)

The statistics suggest that generally, the sea level is rising. This is consistent with the expected increase in the water volumes due to thawing land ice.

If the rise in the sea level remains constant, i.e. a rise at the same pace, as was the case for the 20th century, a further rise by about 20cm can be expected by the end of the 21st century. However, with increased thawing of land ice, the volume of fresh water flowing into the seas will increase, resulting in a still higher rise of sea levels.

Consequences of a rising sea level and extreme storms

The effect of a rise in sea levels can be imagined very clearly. The areas that would be affected potentially can easily be identified: the low-lying coastal regions. These usually have a dense population. The estuary areas of large rivers with correspondingly extensive deltas would be particularly threatened.

A direct effect of rising sea levels can be flooding, while indirectly, salinization of the ground water and the coastal ground could result. The level of the deltas, which even now lie at almost sea level, would fall even more: for one, weirs prevent sand from flowing to the deltas, for another, sand is exploited for use as building material, not to forget the falling ground water levels [109]. One example of a very fragile area in this respect is the Nile Delta in Egypt, which lies a mere two meters above sea level and is one of the oldest agricultural areas in human history. The population density in this area can be up to 1600 persons per square kilometre.

Egypt has limited space for resettlement, since even now the population of Egypt, now 100 million people, is concentrated on a thin strip left and right of the Nile River and in the Nile Delta. Parts of the country far removed from the Nile are desert regions and practically inhabitable. River deltas offer outstanding farming conditions, since the alluvial sludge provides fertile soil and irrigation is easily available.

In Bangladesh, flooding in the monsoon season is a recurrent natural catastrophe even now. With a rising sea level, not only will the water masses increase during flooding, but the damages caused by greater and permanent salt-water flooding will also ruin the lands and ground water: rice, the staple diet in Bangladesh, will not grow in salt-brine fields. The present population of Bangladesh is about 165 million people, living just above sea level in an area of 147,570 km^2. The population density is 1111 persons per km^2. This makes Bangladesh the most densely populated territorial state in the world. Although population growth has meanwhile fallen considerably, it was still calculated to be 1.1 % in 2016. Accordingly, assuming stable growth, doubling time of the population is 64 years (70/1.1 = 64). At the same time, large-scale loss of the living space and arable land due to flooding and salination of the soil is expected in the coming decades. Some parts of the country could be lost permanently to the sea. Ultimately, tens of millions of people will look to another country for living space. India has already secured its border to Bangladesh with walls and fences.

The term "rising sea levels" sounds to me like a gradual process during which the sea level rises and the water slowly creeps its way up to the shoreline. This mechanistic idea is not completely wrong, of course, and when the sea level rises by several meters, it is obvious that low-lying coastal regions will sink below sea level. Dykes are constructed to prevent this. This has been common practice in Holland for centuries now. But what the Dutch are also aware of is that the dykes must not only be slightly higher than sea level, but that they must withstand extreme flooding to protect the land and people.

When we feel the results of rising sea levels in the next few decades, then most probably indirectly as the result of extreme weather situations. In 2005, the fierce hurricane Katrina led to large-scale flooding in the delta of the Mississippi river in the south-west of the USA, even though the normal sea level was still several meters under the ridges of the dyke line. The Americans have since constructed very sophisticated coastal protection systems. However, every engineer finds it a nightmare to erect a building foundation in the geologically unstable muddy ground of deltas. It is a very complex undertaking to construct water protective barriers when they are to have a solid anchorage, since this requires going down deep into the ground before hitting on solid ground.

Not only storms, but also earthquakes with tsunamis can cause flooding, such as the tsunami on 22 March 2011 that hit Japan and that of 26 December 2004 in the Indian Ocean, which now remain in collective memory. But Europe is not safe from tsunamis. On 1 November 1755, the Portuguese capital Lisbon was destroyed by a tsunami.

When considering the effect of thawing glaciers in this chapter, the "Storegga event" is a case in point. About 8000 years ago, at a time of forceful glacier melting, there was a case of a large-scale slide of the glacier shelf in the North Atlantic on the Norwegian coast, the so-called 'Storegga slide'. The huge undersea movement caused an enormous tsunami, traces of which can still be found on the Atlantic coastlines of countries in northern Europe [110].

Similar events could result from the loss of land ice. The weight of land ice in the Antarctic or in Greenland has pushed the land mass several hundred meters into the earth's mantle. When this ice thaws, the land mass will gradually rise [111] (post-glacial rebound). When the land mass rises, this causes active geological structures, such as volcanoes and magma layers to rise, too. Added to that, the rise of land masses can cause further geological surface tension, resulting in faults and releasing magma, due to the motion of the earth's mantle. In a few words: it seems plausible that land ice loss will result in geological activity. This could lead to volcanoes erupting, to earth and sea quakes and tsunamis.

The higher the sea levels, the greater the impact of storms and floods. When I sit in the bath and slowly let water run into the tub, I won't flood the bathroom as long as I lie quietly in the water, even if the water level is only just below the top rim of the bath. But even when the water is far below the top rim, if I move a lot, turn around, sink my head into the bath or wave my legs wildly, the water will spill over the top of the bath. My bathroom will be the scene of a flooding catastrophe of a magnitude that increases in direct proportion to how wild my movements become and the initial water level in the bathtub.

There is no need to look in far-off countries in order to identify threatened areas. Hamburg, for example, lies six meters above sea level. Although it is about 80 kilometres from the North Sea, the tides are clearly perceptible in the Elbe river running through Hamburg. From my office I have a view southwards over of the Elbe river to the dockyards of Hamburg Harbour, the third largest in Europe after Antwerp and Rotterdam. Even as a landlubber from southern Germany I am able to see whether the tide of the

Elbe is high or low. The tides need to be considered for large vessels with draught when they arrive or depart.

In mid-February 1962, the stormy and rainy west-wind weather since the previous December, which had soaked the dykes surged to full-fledged gale force weather blowing from the north-west into the German Bight ('Deutsche Bucht'). If you look at a map of the Elbe estuary, you will see that this forms a funnel opening towards the North Sea. The hurricane Vincent thus blew directly into the funnel of the Elbe estuary [112].

The north-west winds that blew prior to the hurricane prevented the midday high tide in the Elbe from flowing back into the North Sea during the following low tide. The gale-force wind that blew into the Elbe estuary increased the flood to a storm flood. The dykes along the entire German North Sea coast were badly damaged, agricultural land was flooded with sea water. Nevertheless, the German federal state Schleswig-Holstein, which extends from the lower course of the Elbe River and the state of Hamburg northward to Denmark and thus occupies the southern third of the Jutland Peninsula, experienced material damage only. The inhabitants of the coastal region had learnt to live with unfavourable weather conditions and organised costal defences at community level, so that there was a commonly felt sense of responsibility and everyone knew what to do for personal protection and for the protection of houses, cattle and the dykes.

It was quite a different matter in Hamburg with its 1.8 million inhabitants, where the gale-force winds had forced the masses of water to flow. Here, the bomb holes in the dykes had been filled makeshift with rubble after the war, the inner dykes were much too steep, and buildings and factories were situated in the dykes. The dykes broke in over 60 places. All the Hamburg urban districts south of the Elbe river and lower-lying regions towards the North Sea were flooded. The floods caused 315 deaths, and tens of thousands of people were faced with homelessness [112].

Hamburg has since given flood control considerably higher priority. Documentaries on the consequences of a worldwide rise in the sea level show blue sea in the place where Hamburg currently lies. Worrying.

The same documentaries show Holland, too, having sunk into the sea. No other country has developed greater competency regarding water management and coastal protection than Holland. Approximately 25 percent of Holland's land mass lies below sea level. The Dutch nevertheless manage to provide effective protection against storm floods and even to gain more land. This is not only achieved by increasing the height of the dykes, even if this is a (very important) part of the Dutch coastal protection mechanism. What the Dutch also have is a sophisticated water management system, which they have had for hundreds of years now. The one purpose of the picturesque windmills that have been built since the 16th century in the Netherlands is their use as grain mills, but their chief purpose has always been for the wind-driven pumps to drain the low-lying tract of land enclosed by dykes, the polders, of water. The purpose is thus not only to construct flood barriers, but to drain the masses of water into specific canals, the polders, while keeping damage at a minimum, this also being the case in extreme situations such as storm flooding. Distinguishing between natural and sea water is crucial, of course, since the fertile Dutch soil combined with plenty of natural water has made Holland one of the most fertile regions in the world and one of the largest agricultural producers worldwide. It is therefore essential to keep the agricultural and cattle-grazing land free of salt from seawater. With rising sea levels (and sinking coastal cities due to ground water depletion), the Dutch know-how in dyke and coastal protection, and indeed of water management, is becoming a much sought-after commodity.

Droughts

It is easy to grasp the fact that the catastrophic effects of storms with flooding are intensified by a climate-induced rise in the sea level when considering the pure mechanisms of this phenomenon (think of the bathtub example). The potential impact on the living conditions in the interior is much more complex. It cannot be said generally that climate change will result in droughts everywhere – at least not as long as the global temperatures do not rise to the level that heat damage comes into play. For certain regions, global warming can even be advantageous: for example, if the climate warms up towards the north providing regions with arable land, this could be very beneficial for Canada, Alaska, the Scandinavian countries and Russia (provided the thermohaline circulation remains stable).

Regional droughts and failed harvests could be a threat, however, particularly in already temporarily dry regions with a high population growth. Droughts and food shortage need not necessarily be connected to global warming; they can also be the result of local environmental destruction and overuse of the land. Lake Chad at the conjunction of Chad, Cameroon, Niger and Nigeria, provides the livelihood for about 38 million people. Because it lacks drainage, there has always been great fluctuation in its water levels, depending on the amount of water that reaches it from its tributaries or rain. In the past few decades, however, its water levels have shrunk from about 25,000 km^2 in the 1960s to about 4,800 km^2 in 2014. At the time of writing (December 2018), the lake has a surface area of 13,500 km^2. Meanwhile, many people are moving southwards from the poor Borno Province in Nigeria, some even becoming members of the militant group Boko Haram [113]. The loss of grazing areas and farmland and the resulting exodus of people from such areas to other regions have led to conflicts with the original population in these areas and between various land users, such as cattle and agricultural farmers [114]. Whether this shrinkage of Chad Lake is a result of the global climate change cannot be said with certainty, since the local climate is characterised by great fluctuation in precipitation.

The Chad basin encompasses four climate zones: the extremely dry Sahara climate (< 100mm rainfall per year), the Sahel-Sahara climate with 100 – 399 mm of rainfall per year, the Sahel-Sudanese climate with 400 – 599 mm rainfall per year, and the Sudanese-Guinean zone with 600 – 1500 mm per year [115]. As can be imagined, small fluctuations in the proportional distribution of these climate zones over a year or a decade result in great differences in the water supply to the lake. Only 100 years ago, in 1908, the Chad Lake experienced greater shrinkage than is the case at present and had dwindled to mere marshland with two small basins [116]. Since Lake Chad has no discharge, the volume of water can only be reduced by evaporation and water extraction. In 1908, the extraction was certainly lower than it is today. In summary, I cannot say whether the lower water level in this region is partly caused by global climate change or is to be explained completely by the enormous pressure from the population with over-exploitation of the lake and local environmental destruction.

There are regular periods of drought in East Africa. Every few years there are years with low rainfall. This is thought to be the result of an "ocean-swing" between East Africa and Indonesia. Warm water on the East African coast and cold water on that of Indonesia result in rain; when the water on the East African coast is cold, the rainfall tends to be sparse [117]. It is quite conceivable that these weather conditions are exacerbated by changes in the global climate. However, during the famine in 2017, mismanagement with too little food storage in proportion to the high population pressure also contributed to this shortage. Somalia, Yemen and South Sudan are war-torn countries; the misery in these countries is particularly severe.

(3) What are the consequences of climate change for the living conditions on earth?

The question of how an increased global temperature will affect the living conditions of human life is a speculative one. Some scientists, such as the American ecology professor Guy McPherson (https://guymcpherson.com) fear that the entire earth will soon become inhabitable for humans and that humans will exist only a few years more. Should you read these lines in 2050 or later, Guy McPherson was not right, at least in view of the dynamics and comprehensiveness of the extinction of human life.

If global climate changes do not result in rapid global destruction, the question is how the living conditions will change in various regions and climate zones. It is not necessarily the case that every change in every place will mean deterioration. Local living conditions may even improve. It is quite possible that fertile and comfortably habitable zones will extend to the north, offering North America and Asia huge new arable areas.

Do we know too little about human-made climate change to talk about possible measures?

We know for sure that the atmospheric content of greenhouse gases has increased significantly in the past 200 years. As already mentioned, the measured CO_2 concentrations have risen from about 280 ppm before the industrial age to above 400 ppm today. We can also observe an increase in the greenhouse gas methane, due to thawing of the permafrost ground and cattle breeding and of nitrogen from combustion processes. Only CFCs, which include extremely potent greenhouses gases, are on the decline, thanks to the Montreal Protocol. However, this reduction is threated by illegal CFC production and emissions [95].

We were also able to objectivize decrease in the Arctic sea ice and have strong indications that the Arctic and Antarctic land ice masses are thawing. There are signs of increases in sea levels from summaries of water level records in the 20th century and satellite data since the early 1990s.

Our knowledge of physics and chemistry allow us to deduce from the rise in CO_2 levels in the atmosphere that the greenhouse effect will result in (1) more solar energy being stored in the atmosphere, leading to an expected increase in temperature, and in (2) a slight reduction in the pH content of the seas due to carbon dioxide absorption. Changes in temperature in the seas and the resulting changes in water density will lead to changes in the extremely complex thermohaline circulations, which we only vaguely understand. The median global temperature of the earth has risen from 13.6 in 1850 to 14.6 degrees Celsius today, the rise in the past fifty years being more pronounced, showing an exponential curve upwards. Since the earth's temperature has changed time and again in the history of the Earth, it cannot be excluded that changes in temperature might be a natural phenomenon. However, it seems plausible that humankind has also contributed to the rise in temperature in an inconceivably short period of time (200 years).

Of course, we cannot forecast the precise development in the earth's climate and what consequences this will have. But does this justify a rejection of the measures as introduced in the Kyoto Protocol and extended in the Paris Climate Agreement and not to take further steps towards climate protection?

A large proportion of the Establishment of the Republican Party in the USA, the most powerful nation in the world, rejects the idea that climate change is induced by humans or at least is of the opinion that measures to protect the environment should not be discussed as long as it is not proven that humans are responsible for changing the climate in such a way that humankind is moving towards a climate catastrophe [118].

Viewed in terms of scientific philosophy, it is impossible to fulfil the demand to prove a process scientifically, at least if one follows the line of contention of Karl Poppers, who as an important member of the Mont Pèlerin Society, should be known in neoliberal circles. His hypothesis is that scientific research looks for falsification by discarding a zero hypothesis (the assumption that there is no effect). We can only but gather evidence against the zero hypothesis that everything will remain as it was (which corresponds to a zero effect) and conclude that there is indeed some change (in our case, there is climate warming). This is something that multitudes of scientific experts on climate have done.

The fact that most members of the Republican establishment are financed by money from American corporate groups is only mentioned in passing. At least it can be said of President Donald Trump that he was already a billionaire when he entered the election campaign and was thus reasonably independent of funding [119]. But the reality is that policies are absolutely in alignment with the tastes of the powerful military-industrial complex. Trump's former foreign secretary of state Rex Tillerson took office in his position in the American administration directly after being on the executive board of Exxon Mobile. The planned budget distribution of the Trump Administration suggests that especially the big players in the military-industrial complex will enjoy growing profits, while the policies on the conservation of human natural living space and, generally, social policies will have to take a back seat [120]. For the American Environmental Protection Agency, whose budget was cut to a third in 2018, a "refocusing on core activities" will continue in 2019. Accordingly, the climate change research program is to be completely abandoned [121]. These developments geared towards the interests of the military-industrial complex should actually lead to strong opposition in a democracy. Apparently the process of dismantling civil society and its disempowerment has made such headway that the oligarchic-plutocratic course of catering to the profit interests of the armament, financial and oil industries is irreversible [122].

6   Human impact on other species

In the early 21st century, the earth's human population is probably larger than any other big land mammal population has ever been before. While plants containing chlorophyll interact directly with the CO_2 via photosynthesis in the atmosphere and determine the climate. On the other hand, practically no other animal species has changed the ecosystems of the earth and its flora and fauna more than humans.

Some livestock species have reproduced very successfully in the human environment and dominate the animal populations in numbers. However, the life of the individual domesticated animal in the human agrarian factories seems to be somewhat dismal. The populations of numerous other species, i.e. wild animals, have generally been on the decline or have even collapsed as a result of human impact. Many animals are becoming extinct, others have only a small residual population. If there are only a few remaining animals from a formerly widely distributed species, the genetic diversity of this species is reduced. When the populations grow in size once again, all the subsequent generations of this species originate from this small residual population. If the residual population was too small, the lack of genetic diversity can become an existential threat for the species. The phenomenon of reduced genetic diversity due to near-extinction has come to be known as "genetic bottleneck".

Humankind as an existential threat to other species

Humankind contributes directly and indirectly to the extinction of species: indirectly through environmental changes and destruction of entire ecosystems, directly by hunting. Mainly large animals are affected by direct hunting. Firstly, they serve humans as a direct resource for food, clothes and utility objects. Secondly, large animals require large spaces to survive, which means that they compete with humans or are reduced by human intervention. Thirdly, the number of large animals is restricted without any human interaction. One can imagine encountering thousands of small animals on a small island, but only few elephants in the limited space. The sea as a habitat is less restricted, which is probably why the largest animals on earth, namely whales, live there. Modern whaling has decimated most whale species to the extent that some whales already now find it difficult to find a suitable partner for mating. Particularly after the harpoon canon was invented in 1863, the whale population was reduced rapidly. In contrast to land mammals such as cattle species, whales cannot be domesticated and thus cannot be bred. Cattle is bred to cover the human need for beef and milk, which is why the populations of cattle has risen enormously throughout the world. Whales cannot be bred for their whale oil or whalebone, which is why their natural stocks have dwindled almost to extinction.

The populations of large animals are more fragile than those of small animals. Nevertheless, one can state roughly that the larger an animal species, the longer its generation length. The individual animal is not replaced as quickly as is the case with smaller animal species.

Whales

Ironically, direct hunting played only a minor role in the first whale species, the Chinese river dolphin, being made extinct by human hand. Anthropogenic environmental changes rather than direct hunting made **Yangtse dolphin** extinct. Fishing deprived the Yangtse dolphin of its essential food source or it died from being caught in fishing nets; the Yangtse dolphin was run over by ships or injured by their propellers; the living space was fragmented by dam projects and became increasingly polluted by the industrial waste in the Yangtse River. Since the habitat of the Yangtse dolphin was restricted to only one river, the Yangtse, the dolphin was not able to move to other habitats. Although it was one the smallest whale species, it was comparatively large in proportion to its habitat. This contributed to the fragility of this whale population: while the section of a river between two dams can be sufficiently large for small smaller species to survive, lack of space and resources in a small habitat quickly become a problem for larger animal species [123].

But let us take a look at other whale species, particularly those that are currently caught in the anthropogenic genetic bottleneck. The **bowhead whale** was one of the first whales that was hunted intensively from the late 17th century, after expeditions in search of the Northeast Strait discovered large populations in the Arctic Sea around Spitzbergen. The thick layer of fat, sometimes called train oil, was a sought-after raw ingredient for producing edible oil such as margarine, lubricants, soaps, soups, ointments, paints, leather care products and especially of lamp oil for lighting. Whale oil was also originally used to produce nitroglycerine. Bowhead whales also have very long baleen, which could be used for fishbone of a very high quality.

Originally, there was such a high bowhead-whale population in the Arctic Seat that English whale hunters called it the "Greenland right whale", (to distinguish it from North Atlantic and South Atlantic whales, which were called "right whales"). Of the once estimated 50,000 bowhead whales (possibly the number was considerably higher), there are only 10,000 left today, mostly in the North Pacific. Meanwhile the North Atlantic bowhead whale was considered to be extinct; however a small population seems to have survived and to be increasing in numbers also thanks to the ice opening allowing immigration of bowhead whales from the North Pacific [124].

The bowhead whale was the very first wild animal species that was legally protected by the then League of Nations in 1935. Nevertheless, several decades are required for their populations to recover. Bowhead whales attain sexual maturity only very late, at 10 – 18 years (females) and 25 years (males). The females have a long gestation period of 13 months and can produce offspring every three to four years. Contemporary bowhead whales were found with harpoon arrows in their bodies from the 18th century, which leads to the conclusion that these whales have a long natural lifespan, and in individual cases, a very long lifespan. Due to this high life expectancy coupled with the extended reproduction processes, the question whether bowhead whales have a menopause, and if this is the case, at what age this sets in, is of particular significance in view of the attempt to increase the population. The generation time of bowhead whales is estimated to be 52 years [124, 125].

Other whale species were also hunted heavily. **Sperm whales** were particularly sought after because of the spermaceti organ found in the head of the whale with its characteristic shape. The spermaceti serves as a receptive organ for sonar signals. The mucous and viscous mass can be further processed as sperm oil. It has excellent combustion properties used for lighting material and was popular as a basis for lubricants. In the 19th century, even before the invention of the harpoon cannon, sperm whales were hunted in huge numbers for this sought-after raw material. From about 1860 onwards, large-scale marketing of mineral oil-based combustion material made hunting sperm whales economically unviable, possibly just in time, before the harpoon cannon was used.

In the next few decades, sperm whale populations recovered. In World War II, sperm oil once again became more important for the production of nitroglycerine and margarine. Since the baleen whale population had shrunk so considerably, sperm whales were once again hunted towards the end of the second world war.

According to estimates made by the International Whaling Commission, there were about 360,000 sperm whales in 2008. The estimated figure for 1864, when whale hunting was initiated, was 1.1 million whales. Since the first wave of sperm whale hunting ceased at the beginning of the industrial revolution, because of competition from mineral oil, sperm whales were more or less spared of the catastrophic decimation of the whale population resulting from industrial whale hunting, particularly in the first half of the twentieth century [126].

Not so baleen whales. Our third and last example of whale hunting is devoted to the largest animal on earth, the **blue whale**. This whale is a rorqual whale, as are finback and sei whales. There was little hunting of rorqual whales before the invention of the harpoon canon in 1863, since first of all, they were fast and escaped the harpoons on the rowing boats, and secondly, when they were killed, they mostly sank quickly and could not be sourced, even though the hunt was successful. (Humpback whales, which also belong to the rorqual whale species, were hunted intensively, since they often keep to the coastal waters and are also slower than other rorqual whales.)

Blue whales have been brought almost to the verge of extinction in the hundred years since the invention of the harpoon canon. New technical inventions in the early 20th century such as explosive harpoons and factory ships, which process the whales at sea, increased the efficiency and thus also the lethal nature of the whale hunters. Whereas the blue whale population was estimated to be about 275,000 in the 19th century before they were hunted, the population today is estimated at 10,000. This population originates from the residue blue whale population, which was an estimated 1000 in the 1960, when the blue whale population had reached its lowest point. The genetic diversity of the modern blue whale is thus definitely reduced, and with a generation time of estimated 31 years, it must be assumed that the blue whales are still in a genetic bottleneck [125, 127].

European Bison (Wisent)

Due to human intervention, large land animals are in no better a situation. Though some livestock animals have experienced a great population increase as a result of targeted breeding and mass animal farming, other related animal species, often the predecessors of livestock, have become extinct. There are over 12 million cows in Germany [128], while their predecessors, the aurochs, have been exterminated, and only a few thousand European bison exist worldwide, all descendants from a residual group of 12 animals. For nature enthusiasts, Bialystok on the eastern Polish border to Belarus is a location worth visiting. The nearby Białowieża Forest is a largely primeval forest complex, typical of central Europa of yore. Apart from the enchanting forest, the Białowieża National Park also houses an unusual treasure: the wisent or European bison, with a population meant to secure future bison generations. As the hunting grounds of Polish kings, Białowieża Forest enjoyed special protection status, which was later continued in the 19th century under Russian administration. The resettlement of European bison in Białowieża was made possible because wisents from herds there were donated to zoos and private persons in the 19th century. Meanwhile the wisents from the area were exterminated, too: in the wake of the first world war marauding soldiers ultimately decimated the animals, which between 1890 and 1910 had been reduced from 1900 animals (1857) to 770 (1915). The European bison living in Białowieża are the offspring of twelve animals kept in zoos and parks which were resettled there and released into the wild [129].

Wisents have meanwhile been released into the wild in many other places: in the Slovenian-Polish-Ukranian Carpathian Mountains, in the Caucuses region north of Sochi, the Chernobyl restricted zone in Ukraine, in east Romania and also in the Rothaar Hills in Germany. Bison are a special attraction in many zoos, wildlife and hiking parks.

All of these resettled animals have one thing in common: relatives in the Białowieża Forest. Without the Białowieża breeding line, European bison would no longer exist today. According to the wisent pedigree book in Białystok, the entire population of European bison originated from the twelve animals kept in European zoos at the time of breeding bison for reintroduction to their natural habitat: seven European wood bison (*Bison bonasus bonasus*) and five Caucasian wisent (*Bison bonasus caucasius*). Mountain bison no longer exist, only hybrid breeds, to which the lineage of one of the five bison of the original bison contributed. These were released in Caucasus in 1940 and had achieved a population of 1400. After the USSR was fragmented, this population was decimated to 24 animals. Meanwhile, there is a population of 500 bison in the Caucasus region.

The success in restoring the bison population should not mislead one into ignoring their fragility, since the entire bison population in Europe originates from only twelve animals, and the pure woodland bison from only seven. For those who cannot imagine the concept of genetic bottleneck or who find it too abstract, there is only one thing to do: pack your bags and off to Białowieża to admire the bison! Not everyone seems to be happy about these wonderful animals being resettled in Germany: the first wild bison that wandered into Germany across the Oder River in September 2017 was shot dead on the day it was sighted by order of the German public authorities of the "Ordnungsamt Lebus" in Brandenburg [130].

We will not know during our lifetimes whether the previously mentioned whales or the wild bison will survive as a species. The only information we might be given will be about the extinction of a species. The largest wild cattle species, the aurochs, became extinct long ago, in the 17th century.

Mammoths

The largest land mammal that humankind ever encountered, mammoths, became extinct about 4000 years ago (only a little while ago in terms of the history of the earth!). Was this also the result of human impact? There are diverging views on whether this is the case [131]. What is certain is that mammoths were hunted. Every now and again, almost completely preserved mammoths conserved by Siberian ice are found. This made it possible to take samples of mammoth tissue that was not fossilized and even fluid blood in order to sequence the genome [132]. Might it be possible for humans, who have driven hundreds of species to extinction or near extinction, to soon bring back to life mammoths using modern cloning techniques? And if so, would that be a good idea? After all, a large animal also embodies its own individual habitat for micro-organisms – and who knows what bacteria thrive in an animal that existed at the time of our forefathers, meanwhile became completely extinct and after revival in our modern world develops its own microbiome?

Protection of endangered species

Without doubt, humankind contributes decisively to causing species to become extinct. At the same time, humans have initiated numerous programmes to protect the species. However, most of the corresponding activities are concerned with measures to protect one particular species or its habitat from direct or indirect threats from humans.

The International Union for Conservation of Nature (IUCN) is the organisation that draws up the famous red list (not to be confused with the German medical vademecum, the red list published since 1933 by the Association of Researching Pharmaceutical Manufacturers VFA). The red list of endangered species was first published in 1962 and is a good reference for quick information about the present status of a specific animal species. The degree of danger for a species is divided into ten categories. These are shown in table 5, where the status of the bowhead whale, the sperm whale, the blue whale and European bison is indicated.

Table 5: Endangerment grading for species of the International Union for Conservation of Nature, IUCN, red- list classification of the high-risk species. The bowhead whale, sperm whale, blue whale and the European wild bison and the Yangtse dolphin are shown. *This list still classifies the Yangtse dolphin CR, although there has been no sighting of this species since 2002. The category CF sometimes includes the note "possibly extinct". (Source: http://www.iucnredlist.org)

NE	DD	LC	NT	VU	EN	CR	EW	EX
				bison				
				sperm whale				
					blue whale			
		bowhead whale						
						*Yangtse dolphin	Yangtse dolphin	Yangtse dolphin

NE = Not Evaluated	NT = Near Threatened	CR = Critically Endangered
DD = Data Deficient	VU = Vulnerable	EW = Extinct in the Wild
LC = Least Concern	EN = Endangered	EX = Extinct

7 Mass extinction

It is estimated that the earth has existed for about 4.5 billion years. Modern man (*Homo sapiens*) came into existence about 300,000 years ago.

The mass extinction that took place hundreds of million years ago can only be reconstructed when it has been established what he forms of life existed in the past. This field of research is called palaeontology. In order to record the past existence of a genus or species, mortal remains, mostly of petrified bones or remains of bones (fossils) of the species need to be found. Unfortunately, the find is rarely a fully preserved skeleton in an anatomically logical position, but sometimes only a bone, tooth or a bone splinter or a petrified imprint. The conclusions that are drawn from these finds regarding the lifestyle, occurrence, dissemination and duration of survival of the species on earth are therefore often highly speculative. One of the first questions that arises when a fossil is found is: How old is it? When did the animal live?

An important indicator is the geological layer, the strata in which the find was made. In principle, one would think that that deeper the layer, the older the find. However, it is possible to access very old layers if the right place is chosen, such as those where geological events such as mountain formations have left rift valleys and ledges that allow layers to be reached (geological outcrops). This allows reference systems for geological strata to be made with a description of the morphological structure and the position of the layers relative to each other and to create an ordinal scale (classification in a sequence without consideration of time difference) of the time periods according to the layers.

The age of plants or animal remains can be determined by defining the isotope ratios. Isotopes are two or more forms of the same element that differ in atomic mass. The ratio of the isotopes of an element in an object (bone, stone) changes over time, since heavy elements disintegrate in a characteristic process of radioactive decay. The carbon isotope [14]carbon, for example, is absorbed by all animals and plants during their lifetimes. When an organism dies, it no longer has an intake of [14]carbon. By determining [14]carbon content, the time when the organism lived can be determined using the half-life of [14]carbon. This is possible for organisms of up to 50,000 years old. For younger finds (< 100.000 years) rapidly disintegrating isotopes such as the carbon isotope 14C, which has a half-life period of 5730 years, have proved useful for determining their age. When finds are older, too many atoms have disintegrated, making it difficult to determine the ^{14}C content with any degree of certainty. For dating palaeontological objects that are older than several hundred million years, slow-decaying isotopes with half-life times of several million years are used [133].

First traces of life on earth

It has been established, albeit controversially, that the first signs of life on earth appeared about 3.8 billion years ago. Anomalies in carbon isotopes and tube formation in stone samples from Greenland were interpreted as signs of oxidation processes in a hydrothermal environment that are similar to traces left by metabolic processes of modern iron oxidizing bacteria in stone [134].

There is somewhat more certainty in evaluating shale samples from the Gunflint Massive in Canada. The traces of unicellular organisms found here have been interpreted as traces of 1.9-billion-year-old cyanobacteria. In contrast to other bacteria, cyanobacteria are characterised by oxygenic photosynthesis. Cyanobacteria are therefore allotted an important role in changing the atmosphere of the earth from a low oxygen content to a high-oxygen atmosphere, a process that is thought to have taken place about 3 billion years ago. (According to this theory, the cyanobacteria must already have existed on earth a billion years longer than the Gunflint traces show – geologists seem to regard hundreds of thousands of years as insignificant. But a billion years seems to me worth mentioning!)

The oxygenation of the atmosphere and the oceans put an end to the then existing anaerobic organisms (to a certain extent also a form of mass extinction, which will not be discussed any further here, however). The resulting supply of oxygen created completely new paths for the evolutionary process, since the resulting oxygen offered more efficient methods of generating energy for existing forms of life and generating new life, due to stepwise oxidation of energy-rich molecules. The ensuing observations are restricted to multicellular organisms, which I sometimes term "complex organisms". However, I would like to expressly acknowledge the prokaryotic single cells for their significant contribution to the evolutionary process, even if they are not considered in the chapters to come.

Emergence of multicellular life

According to endosymbiotic theory, multicellular life emerged 3.5 billion years ago through phagocytosis of bacteria by other unicellular organisms, probably archaebacteria, the absorbed bacteria being transformed into mitochondria (or to chloroplasts in photosynthetically active plants and algae) [135].

When we consider mass extinction, we mostly think of the animal world (fauna), although plants are almost more remarkable from a physicochemical point of view, since plants developed the ability to convert energy directly from the sun. One of the resulting biochemical processes, that of photosynthesis, is vital for the world climate and for all of life on earth. Plants use the energy of the sun for the synthesis of complex molecules. In oxygenic photosynthesis, carbon dioxide is harnessed and converted into oxygen, which developed into the most important reactant in supplying animal life with energy. After transformation into ozone O_3, oxygen is the basis for the creation of the ozone layer. Animals are not capable of such biochemical processes and actually only exploit plants (by eating them) [136]. (However, animal metabolic products can also impair the composition of the atmosphere. For example livestock, especially cows, produce methane gas in great quantities, a potent greenhouse gas that also contributes to climate change.)

Life on earth long remained unicellular and small, until there was a veritable explosion of complex multicellular life in the seas during the Cambrian period: during the 56 million years of the Cambrian (about 541 – 482 million years ago), the basis for most of the major forms of multicellular animal and plant life was created, also of phyla still in existence today, such as chordates, whose sub-phyla form the basis for vertebrates. Trilobites (anthropods) also emerged in the Cambrian period. This was a very successful group in the arthropod-phylum that existed in all the seas of the earth for about 250 million years.

Thus, life on earth achieved a level which allowed mass extinction to be detected in the fossil record. It is difficult to observe a massive extinction of bacterial and viral microorganisms, especially when considering events in the distant past, of which multicellular organisms have left only very few traces. I have thus restricted my account to the five great mass extinctions of multicellular complex organisms.

It is only in the past 200 years that discoveries have been catalogued systematically in palaeontology. Not only interesting fossil discoveries are important, but also linking the insights and classifying new discoveries into taxonomic systems. When tracking the course of species known from the fossil record over a period of time, it becomes apparent that there have been repeated instances of a collapse in the diversity of species: this can be seen when geological layers with a rich variety of fossils of all kinds are covered by layers which seem to be barren and devoid of species – and that worldwide. The Sepkoski curve, a database of species diversity, named after the palaeontologist Jack Sepkoski

(d. 1999) shows many high and low points. The five low points are referred to as the big five mass extinctions [137].

The big five mass extinctions

As already mentioned, I will restrict my observations to the five great mass extinctions of multicellular complex organisms. This serves to provide the basis for an overview of the history of mass extinction on earth, albeit only a very patchy one. The emergence and decay of species on earth is part and parcel of what life is about. For the five mass extinctions set out in table 6 below, it is assumed that in each case, over 50 % of the complex forms of life existing during the respective period became extinct.

Table 6: The big five mass extinctions of complex species

Time	Mass extinction event
over 444 million years ago	**Ordovician-Silurian** mass extinction
over 372 million years ago	**Late Devonian** mass extinction (Kellwasser event)
over 252 million years ago	**End Permian-Triassic** mass extinction
over 201 million years ago	**End Triassic-Jurassic** mass extinction
over 66 million years ago	**End Cretaceous-Palaeogene** mass extinction

The history of life is fascinating, but as a layman in this field, I find it difficult to grasp the timeframe. Since most readers will probably also not be experts, I will provide a rough explanation of the processes through the eyes of a layman. I trust that the experts among you will forgive any inaccuracy that might occur. Although the theories and insights that we owe to palaeontology and geology are praiseworthy, the timeframes are certainly not precise. The events took place so long ago and have left too few fossil traces to make greater accuracy possible. These events cover much longer periods of time than the centuries or millennia that the human mind can comprehend. In this chapter, I will usually indicate the timeframes in millions of years before our time. Once more for the records: modern humankind (*Homo sapiens*) has existed for a mere 0.3 million (300,00 million) years.

Geologists have divided the history of the earth into eras and given them names. These are helpful in providing orientation of the 4600 million years of the history of the earth. The interesting part of this history for multicellular complex life actually began 541 million years ago with the Palaeozoic era, which began with the explosion of species diversity in the Cambrian era. I have set out the respective eras in table 7 below. I have also taken the liberty to provide rounded dates for each era, except for our present time (quaternary = the era in the last 2.6 million years). Here I have considered the figures in the decimal points (hundred-thousand years). Precise estimates are not the main consideration in view of the enormous length of the periods.

Table 7: Geological era of the last 541 million years (phanerozoic eon). The big five mass extinctions have been indicated with the figures 1-5 in small print next to the relevant era

	Earth age	Earth era per geological strata	Time in millions of years	Beginning time in millions of years
Phanerozoic (age of visible life) Duration 541 million years	Cenozoic (Present earth age) since 66 million years ago	Quaternary		2.6
		Neogene	20.4	23
		Palaeogene [5]	43	66
	Mesozoic (Middle earth age) Duration 186.2 million years	Cretaceous [5]	79	145
		Jurassic [4]	56	201
		Triassic [4] [3]	51	252
	Palaeozoic (Early earth age) Duration 288.8 million years	Permian [3]	47	299
		Carboniferous	61	360
		Devonian [2]	59	419
		Silurian [1]	25	444
		Ordovician [1]	41	485
		Cambrian	56	541

[5] Mass extinction at Cretaceous-Palaeogene boundary
[4] Mass extinction at Triassic-Jurassic boundary
[3] Mass extinction at Permian-Triassic boundary
[2] Mass extinction in Late Devonian era
[1] Mass extinction at Ordovician-Silurian boundary

When describing mass extinction, the terms genus and species are used repeatedly. These are terms used in biology to express taxonomic ranking, the genus ranking above the species. The family ranks above the genus, and several levels above the family, the phylum. A genus can have a number of species. *Homo sapiens* is the only surviving species of the genus *Homo*. There are two species from the genus *Pan* (chimpanzees): *Pan troglodytes* (chimpanzees) and *Pan paniscus* (Bonobo or pygmy chimpanzees). The chimpanzee and the genus *Homo* belong to the primate family. Gorillas and orangutans are also classified as belonging to this family. Gorillas and orangutans were previously each classified into a genus with only one species. Meanwhile, gorillas are classified as two species, the western and eastern gorilla, and orangutans as three species, illustrating that the classification into genus and species depends on the relevant definition. The primate family thus comprises four genera and eight species, one of which is the *Homo sapiens*.

The definition of the terms genus and species is itself subject of lively debate and is constantly changed. While the taxonomic classification was once almost completely based on phenotypic comparisons, genome comparison plays an ever more significant role today. In simple terms, let us say that the reproductive capacity is central for the definition of a species. However, this does not mean that the distinction made between species and genus is sharp: horses, zebras and donkeys, for example are classified in the genus *Equus*. As is known, horses and donkeys can cross-breed, producing mules or hinnies, whose reproduction capacity is very restricted, however, since horses have 2 x 32 chromosomes and donkeys 2 x31. Zebras can also cross-breed with horses or donkeys, producing the usually sterile zebroids.

All these examples of genera and species were insignificant in the five mass extinctions described below, since these genera did not exist at that time. The extinction of species was always part of the evolutionary process.

(1) Ordovician-Silurian mass extinction (450–440 million years ago)

The Ordovician era followed the Cambrian era (when life exploded) about 480 million years ago, and was in turn followed by the Silurian Era. All of animal life existed in water in the Ordovician era, i.e. in the oceans and seas. The flora consisted of green algae in water and the first traces of moss on land. The great variety of sea fauna was made up of shells, corals and invertebrate marine animals, the echinoderms (*echinodermata*), but there were also primitive nautiloids, the cephalopods (*cephalopoda*). When I consider the amazing capacity of octopuses living today to learn and solve problems, I tend to speculate that remarkably intelligent creatures must have existed on earth half a billion years ago. In terms of numbers, however, the trilobites were dominant. These were arthropods, (most easily comparable with the woodlice in appearance) that originated in the Cambrian era, were to be found frequently in the Ordovician era, and existed for a very long time (270 million years), so that trilobite fossils can be found in great numbers everywhere worldwide.

The average CO_2 content in the Ordovician era was about 4200 ppm, thus ten times the concentration today (and 15 times that of 200 years ago). This is about the same as the upper limit that is tolerable by labour protection standards (see table 3 in the chapter on climate change). A human is thus capable of surviving in such a high CO_2 concentration. However, the low level of oxygen concentration in the atmosphere of 13 % (today 21 %) would be problematic. This is the limit set by labour protection regulations in those areas where the oxygen level is reduced because of fire hazards (however, with the CO_2 concentration remaining the same). People working the area are prone to tire easily when the oxygen concentration reaches such level; with a decrease in oxygen to under 13 %, serious bodily harm leading to death could result [138].

Information on the loss of species through the Ordovician-Silurian mass extinction are only rough estimates, of course. But what can be said is that of the many families, genera and species existing 450 million years before our time many no longer existed 10 million years later. An estimated 80 % of the species, 60 % of the genera and about 100 families (25 % of the previously existing families) no longer existed [139].

There a various theories regarding the cause of the mass extinction, among others, that gamma rays from a hypernova (supernova of a previously very large star) destroyed the ozone layer, allowing lethal ultra-violet rays to reach the earth and causing death and destruction. However, there is no proof in astronomy of such a hypernova 450 million years ago. Forms of life in deep layers of water would have been protected to some degree, but the favoured ecological niches and crannies were probably the shallow-water zones of the original continents which would have been severely damaged.

Volcanic activity could have caused great change to the atmosphere and the climate. The drift of the southern continent Gondwana through the South Pole caused glaciation on the continent and also of the shallow-water areas, which were the most important habitats for life in the Ordovician Era. Can a continental drift be a reason for sudden mass extinction? The Ordovician-Silurian mass extinction should not be imagined as an event at one particular point in time (although developments taking place over millions of years sound like a fleeting event in the mouth of a geologist). On the contrary, it was a process that is considered to have taken place over a period of 10 million years (once more for the records: humans have existed on the earth for 300,000 years) – thus sufficient time for the inconceivably slow drifting continental shelf Gondwana to have crossed the South Pole. Continental shelves today drift at a rate of 1 – 20 cm per year. A shelf drifting at a pace of 10 cm per year would cover 1,000 km in 10 million years.

(2) Kellwasser event (Late Devonian mass extinction, about 372 million years ago)

The Devonian era followed the Silurian about 419 million years ago and was followed by the Carbonian era 359 years ago. The complex plant world, which already was generated in the Silurian era, continued its development and created ferns and other plant growth, which sprouted well above the surface of the ground. In the final phase of the Devonian era, extensive swamp forests came into being from which developed the oldest coal beds on earth.

Fossilised ammonites are my childhood memories of fossils, since my father had an ammonite fossil displayed in his study and ammonites were also depicted in the brochure of the Bad Dürkheim Natural History Museum in Germany. To me they were snail-like fossils. But when I now look up "ammonites", I learn that they were cephalopods with a ribbed plan-spiral-flat-coiled shell. Well, now I know! These ammonites – my personal embodiment of fossils – also came into being in the Devonian about 407 million years ago and dominated the face of the earth for about 350 million years, until they fell victim to the most recent of the five mass extinctions (more about this later).

The oxygen content in the atmosphere in Devonian was about 15 % (it is 21 % today) and the CO2 content about 2200 ppm (today, 410 ppm, and about 280 ppm 200 years ago).

The Devonian is sometimes called the age of fish, since a great variety of species, forms and size developed during this era. [137]. The lobe-finned fish, the *Sarcopterygii,* include the six lung-fish species and two coelacanth species still found today: the Comoros and the Indonesian coelacanths. Towards the end of the Devonian, the first amphibians started to move from water to the surface of the earth for short periods of time. During the same era, land plants experienced developments and sizes unknown until then: before this time, plants grew a maximum of 30 cm above the ground. The trees in the Upper Devonian, on the other hand, grew to a height of 30 m.

The Late Devonian mass extinction is a two-phased one: the so-called 'Kellwasser' event about 372 million years ago and the 'Hangenberg' event (only) 13 million years later, the latter marking the end of the Devonian about 359 million years ago. (Once more let us recall that modern humans, *Homo sapiens*, have existed for about 300,000 or 0.3 million years). Among others, the armoured fish (*placodermi*) that were found in the Silurian era became extinct. The trilobites, which were widespread in the Ordovician and Devonian, were decimated to four families in the Late Devonian (taxonomically, family lies above the genus). At least these continued to exist another 90 million years in the Carboniferous and Permian eras, until they became victims of the largest of all mass extinctions at the Permian-Triassic boundary.

The cause of the Kellwasser and Hangenberg events can be nothing more than speculation. The long duration of the processes with two main phases and an interim period of 13 million years seems to make a one-time causal event unlikely. The Late Devonian mass extinction was probably a multi-factor event involving powerful and changing atmospheric conditions, which gave many species little opportunity for adaptation. Possibly, a succession of catastrophes such as asteroid impacts or major volcanic eruptions with consequences for the earth's climate played a role.

The oxygen content in the seas decreased as a result of the process of photosynthesis from plants. The photosynthesis on the now green land masses could have reduced the CO_2 content in the atmosphere and thus have weakened the greenhouse effect, resulting in low temperatures and ice formation. The size of the new plants on land with complex and deep root systems could have led to the surface land area being remodelled. The soils probably became more mobile and strongly permeated with organic substances from dead organic matter. The effects of the weather caused this soil to be washed into the watercourses, which could have caused over-fertilization with eutrophication of the water: the over-supply of fertilisation and nutrients would have led to the algae blossoming, causing large masses of organic material to sink into the water and decay there, this again resulting in decomposition gases being released and oxygen being used up. The many conditionals used in my descriptions show that just as fascinating these theories are, so highly speculative are they [140].

(3) Mass extinction at the Permian-Triassic boundary (252 million years ago)

The Permian followed the Carboniferous era about 299 million years ago, followed by the Triassic approximately 252 million years ago. The Permian-Triassic boundary marked the greatest mass extinction ever in the history of the earth.

Thanks to the rich green plant world during the Carboniferous, the oxygen content of the atmosphere was 35 % (the figure for today: 21 %), which not only supported the development of lush flora, but also of enormous insects (dragonflies with a wingspan of 70 cm, centipedes of 2-metre length). The carbon stored in the forms of life in the Carboniferous was deposited in the soil after they died and decayed, forming the coalbeds that gave this era its name.

During the Permian era, many amphibian animals developed from the lungfish that flourished in the carbon. Of these amphibians, especially the amniotes (tetrapod vertebrates) could increasingly survive out of water and were also no longer dependent on water for their reproductive process.

The Permian also saw the oxygen level gradually falling to about 16 %. The insects again became smaller, but continued to develop well, and were probably the most successful class in evolution. (Although today, we read a lot about human-induced insect demise – even the success story of insects cannot go on forever.) The vertebrates, which also had become terrestrial creatures, developed well in the lower oxygen level of the Permian. Amniotes still surviving today are turtles; they developed about 220 million years ago in the Triassic, thus, 30 million years after the Permian-Triassic mass extinction described in this section.

Amniotes developed in two directions: reptiles and birds developed from the sauropsida clade and mammals from synapsids. Huge vertebrates already existed in the Permian; the diadectomorphs, a group that became extinct 272 million years ago had reptile-like and amphibian characteristics, with very bulky bodies and were as much as three meters long. The therapsids, ('mammal-like reptiles') were forerunners of mammals and already had developed some impressive and fearful species, such as the gorgonopsian. Gorgonopsians were almost two meters tall with sabre-like mighty fangs. However, the complete group of gorgonopsians became extinct in the Permian-Triassic boundary mass extinction [141].

The Permian-Triassic boundary about 250 million years ago is also regarded in geologic timescale as being the transition from old earth time (Palaeozoic) to middle earth time (Mesozoic). The greatest mass extinction on earth took place in the Permian-Triassic boundary. Approximately three quarters of land- bound species and about 95% of marine species were lost, among these, the last four trilobite species that had survived the Kellwasser event, and also many insect species that had been otherwise little impacted by mass extinction events. The very successful trilobite group of marine anthropods was extinguished forever, after having shaped the more complex life on earth for about 300 million years [137].

One of the few large animals that evolved in the Permian and survived the mass extinction was the plant-eating lystrosaurus, which was about as large as a modern pig and dominated the early Triassic. There is much speculation about how the lystrosaurus group managed to survive the mass extinction. One possible reason is that the animals were able to compensate the loss of habitats because they could cope better with the high levels of CO_2 in the atmosphere that developed at the Permian-Triassic boundary and that they also had sufficient alternative food sources, since they were not highly specialised, but flexible plant-eaters.

The Permian-Triassic event occurred about 252 million years ago in an extremely short period of time of approximately 60,000 years (compare the period of 13 million years that lay between the Kellwasser and Hangenberg events in the late-Devonian mass extinction) [142].

In this case, too, we can only speculate about the causes. There were probably several. The living conditions probably changed so rapidly that most organisms could not adapt in their evolution and so became extinct.

A contributory factor for the Permian-Triassic event may have been meteorite striking the earth, although this was regarded as rather improbable until recently, since there were no traces of iridium in the relevant geological strata that are regarded as typical for meteorite impacts. In 2006, however, satellite observation of the Wilkes Land region of Antarctica revealed widespread rock compression below the ice, such as is typical for meteorite craters. The Wilkes Land crater has a diameter of 500 km, the diameter of the possible meteor being an estimated 50 km. However, the rock compression could have had other causes [143]. Direct rock samples have not yet been made, since the rock is difficult to access, due to the two- to three-kilometre ice layer covering it. The assumed age of the crater of 250 million years thus needs to be regarded with some caution since the figure 250 million is often justified by referring to the Permian-Triassic event. To conclude that the meteorite caused the event is thus circular reasoning and must be considered invalid.

Another possible cause could be something that created the Bedout formation off the northwest Australian coast. However, here, too, there are diverging opinions about whether the Bedout sub-basin is an asteroid crater or whether its origins are volcanic. Determining the time also requires some research. In other words: it remains unclear whether a meteorite impact was the cause of the mass extinction at the Permian-Triassic boundary.

But even without taking any extra-terrestrial causes into consideration, there were several activities at the Permian-Triassic boundary that could have influenced the living conditions dramatically. The Siberian Traps is a huge volcanic river basalt deposit. This deposit can be found in three-centimetre thick layers that represent the mass extinction 252 million years ago covering an area of about 2 million km^2 today, formerly 7 million km^2, in 3 km thick layers. In order to imagine how enormous these layers are: 7 million km^2 is about 20 times the size of Germany (357,000 km^2) or roughly the size of Australia. These huge magma masses originated in a few hundred thousand years, a short period of time in geologic terms [144]. Volcanic activity and also the stored carbon sites that were ignited caused huge masses of CO_2 to be released into the atmosphere, resulting in the atmosphere being heated (greenhouse effect) and to acidification of the oceans. The temperatures of the oceans increased rapidly (by up to 8 degrees Celcius, 46° F, on the surface layers), reducing its oxygen content. An oxygen-rich pH level-balanced ocean with optimised living conditions was transformed into a hostile, anoxic acidotic, murky brine.

This induced a strong increase in methane content in the atmosphere, probably due to the release of the frozen methane hydrate stored in the oceanic shelves and possibly also due to the distribution of anaerobe bacteria, which transformed organic material into methane by means of a new metabolic effect [145]. The increased greenhouse gas methane caused increased warming of the water by another 5 degrees Celsius (41° F). According to oxygen isotope measures taken, the surface temperature of the water increased to more than 40 degrees Celsius (over 104° F) [146]. Apart from the somewhat cooler moderate zones and the polar regions, survival was not possible for most organisms in large regions of the earth.

(4) Mass extinction at the Triassic- Jurassic boundary (about 201 million years ago)

The Triassic followed the great mass extinction 252 million years ago, at the end of the Permian. The fauna that now appeared was so distinctive that geologists view the start of the Triassic as more than simply the beginning of a new period: it is regarded as the dawn of a new era, the middle earth age (Mesozoic).

The Triassic was characterized by the new super continent Pangaea, which was formed by the southern continent Gondwana merging with the north continent Laurussia in the Permian. The overheating of the planet that had led to the mass extinction at the close of the Permian could still be felt in the Triassic. In most areas of the earth, the climate was tropical or subtropical. The formation of the super continent had resulted in a reduction of the coastal habitats that formerly had been vital for life. Instead there were now large continental areas, mostly characterized by deserts, not least because precipitation did not stretch into the interior and while at the same time, the low-pressure areas on the coasts attracted hot, dry air from the interior.

Plant life on land changed, although many plants from previous periods existed in the Triassic. Some of them, such as tree ferns, palm ferns and the ginkgo continue to do so until this day. At the same time, however, the gymnosperms and the predecessors of the flowering plants (angiosperms) prevailed against the formerly dominant ferns. Pine-like trees had been virtually decimated by the mass extinction at the end of Permian. However, some species recovered in the Triassic and their successors still populate our forests and heathlands today.

During the Triassic, extensive coral reefs were formed once again. In the former periods, the coral reefs had largely been destroyed as a result of the extremely high acidity of the water from the high CO_2 concentration in the atmosphere. There were also conodonts, minute eel-like chordates, little known among laypersons, marine creatures measuring up to 40 centimetres, that became extinct once and for all at the end of the Triassic about 201 million years ago, after having played a significant role in life on earth for about 340 million years since the Cambrian (about 541 million years before our time).

Only two groups of the strongly decimated forerunners of the land mammals, the therapsids, could survive into the Triassic: the dicynodonts (lystrosaurus, among others) and the cynodonts. Mammals developed from the cynodonts ("dog teeth"). The therapsids were forced very much into the background by the eureptiles (forerunners of reptiles and birds), which flourished during the Triassic.

The Triassic also ended with mass extinction, the Triassic-Jurassic mass extinction 201 million years before our time, "a mere" 50 million years after the greatest mass extinction of complex life on earth, the Permian-Triassic mass extinction (251 million years ago). As always, the impact of a meteorite is among the debated reasons. Meteor craters that seem to suggest this are the Well Creek Crater in the US state of Tennessee, the Red Wing crater in North Dakota and the Rochechouart Crater near the city of Chassenon at the margin of the French Massif Central. What I notice is that all the craters are found in regions of the world (USA and Europe) in which there are many geologists, which leaves room for speculation about further craters in lesser-known and less well- mapped regions.

The favoured hypothesis for this mass extinction at present is that the global climate was destabilised as a result of strong volcanic activity caused by rifting of the Central North Atlantic Ocean. Carbon-isotope ratios suggest a rapid CO_2 increase within a few hundred-thousand years in the late Triassic [147].

(5) Mass extinction at the Cretaceous-Palaeogene boundary (about 66 million years ago)

The dawn of the Jurassic 201 million years ago brought the age of the dinosaurs, an age covering 165 million years, spanning the Jurassic and Cretaceous eras, and which suddenly ended 66 million years ago with the fifth big mass extinction. (We recall that *Homo sapiens* have existed for a mere 300,000 years.)

Almost unnoticed, in the shadow of the dinosaurs, the first mammals entered the stage. These originated from several cynodonts that had survived the most recent mass extinction. As long as the dinosaurs dominated the earth, the mammals remained small. While the dinosaurs were the largest land animals ever to have lived, our predecessors living at the same time did not grow larger than that of a rat in size.

The era of the dinosaurs ended abruptly with the mass extinction about 66 million years ago at the Cretaceous-Palaeogene boundary. This mass extinction is thought to have been caused by a massive meteorite. A crater, the Chicxulub Crater, with a diameter measuring 180 kilometres was found in 1991 in the northern ocean basin that edges on the Yucatan peninsula in Mexico. There had been a hypothesis of a meteorite impact having caused the extinction of the dinosaurs since the 1980s, after iridium traces were found in geologic strata from the Cretaceous-Palaeogene.

The dinosaurs also fell prey to the mass extinction. However, the view that the dinosaurs were completely exterminated is now regarded as being outdated. In actual fact, the dinosaurs are classified as an extinct suborder of the reptiles. However, the offspring of certain dinosaurs, namely the theropod dinosaurs, still exist worldwide: birds. This of course leads to the question what exotic suborder of dinosaurs, surely only known to experts, gave raise to birds. In other words, what dinosaur belonging to the theropods is the forerunner of birds? One way or another, carnivorous, mostly upright dinosaurs with strong legs and considerably smaller arms have indeed become very popular in our modern pop culture. One particular species of theropod dinosaur that still fascinates children today was introduced to me before I could even read or write by "Maestro" in the wonderful animated television series "Once upon a Time" produced by Albert Barillé: the *tyrannosaurus rex*.

The sixth mass extinction of complex species

The five mass extinction events are only examples of the appearance and disappearance of species on our earth. How great are the chances that humankind will come to experience a mass extinction of complex species?

If we were to break down the probability over time, the chances seem to be only slight, since *Homo sapiens* has existed on earth for a mere 300,000 years, a proportion of one in 220 of the time since the most recent mass extinction took place 66 million years ago.

Nevertheless: according to everything we know about the development of biodiversity in the past hundred thousand years, we could be right in the middle of the sixth mass extinction of the phanerozoic. Not only right in the middle, but actively involved! This sixth mass extinction is anthropogenic – it is human-made. The question is whether humankind will survive its self-made extinction. The destruction of the ecosystems of the earth could also eradicate our own basis of existence. But could the reduction of biodiversity also have a direct – and catastrophic – impact on humans? Or, to phrase the question cynically: Can the mass extermination of wild animals leave us unmoved, when we view this unsentimentally and brutally? True: the extinction of European bison would have had no direct damaging consequences for our species. After all, we need only few livestock species as fuel suppliers. However, there are signs of a dangerous decline of undomesticated livestock that are important components of global food world supply: fish. There is simply too much fishing taking place. We are emptying our seas of fish [148]!

Comparison of humans, livestock and wild animal masses in the Anthropocene

But what is the role of wild animals in times of industrial agriculture and factory farming? Do they have a role at all? Alone because of its growing population figures, *Homo sapiens* has an increasing impact on the composition of ecosystems on earth. In his article "Harvesting the Biosphere: The Human Impact", Vaclav Smil undertook an attempt to estimate the ratio of wild mammals and domesticated mammals in the Anthropocene (age of humans) by ordering the mammalian biomass in three categories, as an anthropomass (mass of all existing humans) and zoomass (mass of all existing land animals) and mass of wild animals [149]. Of course such estimates are inaccurate, but the comparison of the estimates for 1900 and 2000 in particular reveals an undeniable development, one that could not be more dramatic. (Table 8).

Table 8: Comparison of human, land mammals and domesticated land mammals

	Humans (Mt C)	Wild land mammals (Mt C)	Domesticated land mammals (Mt C)	Total
1900	13	10	35	58
2000	55	5	120	180

Mt C = millions of tons of carbon dry mass

Let us look at the calculation of global carbon dry mass for the 6.1 humans on earth in 2000. Smil assumed a global average body weight of 50 kg per person. For the world population of 6.1, this adds up to 300 million tons of human flesh for the year 2000. Assuming that slightly more than 60% of the human body is composed of water, about 40% x 300 Mt = 120 Mt dry mass remains, of which about 45% is made up of carbon, a calculated 45% x 120 MT = 54 Mt C. Smil continued the calculation by using 55 Mt C as the reckoning factor in order to compensate the previous rounding of human dry mass of slightly below 40% to 40%.

In the original table, there were also columns for elephants and for livestock and no total sum. I assumed that elephants are already included in the mass of wild mammals and livestock in the domesticated land mammals.

All in all, the carbon dry mass of land animals tripled from 58 Mt C to 180 Mt C. (The column for the year 2000 in figure 6 should actually be three times the width of that for the year 1900.) But: the dry carbon mass of wild mammals halved from 10 to 5 Mt C. However, that of humans quadrupled from 13 to 55 Mt C, while that of domesticated mammals more than tripled from 35 to 120 Mt C (table 8 and figure 6).

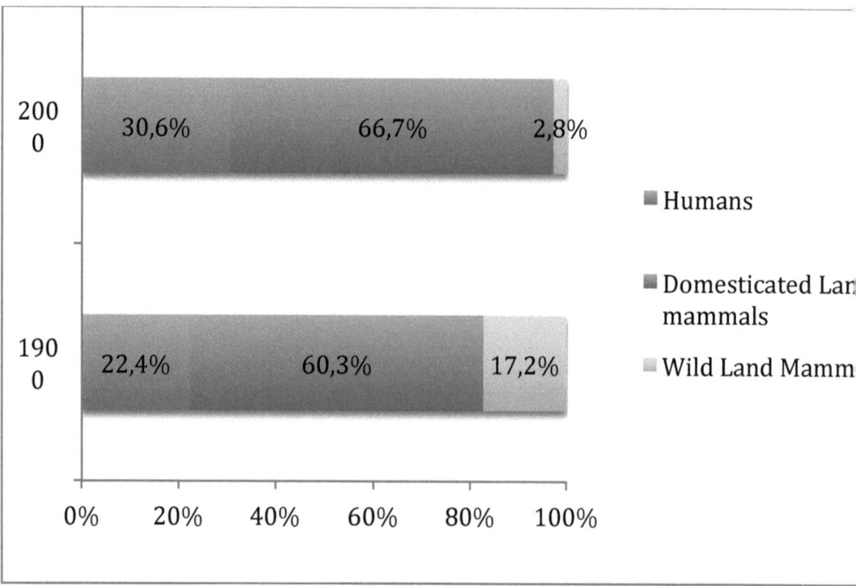

Figure 6: A comparison of carbon mass of land mammals for humans, domesticated land mammals and wild mammals in 1900 and 2000. [149] Source: Smil et al. Population Development Review 2011

Ten thousand years ago, most large land mammals were wild. Estimates of the ratio of domesticated mammals to the total number of all large animals worldwide at the time can only be highly speculative. A rough estimate of the proportion of humans and domesticated vertebrates of the total biomass of vertebrate 10,000 years ago reveals this proportion to be 0.1%. The figure for today is over 97% [150].

Genetic bottleneck phenomena and historical demographics

For many wild animals such as the wisent and the blue whale, the lack of genetic diversity could become fatal even though short-term survival seems to have been secured. A few generations after almost having become extinct, populations that originate from only a few individual members are fragile in the face of plagues. The reduced genetic diversity after a genetic bottleneck decreases the probability that there are animals in the population that are less prone to succumb to epidemics and survive them. In view of the population of 7.5 billion worldwide, this should be no problem for *Homo sapiens*, shouldn't it?

If the genetic variability of a species is to be examined, the mitochondrial DNA is examined, since it is passed on directly from the mother to her young and thus no blending of the genes of the two parents takes place. The stronger the genetic variability of the mitochondrial DNA of a species is, the higher the number of mothers from which the individuals of this species originate.

The unexpected lack of genetic variability of the human mitochondrial DNA implicates that the humans living today are the offspring of a very small population of about 1,000 to 30,000 individuals who had survived a catastrophic mass extinction of our species around 70,000 – 80,000 years ago. Was this triggered by a natural catastrophe or was it the consequence of a gradual reduction in the population due to long-term hostile living conditions [151, 152]?

In the late 1990s, it was suggested that the eruption of the Toba volcano on Sumatra about 70,000 thousand years ago and the subsequent volcanic winter was the cause of such a mass extinction [153]. According to this hypothesis, only few members of the *Homo sapiens* species survived the catastrophe in the tropical forests of Africa. The fact that this narrative appears to be plausible should not lead one to ignore the fact that it contains many speculative elements. Ice core extracted from the vicinity of the North Pole reveals obvious interruptions in the ice formation about 71,000 years ago, but such a phenomenon cannot be established in the Antarctica. Tool shards were found directly above and below the Toba tufa layers in Jwalapuram in southern India. This speaks in favour of ongoing human settlement in the region that was not disturbed to any mentionable degree by the Toba eruption [154]. A controversial point is the species that constructed these tools. It is quite feasible that apart from *Homo sapiens*, it may well have been members of the *Homo erectus* or the *Homo neanderthalensis* species. The 'Out-of-Africa-I' hypothesis refers to the spread of *Homo erectus* from Africa to the Eurasian continent and the Indian sub-continent about 1.8 million years ago. That it was the *Homo sapiens* who originally constructed the tools 70,000 years ago would be a contradiction of the 'Recent-African-Origin' hypothesis, according to which *Homo sapiens* settled in Eurasia about 40,000 years ago, which means that at the time of the Toba eruption, there were not yet any *Homo sapiens* living on the Indian sub-continent.

Whereas it was earlier thought that *Homo sapiens* have existed as an individual species for about 200,000 years, new studies of *Homo sapiens* fossil finds from Morocco, dated at about 300,000 years, suggest an earlier existence of modern humans [155, 156]. The sites of the oldest fossil findings of *Homo sapiens* to date are Ethiopia, South Africa and Morocco. This verifies the theory valid to date that Africa is the cradle of civilization. Apparently, *Homo sapiens* spread throughout the African continent at an early stage in their history. Most maps of the world found in *Homo sapiens'* settlements show arrows starting in Ethiopia and pointing in the direction of the Arabian Peninsula and from there in the direction of Europe and Central Asia. These maps seem to suggest that the regions in Europe that were probably more heavily impacted by the Ice Age 70,000 years ago were settled by *Homo sapiens* 40,000 years ago, and Eurasia and Asia about 60,000 to 25,000 years ago, thus considerably later than the genetic bottleneck 70,000 years ago.

In accordance with the common Recent-Africa-Origin theory, the successors of the original population from the genetic bottleneck left Africa to form settlements throughout the world. [157].

In terms of time, the genetic bottleneck occurred about 70,000 years ago during the last Ice Age in Europe, which began about 115,000 years ago and ended about 11,600 years ago. A gradual decline in the human population due to inhospitable living conditions is thus also conceivable without any catastrophic event worth mentioning in itself having occurred. However, this would imply that the living conditions in Africa were just as strongly impacted, making life there difficult for the *Homo sapiens* population living there. Perhaps it was simply the local processes that make an existence so difficult there, or the social structures of the *Homo sapiens* at the time were such that reproduction dwindled.

Assuming that the Recent-African-Origin hypothesis coincided roughly with the timelines explained above, the population decline leading to the genetic bottleneck of the *Homo sapiens* must have occurred on the African continent. Changes in the climate could have been contributory factors, of course, and floods might have reduced food supply for our forefathers. A genetic bottleneck need not necessarily occur as a result of mass extinction; it can simply be the result of low fertility. But perhaps there was no genetic bottleneck for the time 70,000 years ago, as postulated. Perhaps the *Homo sapiens* population was sustained at a low level for thousands of years without any mentionable increase in its numbers.

We don't know. The only thing we do know is that our biodiversity is lower than could be expected after the 300,000 years that our species has spread over the planet.

Unfortunately, there is only a very thin data base for estimates of prehistoric demography. There are no records, and the very rare fossil finds allow no more than assumptions about the existence of a species, which is difficult enough, since it requires a distinction being made between a specific species and other related species. Put very simply, it is just not possible to make a direct estimate about the size of the population from fossil discovery.

But at least modern genome comparisons enable an estimate of how closely related the individuals are, which in turn makes it possible to draw conclusions about the size of the population from which the individual originates: by estimating phylogenetic distances (the lower the genetic variability, i.e. biodiversity, the closer the relationship) it can be assessed how many common generational forerunners the people living today had. One estimate of the size of the world population of the direct forefathers of *Homo sapiens* (*Homo erectus* and *Homo heidelbergensis*) 1.2 million years ago calculated the human population to be 18,500, but no more than 26,000 individuals [158]. Because of the enormous timespan involved, it appears to me not to be logical to compare this estimated figure – 18,500 individuals that might have lived 1.2 million years ago – with the estimated 1,000 to 30,000 individuals living 70,000 years ago. Another point is that the *Homo erectus* was spread far beyond Africa, as the terms used for corresponding fossil finds clearly show (Java man, Peking man).

Modern *Homo sapiens* probably originate from a small fraction of the *Homo erectus* living throughout the world 1.2. million years ago. According to the Out-of-Africa hypothesis, our *Homo-erectus* forerunners must have belonged to the population spread over the African continent. Corresponding *Homo-erectus* discoveries were made in Algeria and South Africa.

An obvious and plausible explanation for a genetic bottleneck induced by mass extinction is a widespread fatal epidemic. Then that would mean that our forefathers were those individuals that survived this. In view of the very thin population density 70,000 years ago, these forefathers could indeed be survivors, that means, individuals that were infected, but that survived the disease, or that belonged to groups that completely escaped the epidemic.

The Palaeocine-Eocine Thermal Maximum (56 million years ago)

The Palaeocine-Eocine Thermal Maximum (PETM) is not counted as one of the five big mass extinctions in the history of complex life. I would nevertheless like to look at the PETM, since it is often used by climate experts as a comparison in the history of the earth for a rapidly progressing greenhouse effect.

But why is it that the PETM is not viewed as one of the big mass extinctions? Well, first of all, it occurred a mere 10 million years after the previously discussed mass extinctions, which also killed off the dinosaurs, that means, in a period of hardly worth mentioning. (Just think of the Late Devonian extinction about 372 million years ago, which occurred in two waves about 13 million years apart, according to the palaeontological findings.)

According to palaeontologists, the organisms whose extinction characterised the PETM appear anything but spectacular to the layperson. Everyone knows dinosaurs, but who has ever heard of the "benthic foraminifera'? These are the unicellular eukaryotes whose fossilised shells have left many remains of their existence, but because of their unicellular nature are of no interest in connection with mass extinctions of complex life. Dinosaurs are the stars of children's books and Hollywood blockbusters, and can be bought as cuddly toys or as models at zoos. Similar products of benthic foraminifera would not sell nearly as well.

The benthic foraminifera population existed at all levels of the seabed. This form of life experienced mass extinction with a 30 % to 50 % loss of the species 56 million years ago [159].

During the PETM, the CO_2 concentration in the atmosphere rose from about 800 ppm to over 2000 ppm in a very short timespan of about 10,000 years and the temperatures rose by about 5 – 8 degrees Celcius (41 – 47 degrees Fahrenheit). At present, the CO_2 concentration is a little over 400 ppm. Two centuries ago, it was only 280 ppm [160]. In the chapter on human-impacted CO_2 concentration increase, we calculated an estimated 0.5 % increase per year. Assuming a stable CO_2 increase of 0.5 % from now on, the CO_2 concentration would be about 560 ppm in 2083, that is, about double that before industrialisation – doubling the CO_2 concentration in a little more than 300 years.

Of course the PETM cannot be compared one-to-one with living conditions today. The Pole caps were not frozen and the entire earth was very hot with vegetation corresponding to the warm and humid tropical climate or dry deserts. The combination of a tropical climate and a high carbon content generated a veritable explosion of the plant life on earth and turned the land masses into a green hell. The effects in the oceans, however, were more hostile to life. Many zoo plankton species were simply not made to endure the high water temperatures; also, the water became increasingly acidic as a result of the carbonic content. One result was that the shells of the benthic foraminifera were destabilized. For the land mammals and reptiles, the PETM was a good time, however. The primates, for example, flourished

How did this scary rapid increase in oxygenated greenhouse gases such as CO_2 and methane come about? There are various theories in which the release of organic carbon played a significant role. In the lush vegetation a high quantity of CO2 could have been released during widespread forest fires, as well as by the burning coalbeds. The increased in temperature could have resulted in methane being released in the methane-hydrate fields located in the permafrost and the oceanic continental shelves, which in turn reinforced the greenhouse effect. The PETM did not last particularly long in geological dimensions. After lasting for a period of only 3 million years, the temperatures again fell 53 million years ago, and 34 million years ago, the pole caps were again completely frozen. Again, how this occurred is open to speculation. One hypothesis is that the freshwater fern containing chlorophyll (azolla) completely swamped the oceans 49 million years ago, which removed huge quantities of carbon from the biosphere as the plants rotted and fell to the sea floor. The withdrawal of the greenhouse gas CO_2 from the atmosphere would have resulted in a cooling of the planet, so the hypothesis.

In the past history of the earth, there have always been times during which CO_2 concentrations and temperatures were significantly higher than those of today. At times, there were periods in which life flourished and even exploded, such as during the Cambrian. Why, then, are we so concerned about the human-induced rise in CO_2 levels? What makes this development unique is that it has occurred so rapidly. Even in geological time frames of a rapid increase of CO_2, such as the PETM, the rate was several ten powers slower than that we are experiencing. This rate of rising CO_2 levels is much too rapid to allow the human species (and other species) to be able to adapt their evolutionary processes. An adaptation by means of (bio)technological progress and intelligent solutions might be a viable option.

Extraterrestrial threats

The last mass extinction 66 million years ago, which also led to dinosaurs ceasing to exist, was probably caused by the impact of a comet whose dimension is estimated to have been about 10 to 15 kilometres measured by the approximately 180-kilometre diameter of the Chicxulub Crater, located at the Yucatan Peninsula. Could humans also be exterminated by a comet impact? Often, there are articles in the popular press about comets which, so it is claimed, could impact the earth in the near future, since their orbits cross that of the earth. A present popular candidate for a potential collision with the earth is the comet "Bennu", which is expected to cross our orbit in about 2135.

My attention was drawn to Bennu by an article in the regional German popular daily, *Hamburger Morgenpost*, which you can find in cafés in Altona. The article also reported on initiatives taken by American space organisations to develop ballistic defence missiles that could shoot down a comet while still in orbit. Of course comets whose orbits cross that of the earth offer arms lobbyists the opportunity for solid arguments for developing and producing long-range missiles with powerful explosive devices. On the surface, the fact that it might be possible to prevent the impact of a comet could be a comforting thought for those who feel panicked about a comet impact. However, we must also consider that a huge self-initiated human-made blaze can wipe human life off the fact of the earth.

But how dangerous is Bennu and who decides this, and how? Astronomers repeatedly find asteroids whose orbits around the sun suggest the probability of their crossing the earth's orbit. However, even with data from week-long observations, it is hardly possible to predict whether an object could come dangerously close to the earth in a few years, decades or centuries.

If the dinosaurs became extinct 66 million years ago because of a meteorite impacting the earth, the same can happen to us at any time, can't it? Of course something like that could happen to us, but the probability that we will experience such an event (and then not survive it) is very small, given the short lifespan we have roamed the earth as a species. The longer the period of time, the higher the probability that a large and dangerous meteorite impact will fall into this time-span. This is obvious: dinosaurs dominated the earth in the Upper Triassic about 235 million years ago and became extinct 66 million years ago. This means that dinosaurs existed on the earth for about 169 million years. (The birds and reptiles existing today are the offspring of dinosaurs.) When we consider individuals of the *Homo rudolfensis* species to be the first *Homo* species, then the *Homo* species that belongs to the primate family is 2.5 million years old. This corresponds to 68th of the existence of dinosaurs on earth. Modern humans, the *Homo sapiens*, have been in existence for about 300,00 years. This is a fraction of one 563rd of the time during which dinosaurs existed on earth.

Taxonomers will forgive me for having compared the time of existence of different taxonomic ranks. The point that I wanted to make was that we humans have not existed for that long. If we want to increase the probability of being exterminated by a meteorite impact one day, we have to survive long enough on earth without being killed off by other factors, such as our own weapons of mass destruction.

8   The nuclear threat

Is there any other species on earth that has put its own existence at stake through admirable achievements?

The balance of terror

The Cold War reached a decisive phase in 1983. Although it nearly led to a nuclear war, in contrast to the Cuban Crisis 20 years previously, it went largely unnoticed by the general population. What has remained etched in my memory are the television images of the peace movement that protested against the stationing of American Pershing II nuclear medium-range missiles in Germany. Someone explained to me that these protests were unreasonable, since the Pershing II missiles were necessary to balance the Russian SS-20 medium-range missiles in. And also, so I was told, the protest movement was unruly. I cannot say exactly who explained this to me. Perhaps it was only the result of my own perception of the television images and the comments, as well as my regularly reading the German daily "Bild Zeitung" (German tabloid with Transatlantic-neo-conservative spin), which was more appealing to the ten-year boy that I was than the peace-movement's text-laden leaflets.

Stationing the Pershing II missiles was part of the NATO double-track decision of flexible response in 1979, according to which the nuclear arsenal should be complemented to include nuclear cruise missiles to balance the Russian SS20 missiles. Prior to this, NATO and its member state Germany had rejected the Russian proposal to reduce the number of SS20 missiles from 250 to 162 and to withdraw them to east of the Urals. The major part of the German population (and of other NATO states) was against stationing American nuclear weapons in Europe. Nevertheless, the German parliament, the Bundestag, voted in favour of this proposal in November 1983.

The American-Russian bilateral INF (Intermediate-Range Nuclear Forces) treaty banned land-based intermediate range nuclear missiles on both sides. Such intermediate-range missiles posed a particular threat to European Nations. It did not include sea- or air-launched missiles, but nevertheless was one of the most important initiatives for nuclear weapon reduction. In February 2019 the US withdrew from the treaty, after the treaty had already been undermined by the stationing of allegedly defensive US-missiles in Eastern Europe, close to Russia.

In March 1983, US President Ronald Reagan announced the Strategic Defense Initiative (SDI), a programme for the development of a satellite-supported system against ballistic attack from the Russians. Such a programme would have disturbed the balance of nuclear weapons, which is why the Russian view was that the SDI meant a massive security threat. The threat of a nuclear war would have increased considerably with the SDI system, since the USA intended to move the balance of terror in favour of the USA. America would have been in a position to destroy the Soviet Union in a first strike and to ward off a nuclear counter-attack. With no second-strike option, (or at least not one that was secured) the Soviet Union would also have had an added incentive for a massive first-strike attack.

The memory of SDI seems to lie in the distant past, yet the balance of terror is again endangered. In 2001, the then US President George W. Bush cancelled the unilateral ABM (Antiballistic Missiles) Treaty. This treaty limited the further development of antiballistic missile system and thus secured the nuclear balance. If one side feels itself in a position to deter opponents' missiles, the danger of a nuclear war increases.

Allegedly in order to be prepared for an Iranian nuclear attack (which is nonsense, of course) NATO is currently constructing missile station sites in Poland and the Czech Republic. This represents a two-fold threat to Russia: firstly, defence missiles would be in a position to intercept Russian missiles and to deprive Russia of the second-strike option that is essential for the balance of terror, and secondly the Russians would have less reaction time to deter a NATO offensive, since the missiles are stationed very close to the most important Russian cities. The pretended defensive, protective missiles thus increase the danger of a nuclear war [30]. Meanwhile the Russian side has reacted by developing ground-based cruise missiles that have the capacity to intercept the American defence missiles. Furthermore the Russian S-400 antiballistic missiles seem to be superior to the American Patriot system. Though this does restore the nuclear balance, decades of disarmament talks seem to have been in vain. After the American cancelled the ABM treaty in 2001, in February 2019 another treaty lost its value, namely the INF-Treaty signed in 1987.

It could be argued that the Russian cruise missiles can also cover large distances and are thus not medium-range missiles. Whichever view you take: the INF-treaty that was celebrated as such a great success in the late 1980s is now hardly worth the paper it was written on. To make things worse, Donald Trump rejected the proposal from the Russian President Putin to extend the START (Strategic Arms Reduction Treaty) agreements, which expire in 2021. These treaties foresaw a bilateral 50 % reduction of nuclear weapons with reciprocal verification concessions.

The START treaties are the most comprehensive arms reduction treaties ever (or will have been). Unfortunately, Donald Trump has the support of the Senate, where some Republican senators even demanded that START be completely cancelled as, in their view, the Russians contravened the INF-treaty. The Russians in turn have refused to negotiate on this treaty as long as the ABM treaty is inactive.

Those who expect reason to set in at some stage that will allow both sides to return to the negotiating table should consider the logic of power and economic common sense. For the American military industrial complex, a new arms race offers an attractive perspective: apart from major contracts for the construction of new missiles, another prospect is that of new arms developments, which, with the corresponding reasoning, would not fall under the provisions in the existing treaties on ballistic missiles (such as hypersonic weapons).

Since the turn of the century, (or actually already since 1990), the overall strategy of the last remaining superpower has been to shift the former balance of terror into one in which the US dominates the options for destruction by removing the defence potential of the victim (the opponent). The Prompt Global Strike (PGS) strategy submitted in written form in 2003 is aimed at putting the USA in a position to reach any target on earth within an hour and destroying it. The reaction time available to any attacked party (or one which feels threatened with attack) would be reduced even further.

Since the decision-making timespan is gradually moving into a zone which is too short for human decision-making processes, it can be assumed the decision-making algorithms for a counter attack will become increasingly automatic. Should it come to destructive war with weapons of mass destruction, it could well be will be initiated by a computer error.

Apart from launching devices throughout the world (drones, US military bases and ships), hypersonic weapons play a decisive role in the PGS strategy. These are extremely fast missiles which can withstand temperatures of over 1000 degrees Celsius (1800° F) and fly at five times the speed of sound. The Boeing X-51 "Waverider" exceeded mach 5 (i.e. over 6174 km/h, 3836 mph)) during a successful trial flight in May 2013 and covered about 425 kilometres (265 miles) in six minutes. Such a missile launched from a base in Poland could reach Moscow in in about a quarter of an hour. Launched from US outposts in Estonia, a missile of this kind would cover the distance to St. Petersburg in five minutes.

Stanislav Petrov

Stanislav Yevgrafovich Petrov died on 19 May 2017 aged 77. He lived a quiet life in a small town close to Moscow. Perhaps you know his role in the story of what happened in September 1983 – it was referred to in popular culture – but perhaps not. Petrov was a Soviet officer, married and had a son. A truly common life. But Petrov prevented a nuclear war.

Here is the background leading up to this event: in autumn 1983 the Cold War tension between the two world powers Russia and the USA was particularly high, since NATO had planned a major manoeuvre, "Able Archer", for the end of November in-cluding a simulation of a nuclear war. The preparation was kept secret, so that Soviet intelligence services only had some indica-tors and rumours to go on, causing anxiety in Moscow of a NATO major attack.

Tension had already escalated due to the NATO Fleetex ma-noeuvre in the Pacific region in April 1983. Targeted NATO scouting missions that violated Russian airspace in the Kamchat-ka Peninsula area and Sakhalin Island were part of the manoeu-vre and were designed to induce the Soviet Union to activate the radar equipment to detect the NATO planes, making the detec-tors visible to NATO intelligence (and thus allowing them to be recorded as targets during potential nuclear attacks).

On 1 September 1983, Russian radar detected a large aircraft and ordered it to be shot down by a Russian fighter interceptor. Whether it was obvious to the Russian side at the moment of attack that the plane was a civil Boeing 747, that of Korean Air Lines Flight 007 from New York to Seoul, remains contentious to this day. On the same day, a four-engined military Boeing RC-135 aircraft was among the NATO military planes scouting the airspace around Sakhalin Island. Theories on the incident range from the plane being intentionally shot down by the Russian military to the passenger aircraft being accidentally shot down after being defined as a military target by military aircraft. Another theory that is debated is that the aircraft was really a spy plane. Speculation even goes as far as claiming that an air raid involving several Russian and American aircraft took place, during which the Korean Air Lines Flight 007 was shot down in collateral damage by Japanese armed forces or an American warship (similar to Iran Air 655 five years later). I believe that the Russians regarded the aircraft as a military target. A radar cannot always show the difference. When the decisions are made on the basis of misinterpretations, disaster is imminent.

Deciding which side is to blame is not the purpose of this book, but it remains to be said that the accusations from both sides increased the tension between the two power blocs.

Three weeks after this incident, on 25 September 1983, Stanislav Petrov had to stand in as duty officer to work a night shift for a colleague at the Soviet command centre of the 'Oko' nuclear early-warning system south of Moscow. In his capacity as duty officer, Petrov held responsibility for the command centre. Shortly before midnight, the alarm went off signalling a missile attack on Soviet Union national territory. A satellite had detected a missile launched from an American missile silo. Petrov had only a few minutes to make a decision. After 20 to 25 minutes, the missile would hit a site somewhere in the Soviet Union. The strategy for both sides at the time foresaw that in case of an attack involving intercontinental missiles, a large-scale devastating counter-attack (mutual assured destruction) would be initiated. Since a first strike could mean the destruction of the missile silos, the own missiles for a counter-attack were required to be fired before the first-strike missiles hit their targets. This decision had to be made according to the available satellite data. The Oko system had just signalised that a missile had been launched from the American mid-west.

In the tense situation at the height of the Cold War, a missile alarm on 25 September was not completely inconceivable. The shooting down of the South Korean passenger flight had already shown the willingness of the two sides to take action.

There were 200 people stationed at the control centre near Moscow that night. Stanislav Petrov was the commanding officer. His first reaction was to ensure that everyone remained calm by ordering those present to sit down and continue working. Petrov analysed the situation by drawing an analogy with a teaspoon: "Nobody would empty a bucket with a teaspoon." Why would the USA undertake a destructive strike against the Soviets with only one missile? He reported a false alarm. The sirens were switched off.

A moment later they set off again. The satellite system showed another missile launch and then another three. Stanislav didn't budge from his decision: false alarm. Interception was not possible. According to the concept of mutual assured destruction the response would have been an all out counter-attack involving direct and total destruction with all mobilised nuclear missiles. If it had in fact come to a genuine attack, the counter-offensive potential of the Soviet Union would possibly have been fully available until the American missile struck. Added to that, Petrov would have had less time than the required 25 minutes, since his role as commanding officer would have been to report a missile strike to the military high command and the state leaders, in whose hands the authority lies to order a nuclear attack [161].

The story of the Petrov-almost-War became public worldwide only in 1990. However, more disturbing than the incident itself is the fact that this is no exception. The Wikipedia article "list of nuclear close calls" (early March 2018) listed 11 almost-nuclear catastrophes between 1950 and 2010: one in the 1950s, five in the

1960s, including the Cuban crisis, one in the 1970s and two in the 1980s. After the end of the Cold War, there were further close calls, for instance in 1995, when a Norwegian research missile collecting material on the polar lights set off an alarm, ultimately resulting in the then Russian president, Boris Yeltsin, becoming the first state leader to activate his key for the 'nuclear briefcase' The Wikipedia article only lists the few close calls that became public. When we think of the effort to maintain confidentiality that can be expected in matters concerned with nuclear weapons, we have to assume that his is only the tip of the iceberg.

The British-born satirist John Oliver presents the very successful and informative American satirical show "Last Week Tonight". One of the shows dealt with the security (or non-security) of American nuclear weapons and the sometimes careless way of handling them. In this show, we learn about the B52 bomber crash over Goldsboro in North Carolina in 1961, which broke apart in the air and lost two hydrogen bombs. One fell to the ground and made a crater several meters deep without there being any danger of explosion. The other floated gently to the ground on a parachute, where it almost detonated (three of four mechanisms were activated). John Oliver comments the close nuclear catastrophe in North Carolina with the smug remark: "You might be thinking: Ok, we nearly blew up one of the Carolinas, but that is why we have two."

Because there is such a large arsenal of nuclear weapons in the USA and in Russia, it must be assumed that it is difficult to maintain an overview of the weapons, their storage sites and their operational readiness. As John Oliver illustrates this situation, at times, nuclear weapons are flown across the country without the landing basis being appropriately informed. As a result, what can occur is that a B-52 nuclear bomber can stand around for hours on an airfield without anyone working at the airfield knowing anything of the dangerous cargo.

The conclusion is obvious: if there are so many nuclear warheads that even the armed forces cannot maintain an overview, then the number of warheads that exist in itself constitutes a threat. John Oliver ends this topic by drawing the conclusion that the number of nuclear warheads should be reduced to a size that can be monitored and for which a sufficient number of qualified persons can be found to control the arsenal [162]. Nuclear accidents, meaning the threat from a country's own weapons are a genuine threat. And the fact that a nuclear war can also be triggered by accident can be clearly seen from the examples mentioned above.

Counting warheads

The International Campaign to Abolish Nuclear Weapons (ICAN) promotes international treaties on nuclear disarmament with the intention of abolishing nuclear weapons. It was awarded the Nobel Prize in 2017 for the engagement. This honour should not hide the fact that the organisation is miles away from achieving this goal. Part of the laborious effort lies in maintaining an overview of which countries have how many weapons (ICAN has no access to information on the location for reasons of military confidentiality). At present (March 2018), nine countries have a total of 15,000 nuclear warheads between them. The information in Table 9 below is taken from the ICAN website [163].

Table 9: Official and factual nuclear powers with estimated number of nuclear warheads according to the International Campaign to Abolish Nuclear Weapons (ICAN)

	Country	Nuclear weapon programme	Number of nuclear warheads
Official nuclear powers	USA	The first nuclear power and the only one to have used nuclear weapons (Hiroshima and Nagasaki bombs 1945). The USA spends more money on its nuclear arsenal than all the other nuclear powers combined.	6,800
	Russia	The second nuclear power (since 1949) with currently the largest arsenal of nuclear warheads. Heavy investment at present in its modernisation.	7,000
	Britain	The third nuclear power (since 1952) has four nuclear submarines with 16 trident missiles borrowed from the USA.	215
	France	The fourth nuclear power (since 1960) with emphasis on nuclear submarines armed with M45 and M51 missiles, but also has the capacity for nuclear air attacks. Land-based arsenals have been reduced.	300
	China	The fifth nuclear power (since 1964) has a few hundred air-, land- and marine-based nuclear weapons. China has promised never to use nuclear weapons for an atomic first strike.	270

	Country	Nuclear weapon programme	Number of nuclear warheads
Factual nuclear powers	Israel	The sixth nuclear power (since 1967) does not admit officially to possess nuclear weapons, but nor does it deny this. Israel did not sign the Non-Proliferation Treaty.	80
	India	The seventh nuclear power (since 1974) possesses only short- and mid-range missiles, but is developing intercontinental missiles. India did not sign the Non-Proliferation Treaty, but has pledged never to deploy weapons for a first strike.	110–120
	Pakistan	The eighth nuclear power (since 1998) developed nuclear weapons in the 1980s and tested them for the first time in 1998. Abdul Kadir Khan, who is regarded as father of the Pakistani nuclear programme, gained relevant competences during his physics studies in Holland. He is accused of having passed on his knowledge to Libya, Iran and North Korea. Pakistan expressly reserves the option of a first strike.	120–130
	North Korea	The ninth nuclear power (since 2005) conducted its first nuclear weapon test in 2006. It is assumed that the weapon was developed with the assistance of Pakistan.	< 10

According to the Treaty on the Non-Proliferation of Nuclear Weapons, official nuclear powers are states that exploded a nuclear device before 1 January 1967. These states are the USA, Russia (as the successor state of the Soviet Union), Britain, France and China. Factual nuclear states are those that are not listed as nuclear states in the Non-Proliferation Treaty (NPT), but that possess nuclear weapons, namely, Israel, India, Pakistan and North Korea. The three states Israel, India and Pakistan did not sign the

Non-Proliferation Treaty, while North Korea withdrew from the treaty in 2003.

Belgium, Germany, Italy, the Netherlands and Turkey do not possess nuclear weapons, but all have American nuclear warheads stored on their territory and the infrastructure to deploy them. In Germany, Tornado fighter aircraft are equipped to drop American B-61 atomic bombs, which are known to be stored for deployment at Büchel Air Base near Luxembourg. The so-called nuclear sharing is in fact not compatible with the principle of non-proliferation anchored in the Nuclear Non-Proliferation Treaty, which did not deter Germany from signing the treaty.

None of the nuclear powers and no NATO member state participated in the international ICAN negotiations to promote its cause to abolish nuclear warheads (with the exception of the Netherlands, who then voted against the treaty). In July 2017, 122 member states of the UNO General Assembly voted in favour of adopting the purely symbolic non-proliferation treaty, which was signed by (only) 53 in September 2017.

How to survive a nuclear bomb explosion

The chances of direct survival are increased in direct proportion to the distance from the bomb explosion (invert square law). The impact on the body can be traced back to the following physical phenomena:

- heat
- pressure
- -thermic rays (exposure to ultraviolet rays, visible light, infrared rays)
- -direct exposure to ionising rays (neutron radiation, gamma radiation, X-rays)
- -radioactive fallout resulting from radioactive dust that can also settle far from "ground zero"
- -nuclear electromagnetic impulse (causes disturbance to electric appliances)

Short-term survival

In order to survive immediately after an attack, avoiding exposure to heat and pressure from the bomb is absolutely vital. Survival is most likely in a solidly constructed concrete building or far below ground. Generally, chances of survival increase in direct proportion to the distance from the detonation. Under no circumstances should the explosion be observed, since the extreme light intensity can cause blindness or temporary loss of sight. Even for those who are far away from the detonation, blindness can result because of the concentration of light beams on the eye lenses. Waves of pressure spread from the site of the bomb explosion. The recommendation is therefore to take cover (in a ditch, for instance), and lie face down with the eyes on the ground and to cover head and eyes with the arms.

Mid-term survival

For those people who have suffered burning from direct heat or bodily damage from the pressure, mid- and long-term survival depends crucially on how well the wounds heal and how much the injuries inhibit the fight for survival after the nuclear bomb explosion or an extended nuclear war. For mid-term survival, it is generally recommended to take protection in a solidly constructed building during the first hours and days after the explosion.

Those people who find themselves in a badly constructed building and can manage to reach a site offering better protection in a few minutes (5 minutes) should do so, even if this means being briefly exposed to strong radiation. Should it take longer to reach better protection (between 5 and 15 minutes), it is considered advisable to remain at the less protective site for the first half-hour after the explosion and then to swiftly move to site offering better protection [164].

The thicker the walls and the more massive the protective material, the better. Those persons who are working in a concrete high-rise office building during the explosion will find greatest protection in a cellar or in the middle of the building (window-free central elevator or stairwell). At home, a windowless cellar offers greater protection than the uppermost building level. As already mentioned, the potential harm from a nuclear explosion decreases with distance from its location. This applies to both the physical and the temporal distance. The greater the protection from the initial damage (heat, pressure, direct ionising radiation), the greater are the chances of survival. Illustration Figure 7 forms part of a brochure available at the US Federal Emergency Management Agency. It shows the parts of building that offer the best protection from radiation, the figures showing the approximate scale of radiation protection.

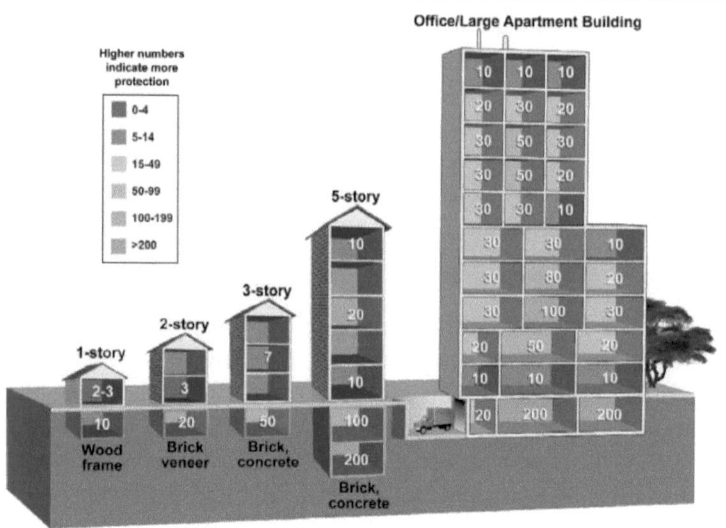

Figure 7: Radiation impact in various rooms in variously constructed buildings. Source: US-Federal Emergency Management Agency [165]

The same also applies for harmful effects of ionising radiation resulting directly from the explosion (neutron, gamma radiation, X-rays): the greatest danger exists immediately after the explosion and danger decreases with increasing time and distance.

After a nuclear explosion it is best to spend a few weeks in a concrete construction, since the radiation is still too great in the days and weeks after the detonation. The greatest fallout is to be expected in the first few hours after the explosion, which is why spending any time whatsoever outside should be avoided at all costs. The radiation in the radioactively impacted environment falls below a lethal level after about a week. Naturally, it is necessary to for food and drink supplies to be available for a period of two weeks. Tap water could be radioactive, if it is available at all.

In order to avoid being completely unprepared, it is recommended to set aside a room that can potentially serve as a shelter and use it as a storeroom for food and drinking water for at least two weeks. Since it is unlikely that after a nuclear disaster any form of power supply will be available, it is recommended that emergency lighting is set up, and a small battery-operated radio is available to be able to hear news reports. Any form of entertainment, e.g. books, to avoid boredom is also a good idea. Warm clothing should also be provided in the shelter, so that the contaminated clothing can be removed before entering the room. Arrangements regarding use of the bathroom and toilet facilities should be discussed well in advance with the other people using the shelter, ideally before there is any contamination in strategically inconvenient areas. Ideally, a WC might be available, but a contingency plan should be considered, should it not be possible to flush away the sewage. The social organisation of the potential inhabitants of the shelter and the long-term development of the post-apocalyptic society should be clarified. Although there are many dystopic scenarios of such post-apocalyptic societies, I find that it is hardly possible for me to imagine how best to survive as an individual or as a family.

Anybody who was in an exposed position when the explosion took place, for example outside a building, is potentially contaminated and should remove any clothing worn outside and ideally, should take a shower before entering the long-term shelter. So much for the theory. However, this concept is problematic when there is no alternative clothing available. As described before, a solution could be to keep clothing available in the potential shelter. But what are the chances of preparing public places, such as places of work? Well, not too good. At such public places, adequate preparation is difficult, since hardly anybody prepares for a nuclear attack that nobody hopes will ever take place. To be prepared for such an event as a society, we also have to be particularly well prepared with emergency stocks stored in emergency structures at the working place. Or, even better, to work towards developing peaceful coexistence within and between societies. But the precondition for this is a good peace policy under circumspect leadership working towards the interest of the population. Unfortunately, this is not the case.

How is survival possible in a protracted nuclear war (and is it worth the effort)?

There are many scenarios on how and whether it is possible to survive a nuclear war. Even a "local" nuclear war would have a catastrophic impact on life and the world. Climate simulations have been made showing the effect of a nuclear war limited to India and Pakistan with 50 war missiles, each having the explosive power of the Hiroshima bomb:

Fine black soot in the stratosphere would block out solar energy, resulting in a drop in temperatures around the world, and lead to a "nuclear winter" of the type known from previous theoretical nuclear war scenarios. Apart from this scenario, the soot in the stratosphere would cause warming of this layer, resulting in the ozone layer being reduced, which in turn would add to the damage to the earth from the ultraviolet rays. Not only that, but there would also be the radioactive fallout with its consequences for humans and animal life, of course (radiation sickness, which mostly ends in death). There is no doubt that even a limited nuclear war will result in the lives of millions of humans being lost [166].

Nevil Shute's novel *On the Beach,* written in 1953, is set in the vicinity of Melbourne in southern Australia. It relates the story of a nuclear war that has exterminated the population of the northern hemisphere. The lethal cloud with radioactive fallout slowly drifts southwards, resulting the people in the southern hemisphere gradually dying. This is also to be the fate to be met soon by the protagonists of the novel. The novel describes the everyday life of the people in Melbourne in the last few weeks before the lethal cloud reaches the area. These people follow their daily routine in the full knowledge that the cloud will not only mean the end of their existence, but also that of all humanity. Attempts to avoid death are not the subject matter of this novel; the atmosphere among the people is calm and collected. Yet, or perhaps particularly because of this atmosphere, the novel describes an impressive scenario of how people could behave in the last remaining days before the end of human life.

However, it is unlikely that in reality, a nuclear war would lead to such an elegant and dignified eradication of human life. The novel is based on the assumption that a major nuclear war would result in the a lethal radioactive cloud spreading throughout the world, that death would result within hours, or within a few days at most after the cloud had reached the area, and that the radiation would be lethal in the long-term, meaning that finding cover in protective buildings, such as bunkers, would not prevent this fate.

The bombs used in the nuclear war as described in *On the Beach* are cobalt bombs, which result in permanent radioactive contamination because of their long half-life period. It is not known that such bombs were ever built and can be found in nuclear arsenals, although in the 1950s there were certainly such plans.

Disintegration of radioactivity: the half-life period

The term half-life period is used to describe the disintegration time of radioactive isotopes: the half-life is the time required for one half the atoms and the corresponding intensity of radioactivity to disintegrate.

The radioactive ^{60}Co from a cobalt bomb has a half-life period of a little over 5 years. This means that it takes 5 years for the radioactivity to be halved. If the initial quantity is high, the radioactivity is probably still fatal after that period. After 10 years, a quarter of the initial radiation remains, and after 15 years, an eighth. What is the period of time until the radiation is smaller than one percent? Or, to be safe, even a thousandth of the initial radiation? Table 10 shows the disintegration of radioactivity with a half-life period of 5 years over a period of 10 half-life periods (50 years).

Table 10: Reduction in radioactivity for a radioactive source with a half-life period of 5 years, including the number of half-life periods, the corresponding duration and the expected radioactive reduction after the relevant period of time

Half-life periods (t ½)	1	2	3	4	5
Reduction in in radio-activity	1/ 2	1/4	1/8	1/16	1/32
Duration t ½ = 5 years	5 years	10 years	15 years	20 years	25 years
Half-life periods (t ½)	**6**	**7**	**8**	**9**	**10**
Reduction in radioac-tivity	1/64	1/128	1/256	1/512	1/1024
Duration t ½ = 5 years	30 years	35 years	40 years	45 years	50 years

According to this table showing a ^{60}Co half-life period of 5 years, the level falls below the 1/100 barrier between the 6th and 7th half-life period, i.e. after more than 30 years. The level falls to below the 1/1000 barrier after about 10 half-life periods, i.e. after about 50 years. It is all but impossible to survive in a nuclear shelter for such a long time.

Types of radioactivity and their radiation effect

When, due to beta decay, ^{60}Co decays to ^{60}Ni, this results in high-energy gamma quanta, which have an extremely destructive effect on the cell-fission processes. This effect is harnessed by medicine to treat cancer by irradiating tumours with a so-called Gamma Knife. The destructive effect on the cell-fission also explains the devastating effect ^{60}Co has on the human body: tissues, whose function and constant regeneration depends on cell-division processes are gravely damaged (the intestines, skins, blood cell formation in the bone marrow). The person will soon develop radiation sickness, which will soon lead to death.

The most important types radioactive rays are alpha, beta, and gamma rays (ionised radioactive rays).

Radiation results in an energy wave (gamma ray) from the decay of complex atomic nuclei or from particles, the alpha rays, that consist of helium nuclei (two protons and two neutrons). The beta rays lie between the energy wave and the particle radiation. Beta rays are usually listed as particle radiation, since they consist of electrons and positrons, which extinguish each other mutually and become two energy quanta (wave-particle dualism).

What all three radiation types have in common is that they can have an ionising effect, i.e. that they can catapult particles, energy quanta or waves from atoms. This induces further radioactive decay, which can result in chain reactions in nuclear bomb explosions, for instance, or to tissue damage in victims of radiation. Considered in purely mechanical terms, due to their huge mass, it seems logical that the large helium cores of alpha radiation have the greatest potential to destroy other atoms. On the other hand, they cover much shorter distances than beta or gamma radiation. Apart from that, high-energy gamma radiation alone can fragment an atom and stimulate its decay, despite the fact that it does not have the mass of alpha radiation. So it is impossible to determine unequivocally which of the three types of ionising radiation is the most devastating.

Considering the immediate ionising effect and the range of the radiation both play a decisive role when creating protective barriers.

The example we have used, ^{60}Co, is a **beta radiator,** which means that it emits electrons and positrons that mutually extinguish each other by generating energetic gamma quanta when they collide. Radiation penetrates tissue superficially and thus mainly causes injury to the skin (skin burn) and the eye lenses. Radiation can be prevented by means of a thin iron or aluminium sheet.

Gamma rays are not composed of particles, but of electro-magnetic waves (just as ultraviolet and x-rays are, but also light and radio waves). However, gamma rays have much higher energy content than x-rays. Gamma rays can be emitted several hundred metres through air. It is necessary to construct concrete or lead walls that are several metres thick to create effective protective barriers.

The massive **alpha rays**, which, as previously mentioned, consist of helium cores (two protons and two neutrons), create great damage over small areas, but have a very small air range of only a few centimetres. The upper skin layer consisting of dead skin cells or a sheet of paper suffice to offer effective protection, so that the rays cannot penetrate the body from an external source. However, alpha rays are particularly dangerous when they enter the lungs through inhalation or enter the digestive system through the mouth when swallowing an alpha ray emitter.

The fact that an attack by the alpha radiator polonium can be "easily warded off with good protection but is lethal when consumed orally" is what makes alpha radiator polonium suitable as a substance used for murder in the secret service. Polonium became generally known after the murder of the former Russian secret service agent, Alexander Litvinenko, who defected to the British secret service. In early November 2006, Litvinenko complained of symptoms such as vomiting, nausea, stomach pains and breathlessness. In the three weeks leading up to his death, he developed all the symptoms of radiation sickness. Shortly before he died, ^{210}polonium content was revealed in his urine. It is assumed that his murderers added the polonium to his food or into a drink. The former Palestinian leader Yasser Arafat probably also died of ^{210}polonium radiation [167].

Nuclear weapon arsenals are characterised by radioactive fission products with relatively short half-life periods. This means that even areas with very high radiation levels can be re-entered after a few weeks or months without the risk of lethal radiation. (This is why Hiroshima and Nagasaki could be reconstructed and re-settled after the Americans' nuclear bomb attacks.) However, radioactive decay following a nuclear bomb explosion is a complex process in which various sequences of decay lead to many different, partly radioactive, products of decay. Accordingly, radioactive fallout comes in many different forms.

Fission products such as the isotopes of caesium, iodine and strontium in the radioactive fallout have an extended half-life period that induce long-term exposition and enrichment of the food chain.

Strontium, similar to calcium, is metabolised (in the periodic table of the elements, the second main group of earth alkaline metals is found in the square immediately below calcium). Just as calcium, strontium is deposited in the bones. Blood and bone cancer result from the deposits of radioactive strontium (blood formation takes place in the bone marrow). ^{90}Sr, a beta ray with a half-time period of 29 years, plays a distinctive role in radioactive fallout. Due to its long half-life, radioactive fallout with ^{90}Sr results in long-term contamination.

Caesium-137 is used as an alternative to ^{60}Co in radiotherapy of tumours. It thus has a similarly destructive effect on frisson, but also has six times the half-life period of ^{60}Co. Accordingly, caesium-based radiation therapy devices can be used six times longer than those that are cobalt-based. As an ingredient of radioactive fallout, ^{137}Cs causes long-term problems. Similar to potassium, ^{137}Cs is easily resorbed in the intestines and spreads mainly to muscle tissue. High doses of ^{137}Cs can cause radiation poisoning. The biological half-life period (i.e. the time required to halve the caesium in the body through excretion) is about 110 days.

Iodine is automatically associated with the thyroids, and radioactive iodine isotopes are actually used for thyroid diagnostics and therapies (mainly ^{131}I). Unfortunately, iodine isotopes are also contained in nuclear fallout after a nuclear explosion. The pollution caused by radioactive iodine tends to be short- to mid-term (in contrast to long-term contamination with radioactive caesium or strontium), since radioactive iodine isotopes have short half-life periods. ^{131}I for instance, has a half-life period of 8 days and ^{123}I of 13 hours. The potassium iodine tablets that are available by the civil protection to be used when accidents at nuclear plants and nuclear explosions occur should be distributed immediately after the event, if at all possible. The stable iodine isotope ^{127}I displaces radioactive substances and thus dangerous iodine isotopes from the thyroid glands.

The dirty war plans with clean bombs

Maintaining the balance of terror was probably successful, because the nuclear powers knew that they would not be capable of waging a nuclear war without themselves suffering enormous damage. Even with a completely one-sided nuclear war – which is quite conceivable if one side removes the option of the other for a counter attack or forgoes the realisation of a counter attack for humanitarian reasons – the global consequences of the radioactive fallout and the pollution of the atmosphere through dust particles (nuclear winter) would also destroy the "victorious power" or at least cause enormous long-term damage.

In the 1950s, an effort was made to advance the development of clean bombs. The adjective "clean" mostly referred to the fact that the intention was to reduce radioactive fallout. This was a useful argument to justify further nuclear weapon tests [168]. Teller Ulam configurated design "clean thermonuclear bombs" create fewer radioactive isotopes, which are also comparatively short-lived in comparison to classic nuclear bombs. However, these bombs are also not completely free of radioactive fallout.

If we consider the euphemism of the "clean bomb" absolutely callously, it becomes apparent that truly "clean" weapons of mass destruction are targeted at damaging the enemy as much as possible while allowing the aggressor to remain unharmed and being able to use all the resources of the destroyed enemy after the war is over. That means that a "clean" weapon of mass destruction destroys human life without destroying the infrastructure and the ecological system and without causing any global side effects, such as a nuclear winter, for example. As long as the opponent still has enough time to carry out a counter-attack, the idea of a war of acquisition with "clean" weapons of mass destruction would not be successful, since a counter attack using normal "dirty" nuclear weapons would drag the aggressor down into the abyss.

A nuclear war would doubtlessly cause mass mortality. If a nuclear war were existential, would it mean the end of human existence, or can a residue population of *Homo sapiens* survive and then multiply to establish a new population? Let us hope that nuclear weapons are never again deployed. This leads to the one remaining question: Can humans live with nuclear weapons without using them (again) one day?

9 What's so special about *Homo sapiens?*

In the chapter entitled "Cognitive Revolution" of his book *"Sapiens"*, Yuval Harari developed the hypothesis that the acquisition of the cognitive abilities particular to *Homo sapiens* about 70,000 years ago was not the result of massive genetic and biochemical changes, but rather a socio-psychological development. According to Harari, what distinguished *Homo sapiens* from other *Homo* species existing at the time (*Homo neanderthalensis, Homo rudolfensis, Homo erectus*) was the growing ability to tell stories and to believe in what they portrayed. This ability to believe in non-objective, non-material entities became the foundation for co-operation far beyond bonds with family or friends [169].

Communication via sounds (language) is not a characteristic specific to humans: what distinguishes humans from other animals is the ability to communicate non-concrete matters, and thus to create institutions from what are originally only shared ideas. In other words, humans cause imagined reality to become existent, although the ideas themselves are not concrete.

The term "cognitive revolution" implies the rapid onset of a process. However, it seems far more likely that it was a slow and gradual process that evolved during the course of several generations and involved the beginnings of many various small myths in various populations. Meanwhile there are many non-concrete institutions in our world, such as deities, nations, marriage, business, government, money, ideologies. The existence of common ideas allows large groups of humans to co-operate with persons who are alien to their community and with non-related persons and thus to wage war, for instance, to mission for religions and to define standards to coexistence. The common belief in the value of money is the basis of all economy as it exists today. People develop complex machines in large business enterprises.

As a result of co-operation in a non-quantifiable, solely imagined social structure involving common tasks, humans were also able to develop an object that makes the extermination of all of humanity possible: the nuclear bomb.

"Chosen nations" and "clean" weapons of mass destruction

As I have explained in this book, humans are faced with several existential problems resulting from the massive increase in the global *Homo sapiens* population and the corresponding consumption of resources, pollutant emissions and destruction of natural habitats. At the same time, there is a high level of rivalry at various man-made organisational levels: between individuals, between economic classes, between power groups, and – particularly significant for armed battle – between nations and states. A state that believes in its own privileged position in the world could be tempted to take possession of other parts of the world by exterminating the people living there using "clean" weapons of mass destruction. The resulting reduction in the world population would mean that the population of this state would also have more resources available for its own citizens' continued prosperity. Such action is ethically and morally reprehensible, yet the history of man is rampant with genocide.

According to the concept of balance of terror, it seems that the capacity of the "remaining world" to strike back against attack and thus the ability to threaten the assailing nation with the warning that it will also be dragged into the abyss is regarded as a more dependable method of securing oneself against the deployment of "clean" weapons of mass destruction than to believe in the ethnic and moral integrity of human action.

Global elites and "clean" weapons of mass destruction

What is also conceivable is for international elite groups to deploy biological weapons of mass destruction to decimate the world population. My first impulse as an educated person is to declare such a scenario as inconceivable. My argument would be that the concept of humanism is so strongly anchored not only in the educated classes but also in the members of the families of today's power and wealth elites that they would oppose such a terrible crime. – Or would they?

There is a socially accepted speciesism embedded in humanism and the emphasis on the higher value of human life as a matter of course in our society. We breed and kill species other than *Homo sapiens* in large-scale industrially organised factories in order to eat them. When animal diseases occur, slaughtering the entire stock is common practice. When an animal population becomes too large or is classed as a pest, we humans resort to drastic means of decimation (for example eradicating hares in Australia or shooting red deer in Europe).

Meat eating animals, i.e. carnivores, also kill other animals. But the way we humans utilise animal life is of a completely different quality. In the chapter on the estimated volume of livestock and wild animals it was illustrated that there is a constant increase in the volume of livestock (that is, animals that owe their sole existence to the fact that they are useful for us humans). Most large mammals that exist at present would not exist at all if they were not useful to us.

It is not the fact the humans eat meat that distinguishes us in quality from other meat eaters, but the systematic industrial exploitation of other species, which is only possible because of cooperative practices in non-concrete (only imaginary, but as objects non-existent) cooperative entities (networks). We justify this practice ethically and morally by distinguishing ourselves from other species and giving humans a unique position of privilege based on humanistic principles. What is this actually based on?

Do only humans have a consciousness? Many people who have a dog would probably negate this. Do humans have a superior consciousness? Perhaps. Is it intelligence that makes humans unique?

We derive all kinds of privileges and rights for our species from the intellectual superiority of *Homo sapiens*, privileges and rights that we do not grant other species. We measure our superiority by cognitive abilities, in which *Homo sapiens* outrank other species. What we do not consider is that there are many neurological, cerebral and cognitive abilities in which *Homo sapiens* are inferior to other species. If dogs were to develop an intelligence test, *Homo sapiens* would probably fare very badly, since we would not be able to compensate our badly developed sense of smell with our ability to interpret poems. Linguistic ability would not play any role in an intelligence test developed by dogs, just as a good sense of smell plays no role at all in intelligence tests developed by humans.

Ultimately, we have to concede that the privileged special status given to Homo sapiens is simply the result of the factual power of our species over other creatures.

But what if specific humans were to be genetically optimised to humans that are clearly distinguishable from normal humans, to humans that feel just as superior to *Homo sapiens* as *Homo sapiens* do to other species? As a superior species, this *"Homo deus"* could assume the right to exploit *Homo sapiens* and to take over control of its populations [170].

The question regarding the basis of the privileged position of humans cannot be answered with any degree of satisfaction. The unique position of humans, anchored in the world view of humanism as characterised by enlightenment and human rights, forms the present-day basis of the unique position of humans in the society in which I grew up. In many religions, the unique status of humans forms the basis of their theological principles. In a few words: the unique position granted to humans is a product of our ability to believe in non-objectifiable, non-concrete (non-matter) things.

Racism has repeatedly induced peoples to rise above others and led to horrific mass murders. The acquisition of resources that accompanied these atrocities or the exploitation of subjected people were always justified with ideologies explaining the superiority of the own group over the subjected group. Whether the lines of argumentation were based on racist, missionary or democratisation principles, they had one aspect in common: without fail, they relied on our ability to instrumentalise, our belief in non-objectifiable, non-concrete matter.

Eugenics

The fact that since the Neanderthals have disappeared, there is only one remaining species of the *Homo* genus makes it easier for us to reconcile our ethical and moral values with a form of speciesism: it allows us to condone the exploitation of other animals without creating all too much cognitive dissonance. However, we may not ignore the fact that also within the *Homo sapiens* species and against all humane principles, we allow ourselves to declare certain groups of humans valuable while others are declared less valuable, and we then to take brutal action against these. If this division is made according to biologi(sti)cal criteria, we call this racism. The fundamental principle used for the construction of effective enemy stereotypes as an element of war propaganda is to give top priority to the superiority of the own group (formerly based on racism, nowadays on claimed ethical and moral superiority of the own group).

Racist claims to superiority have always been considered be the legitimisation of certain groups of *Homo sapiens* to exploit, displace or exterminate other groups (mention need only be made of the conquest of America by eradicating most of the indigenous population and the subsequent trans-Atlantic slave trade). If moral misgivings regarding such exploitative actions were raised, evasive narratives for the own group's superiority were found, such as a superior religion, for example. Then, one could continue oppressing and massacring other people (at least now acknowledged as humans) to save their souls. The resources were then acquired for the own use of the superior group and, at the same time, they could regard themselves as good people (at least better than the other, inferior group).

In the Cold War it was the superiority of the own societal or state form that dominated the divisive narrative. Meanwhile, the (own) ethical and moral religious higher values are used to diminish the value of other groups (nations, countries). Wars fought by western powers for the acquisition of resources are not justified to the public with the acquisition of commodities or defining the routes of pipelines, but with the objective to pave the way towards democracy and humanistic enlightenment to the country under assault.

In order to contain the rising cognitive dissonance at least partially, enemy stereotypes are shifted to individual persons or dominant groups in the country from which the population needs to be freed (Saddam Hussein, for instance, or Muammar al-Ghaddafi). The construction of enemy stereotypes is particularly effective when directed against specific persons. Directing hatred in the population towards abstract groups (Muslims, communists) requires a higher measure of constant propagandist effort [122].

Twentieth-century racism, which culminated in racist mass murder in my country (Germany) and in conquered areas, particularly of the Soviet Union, was also fostered by scientists. Racist theories and scientific projects aimed at breeding better humans in the first half of the 20th century were wide-spread, and were not only found in Germany. The renowned "Cold Spring Harbour Laboratories" on the east coast in the USA had declared eugenic objectives. The eugenic concepts of the German National

Socialists were based on selection, in the most brutal manifestation by the "eradication of unworthy life". Ultimately, the objective was the movement was the optimisation of humans to create a better species.

At present, there is a new eugenic movement on the horizon. This will not be based on brutal selection, but on targeted genetic modifications of the human genome. At first, only the human predisposition to certain illnesses will be corrected by genome modification, but it will not be long before the targeted creation of more positive characteristics promising certain advantages will have established themselves large-scale.

That makes the role of the sciences at least as prominent as in the selective murderous eugenics of the 20th century. The societal, ethical and moral problems and questions that will develop with the genetic improvement of humans could unravel our humanistic, i.e. human-centred, global view. At present, the inequality of humans worldwide is social and economic in nature. The equal value of the biology of all humans is a fundamental pillar of humanism. Racism and humanism appear to be incompatible. (Unless one recognises the social Darwinism and eugenic nature of "evolutionary humanism" as a form of humanism.) However, it appears that the oppression and exploitation of other animal species are absolutely compatible with our form of humanism: we derive the legitimisation to exploit other species from our self-declared superiority. Should various species of the genus *Homo* exist one day, this could lead to similar exploitative hierarchies.

It is only a question of time until humans consciously intervene in the evolution of their own species. But simply allowing this improvement to occur could result in grave social upheavals, when biologically superior human species have to coexist with inferior human species. In his book "Brave New World", Aldous Huxley described a fictional society that is structured according to genetic classes. However, in this fictional society, each person's acceptance of class membership is anchored genetically, so that though the individuals are not free, they are content.

A decisive issue is also whether genetic improvements will mainly be made through the germline editing (producing so-called "designer babies"), or whether a living *Homo sapiens* can be improved. (Can I enhance my intelligence during my lifetime using genetic modification, or stop the ageing process and become immortal?)

If the road via germline editing is taken, this would require an altruistic generation of parents who hope to provide an advantage for their offspring. The advantage of this road would be that it would be easier to monitor the improvement of the human species. Theoretically, it would make it possible to gradually improve the human species from generation to generation, a common human project, so to speak. It also would be possible to prevent the oppression and exploitation of the inferior species living at the time by respective superior species, since the inferior species would be the parents or grandparents of the superior species. I could even imagine such a gradual optimisation imaginable in contrast to the horrific fascist-like scenarios that I usually envisage in connection with this topic. But the precondition would be that it be coordinated worldwide.

If, however, we leave future eugenics to "market forces", creating a breed of improved humans would turn into a purely elite project. Genetic optimisation would only be utilised by rich people from the global upper classes. The assumption based on human-rights declaration that all people are free and equal would become obsolete.

Genocide

I studied medicine in the second half of the 1990s, from 1994 to 2001. I spent the whole year 2000 doing my practical year at a hospital, as is required in Germany.

In that year, patients between 90 and 100 years old were from the birth cohorts between 1910 and 1900, those between 80 and 89 were born in the decade between 1920 and 1911 and those between 70 and 79 between 1930 and 1921. In 1940, the birth cohorts between 1910 and 1900 were between 30 and 40 years old, those in the birth cohort 1920- 1911 between 20 and 29 and those born between 1930 and 1921 were between 10 and 19 years old. This means that most patients that I learned to know in 2000 were of the generation that personally experienced National Socialism in Germany, i.e. at an age when they can assume to have been productive and made a contribution to society.

Most of the patients that I learned to know during that year were completely normal people with their own strengths and weaknesses, with good manners and who behaved in the accepted polite and friendly manner.

The second world war began with Germany attacking Poland in September 1939 and led to the death of 65 million people, mainly (about 27 million) in the Soviet Union. The national socialist ideology was social Darwinian and racist, "race" being a collective category for absolutely randomly defined group distinctions and categories of division. Jews and Slavic peoples were particularly caught up in the crossfire of hate propaganda and became the targets of a genocide campaign that was partly industrialised. The holocaust lead to more than 6 million deaths, most of them in Poland and the Soviet Union.

The novel by Jonathan Littell, "The Kindly Ones", originally published as *Les Bienveillantes,* depicts a fictional, but well researched version of the true events of the military campaigns in East Europe and Russia from the perspective of a young SS officer named Dr Max Aue. The plot of the novel tells of Aue's involvement in murdering Jews and other declared enemies or 'life unworthy of life' as part of his duty in the war. He survives Stalingrad and performs his duty, working and murdering in the concentration camp Auschwitz.

The most disturbing aspect of the novel was the strong identification with Max Aue that readers experienced when reading the novel (or at least that I experienced). As the novel unfolds, the motives and actions of the protagonist seem plausible, although monstrous crimes are described, for example the shooting of lined-up civilians from the perspective of Max Aue as an accomplice murderer in his position of commander. The reader, who identifies himself with a mass murderer, is not even given the opportunity to qualify Aue's actions by putting them in the context of the national socialist ideology, since when Aue murdered his own mother, he did something that, irrespective of any ideological classification, everyone (both the convinced national socialist and the morally confirmed humanist) could only describe as evil. With his incestuous feelings towards his twin sister, he has human traits that are rejected by many people, not least those with religiously motivated values, this, too, being in keeping with the national socialist ideology. And yet the reader identifies himself (or at least I did) with what can only be defined as an evil person, if he is viewed objectively.

The book, which was highly acclaimed in France and was awarded the highly prestigious French Prix Goncourt, was debated extremely controversially in other countries, including Germany and Israel. Critics regarded it as amoral to describe the holocaust in fictional terms and then to do so in the first person, thus winning the confidence of the reader, although the protagonist is a dangerous criminal. What is even more interesting is the fact is that some critics concentrated on the style that the book was written in, and declared it "of inferior quality". Well, perhaps the German translation was terrible. In French, I did not find the style cloying (at least as a non-native speaker it did not appear to be so). The French critics' comparisons with Tolstoy, Pasternak and Dostoevsky speak against bad writing style and the criticism of it being cheap literature. Obviously, the novel put its finger in an open wound, something unconscious that we only reluctantly admit to ourselves, but somehow know or at least feel.

I cannot speak for the subconsciousness of other people, and in particular of some literary critics, who reacted with raging critiques. I can only ask myself what the cause is of the unconscious feeling of discomfort this book left me with. I became aware of the fact that I might have committed similar crimes if I had been born 60 years earlier and had found myself caught up in similar circumstances. Of course I prefer to think about how I would have fought an unjust system as a resistance fighter or how I would have acted as a hero working undercover to save lives in an evil system. A novel that makes me realise that in similar circumstances, I could become a criminal rather than a hero makes me furious. My impulse is not to want to simply accept a scenario that attacks my perception of who I am. I want to fight against this and emphasise that not everything can be explained by the circumstances, and that I am capable of making morally well-founded decisions for good and against evil (naturally implying that I myself would have acted better).

I think that even I can actually know that I am also capable of evil and amoral actions, but that I actually am not prepared to want to know this. This could be what the Slovenian philosopher Slavoj Žižek meant with the category "unknown knowns".

As described at the beginning, the people of the war generation, who I encountered at the hospital 20 years ago did not appear to be less good people than the generation of elderly people who are now being treated in German hospitals. And I have nothing negative to say about the three of my four grandparents that I met. It does not take truly evil people to make evil actions possible. Every person has the potential for evil. Supplying weapons incites warfare. Nevertheless, I do not claim that those persons who are responsible for producing the weapons and supplying them have more evil traits in them than I do. Money is a universally accepted incentive. German weapons are supplied to countries throughout the world [171] and in the second world war, the Germans would not have had sufficient supplies of oil for the so-called German blitz war without the oil supplied by the Americans [171, 172].

To say that the holocaust is not a unique event could be misunderstood as being an attempt to dilute this atrocious genocide. There can be no doubt that the holocaust had some particularly horrific aspects, especially the factory-like process of human extermination was taken to an extreme in its perverse perfection. Nevertheless, I want to emphasise that I do not view the holocaust as being a unique event in that a crime of such dimensions could not be repeated at any time.

10 Poverty and hunger

An entire book could be written about the nature of poverty and the various definitions of poverty. This chapter will refer only briefly to the conceptional differences between relative and absolute criteria for evaluating poverty.

Relative poverty

Germany is regarded as a rich country. When measured by its gross domestic product (GDP), this statement is certainly correct. Nevertheless, in 2001 the suggestion was made for the first time that a report on poverty and wealth be made. Since then five such reports have been made, the most recent in 2017 [173, 174]. In view of the fact the almost no data was compiled for the small group of super rich in Germany, the frequently used term "poverty report" is more apt than the officially termed "Report on poverty and wealth". Whether the information on the super rich was not provided because there are only few such people in Germany or whether this omission was a result of political influence is left to the reader to decide.

The German writer Bertolt Brecht put this concept of relative poverty in a nutshell:

> Rich man, poor man
> faced each other in a van.
> Said the poor man with a switch / twitch:
> Were I not poor, you wouldn't be rich
> (Bertolt Brecht, 1934)

(Translation attributed to Jens Martens, Kapuscinski Development Lecture, Helsinki, 29 October 2014   Benchmarks for a truly universal post - 2015 agenda for sustainable development source: http://kapuscinskilectures.eu/wp-content/uploads/2014/11/Martens_KDL_text.pdf)

The rich man could have responded: „Were I not rich, you wouldn't be poor".

Existential poverty

Existential poverty that includes famine can repeatedly be found in the records of settled cultures. In the Christian Middle Ages, hunger was one of the four apocalyptic threats in the Revelations to John, the others being war, pestilence and death.

In his work "The Principle of Population", written in 1798, Thomas Robert Malthus predicted a developing imbalance between population growth and potential increase in food production. Up to that point, population growth was exclusively regarded as a positive state, since this was thought to be the essential condition for a more productive society. Due to the increase in the food production worldwide, the gloomy Malthusian prognosis does not completely correspond with modern-day reality. However, the principle that over-population results in famines remains a matter of concern that dominates debates on the future.

Hunger today

The United Nation's Food and Agricultural Organisation (FAO) defines hunger as an extended period of reduced calorific intake of less than 2100 kcal per day. According to statistics published in the World Food Programme in 2015 more than 35 % of the population in the five countries Haiti, Namibia, the Central African Republic and North Korea suffered hunger. This was established for 25% to 35 % of the population of Afghanistan, Yemen, Madagascar, Uganda, Ruanda, Tanzania, Ethiopia, Mozambique, Chad, the Republic of the Congo, Zimbabwe and Liberia. In the two most populous countries in the world, China and India, over 5% (China) of the population suffered hunger and as much as over 15 % (India) respectively. There are certainly many people suffering hunger in countries listed in the category "no data available":

Somalia, Sudan, South Sudan, Eritrea, the Democratic Republic of the Congo, Burundi, Libya, Syria and Palestine [175]. In 2010, two of these states, Libya and Syria, were still listed in the same category (under 5% starving people) as the European countries.

In absolute numbers, the number of starving people worldwide has decreased by about 211 million people (12.9 % of the global population), from 991 million people (23.3 % of the global population) in 1990 to 780 million people (12.9 % of the global population) in 2016. However, the number of starving people in 2017 increased again for the first time in a long while, the present figure being 815 million [176]. About two thirds of the decrease (2/3 x 210 million = 140.5 million) between 1990 and 2016 are due to the improvements in food supply in the highly populated country, China.

China previously repeatedly suffered catastrophic famines. Between 1958 and 1961, between 20 and 43 million people starved to death. Apart from natural climatic adversities, the collapse of agricultural production structures resulting from radical economic reforms were the cause of famine. The "Great Leap Forward" at the close of the 1950s was a structural reform of the Chinese economy designed towards a radical reconstruction of agriculture. The core of this "reform" was the absolute prohibition of private property. Any attempts at resistance were immediately suppressed, and "anti-rightists" were persecuted, jailed and sometimes tortured and killed. Most of the poverty-stricken farmers who were fighting for the survival of their families in a subsistence economy (cultivation of fields mainly for their own food supply) were prohibited from providing for their families, initially resulting in the collapse of agricultural production. The forced collectivisation that the "Great Leap Forward" reform entailed, caused organisational chaos. The farmers, who mostly had only a rudimentary education, were removed from their families and put into collective large-scale farms, where there was complete confusion regarding the areas of responsibility and duties of the individual person. At the same time, the farmers were forced to work in large-scale industrial projects. This in turn meant that agricultural food production was neglected and that the formerly existing more or less functioning subsistence economy was destroyed [177].

The famines in China resulting from the "Great Leap forward" have remained in the collective consciousness of the Chinese people as a huge catastrophe. However, in the 20th century, hunger was the rule rather than the exception in India, too. The Indian economic scientist Amartya Sen is said to have stated that the gigantic surplus mortality in China was completely overshadowed by the regular surplus mortality in India due to hunger [178]. What entered collective memory as a huge catastrophe in China, he said, was a normal occurrence in India in the 20th century.

In 1969, the Indian population was recorded at 523 million inhabitants [179]. After decades of population growth exceeding 2%, the population in India was 870 million in 1990, when population growth fell below 2 % for the first time. Meanwhile (in 2017) the population in India has reached a level of 1.32 billion people. Population growth in the country has fallen to 1.2 %, leading some experts to consider the problem of population explosion to have been alleviated [180]. However, assuming that the population continued to grow at a rate of 1.2 %, the population would have doubled to 2.64 billion people in 58 years (2076) (doubling time according to Al Bartlett = 70/1.2 = 58.3). Between 15 % and 25 % of the population in India is considered undernourished. By extension, this means that about one quarter of the people worldwide who are undernourished live in India.

China took drastic steps to decrease population growth by introducing its one-child policy in 1980. At the same time, it experienced enormous economic development. The proportion of undernourished people in the population was 23.9 % in 1990 and has meanwhile fallen to below 10 % [181].

Table 11 shows a comparison of the population projection in India and China for the next ten years under the assumption that the population of India will grow at 1.2 % and that of China at 0.5 %.

**Table 11:   Demographic development in India and China 2016-2026 (in billions). Projection based on population growth of
1.2 % in India and 0.5 % in China**

	2016	2017	2018	2019	2020	2021	2022	2023	2024	2025	2026
China	1.3079	1.386	1.393	1.400	1.407	1.414	**1.421**	1.428	1.435	1.442	1.450
India	1.324	1.340	1.356	1.372	1.389	1.405	**1.422**	1.439	1.457	1.474	1.492

According to this calculation, the Indian population will exceed that of China for the first time in 2022. The third most populous country on earth is the USA with 324 million inhabitants, followed by Indonesia, which has 260 million inhabitants. In sequence of inhabitants then comes Brazil (206 million) and Pakistan (203 million), followed by Nigeria (187 million) and Bangladesh (163 million) inhabitants.

China, or more specifically, Chinese companies, are buying up agricultural land throughout the world, in particular in Southeast Asia, but also in Africa. The most expansive (i.e. about three quarters) Chinese agricultural land acquisition is taking place in Southeast Asia, including Papua New Guinea.

When considering Chinese land acquisition in comparison to that of other countries (or their companies), its volume of land acquisition is not the largest. The organisation Land Matrix (landmatrix.org) compiles excellently displayed statistics on international land acquisition. China ranks only fourth among the top 10 investor countries (as of March 2018). The USA, which has bought up 9.9 million hectares of land worldwide, heads the list, followed by Malaysia and Singapore before China. The fact that Singapore ranks third shows that nations are not necessarily directly involved in international property trading, but that internationally active businesses based in a certain country, Singapore, for instance, play a significant role. (Why exactly Singapore I cannot say, but possibly for tax saving purposes.) [182]. Since land property always means that exploitable resources can be accessed, it must be assumed that land purchases involve connections between state power structures and major investors.

The African continent is a prominent target for land purchasing, and includes numerous countries where a high proportion of the population suffers from starvation. Land purchasing can also be advantageous for Africa, of course, since many countries have a large, not yet utilised, potential for the cultivation of food products. Foreign investment in these countries can mobilise this potential, thus contributing to allowing the domestic population to provide its own food. Whether such investment is for the good or bad of the country depends on international trade regulations. These should facilitate profit-oriented cultivation without this advantage coming at the expense of the food available to the local population. The local labour market should also be integrated. The former subsistence farmers, who may not be able to compete with large agricultural companies have no other option but to work for international companies. So solid labour protection laws should not be regarded as a luxury in emerging countries. On the contrary, it is particularly important for developing countries that such laws are common practice and are implemented.

In order to prevent the cheap labour being the main investment consideration, it is essential to negotiate international treaties and agreements to protect employees, and mechanisms to implement these need to be put in place. But at a national level, too, governments are not at the mercy of international companies. The land might belong to international companies, but de facto it still lies within the host country's territorial area and is subject to the legislation of this country. If national governments improve labour protection, it is not possible for international companies to simply ignore this aspect when investing in a foreign country. Of course, enhancing national labour rights can be more effective when states in a certain region coordinate relevant laws. However, this requires functioning state and administration institutions, since the companies are not likely to feel responsible for the food supply of the local population. South Sudan, for example, a country plagued by civil war and lacking governance, is one of the main countries targeted by investors, but also one of the main receiver states of the world food programme.

Apart from South Sudan, there were 36 other countries dependent on food supplies in 2017, 30 of them on the African continent. It is particularly worrying that the population growth on the African continent is so high, the projected figures citing growth from 1.2 billion people in 2015 to 2.5 billion in 2050. The current statistics on starvation in the world can be accessed at http://de.wfp.org. When listing the remaining seven non-African countries that are dependent on food assistance, the correlation between hunger and war is striking: Iraq, Syria, Afghanistan, Yemen, Pakistan, Myanmar and North Korea.

For western countries, which claim to be committed to the values of enlightenment, this is particularly shameful: in Iraq, a "coalition of the willing" led to a war that was completely in contravention of international law and turned a previously functioning state into a failed state [37, 183, 184]. In Syria, the west also massively undermined governance, among others, by trafficking weapons from Libya to Syria to rearm the "moderate rebels" with weapons, a step that was beneficial to the radical Islamic opposition. It was only due to the support from Russia and Iran that the Syrian government troops were able to regain control in the country, which probably prevented a further "failed state" after Iraq [50]. Afghanistan was occupied after 9/11, in order to ... I'm afraid cannot say exactly why, but I am quite certain that it had something to do with democracy, drilling wells for water and human rights.

Since 2015, Yemen has been bombarded and starved out by Saudi Arabia, supported by the west (USA, France and Britain), by means of naval blockades, also with German-produced patrol ships [171]. Pakistan, Myanmar and North Korea also depend on western aid for food, without experiencing direct aggression from the west. To be fair, it should also be mentioned that it is in Pakistan that the highest number of murder missions of American drones are recorded [185] and North Korea's harvests, which are not bountiful anyway, are impeded by the American-South-Korean manoeuvres taking place close to the border during the harvesting season [186, 187].

In Africa, 232 million of the 1.2 billion inhabitants of the continent are suffering from starvation. The African continent has the highest proportion of starving people (about 20%, i.e. one in five persons). Demographic projections forecast a doubling of the population to about 2.5 billion people in 2050. Wars also play a decisive role in Africa's severe famines, such as the terrible famines in the South Sudan, which is plagued by civil war and in North-East Nigeria, which is terrorised by the notorious Boko-Haram militia. A state of famine has been declared in the Central African Republic, in Somalia and in Yemen. A country is defined as being in state of severe famine when more than 30% of the population suffers from acute undernourishment and less than 4 litres of water is available per person and day. A country is defined as suffering from famine when more than 15% of the population suffers from acute undernourishment. Such a country is considered to be in a state of humanitarian emergency [188].

But even without decaying states or war, the food supply in large areas of Africa is problematic. The Sahel Zone is a semi-arid vegetation belt that links Sudan to the hostile deserts of North Africa and stretches over an area of 150 to 800 kilometres wide from the Red Sea to the Atlantic. The Arab word "Sahil" means coast (of the sand sea of the Sahara). The climatic conditions are unfavourable for agriculture in this area. The Sahel Zone, especially the broader western region, where the countries Mauritania, Mali, Burkina Faso, Niger and Chad lie, suffered a disastrous hunger catastrophe between 1968 and 1972, which contributed to the term "Sahel Zone" even today spontaneously being associated with hunger. Ethiopia, which, strictly speaking, lies south of the Sahel Zone and does not really have the same climatic characteristics as the Sahel Zone, became the epitome of a hunger crisis in the years between 1984 and 1985. It is estimated that about one million people died of starvation.

While the number of people worldwide suffering from starvation fell between 1990 and 2016, the number of food crises that are clamouring for attention from the media has risen. In 1991-1992 and 2011- 2012, there were acute food crises in Somalia, which is suffering from state collapse and has become a failed state. Food crises were also experienced in the Democratic Republic of Congo between 1998 and 2000, and in the western Sahil Zone in 2012. In these countries, all having to cope with crises and difficult climatic conditions, the food situation remains problematic, even when there is not current hunger crisis.

This clearly demonstrates that war and hunger go hand in hand. However, the unfavourable climatic conditions and unfertile land, but also over-rapid population growth all contribute to hunger being a permanent threat. As already mentioned, it is expected that the population in Africa will double to about 2.5 billion people between 2015 and 2050. At the same time, deserts and semi-arid dry regions are likely to expand. It is difficult to foresee what effect climate warming will have on the continent. Quite aside from the climate, the local exploitation of resources such as water and land for agricultural production is even now causing desertification, dehydration of the soil and soil erosion of large areas of productive land. Large areas of land that have not been effectively utilised to date are being bought up by international agricultural companies. This will without doubt lead to displacement of the local population. If any benefit can be gained from the land purchasing, then it might be found in the hope that the investors develop areas that are currently lying completely or partially dormant and that they will create new areas of agriculturally productive land.

However, plantations require huge quantities of water. In the past few months, there have been repeated reports that fresh water is threatening to run out in Cape Town. South Africa is the richest country in sub-Sahara Africa, and since Libya has been turned into a failed state by a French-American military intervention in 2011, even the richest country in Africa. Perhaps it is a blessing in disguise that water shortage first manifested itself in this country. This makes one hopeful that technical and political measures will be taken to solve the problem of water shortage.

11 Epidemics

When we consider what the four riders of the apocalypse represent, the first and second being conquest and war, the third and fourth famine and death respectively, then it is only the harbinger of disease and death that has not yet been included our spectrum of topics.

The great pestilences of the Middle Ages cost the lives of millions of people. It is estimated that approximately 20 – 25 million people, at least a third of the European population, fell victim to the bubonic plague of the 14th century [189, 190]. The plague is transmitted by rat fleas, and in the case of lung pest, directly aerogenically, via contact from person to person, i.e. it is contagious. In the novel *La Peste* by Albert Camus, the pest breaks out among humans after rats have died. When the body of a rat becomes cold after dying from the pest, an infected rat flea that has housed on the rat looks for a new host – a human, for example.

Spreading epidemics by land and water

Air travel developed in the early 20th century, but it was only after the second world war that airplanes became means of mass transportation. Previously, travel mostly took place on land and water, allowing epidemics to spread mainly along the long-distance land and ship routes. Military campaigns also contributed to epidemics spreading, and the military camps with their bad hygiene provided the best environments for spreading germs.

It is assumed that the pest in the 14th century [191] started in rodent populations of East Asia from where it spread to the estuaries of the river Volga on the Caspian sea, and all over the area that was then under the rule of the Mongol khanate of the Golden Horde. The Silk-Road caravan route passed through the capital city of the Golden Horde, Sarai, which was situated on the banks of the Volga. With a population of over half a million persons, it was one of the largest cities of the time. In 1345, it was ravaged by the plague. (Sarai no longer exists today.)

North Italian merchants held trade posts on the Black Sea, where the Genoese merchants traded in Caffa (today known as Feodosia) on the Crimean Peninsula. When the Tartars lay siege to Caffa in 1347, the pest spread among the soldiers. The corpses were thrown over the city walls into the city, leading to the outbreak of the pest in the residents of Caffa. In view of the impending fall of the city, several inhabitants of the city and Italian merchants fled to Italy by ship – with the plague on board [192].

The version of history telling of the corpses from the pest being dumped in the city is plausible and is a favoured example for an early deployment of biological weapons. We can assume that the route via Caffa taken by the fleeing sailors was instrumental in spreading the plague, but it is probable that the plague reached Europe via various land and sea routes.

The earliest report of the plague spreading to a European city in the 14th century is from Messina in Sicily, where the pest broke out as early as in September 1347, then in Pisa and Venice in January 1348 and in Florence, Genoa and Marseille in March of the same year [193]. The pest reached Europe via ship on route to the well-developed trading centres in Italy. There were certainly also ships with passengers or crew members from Caffa suffering from the pest, but which surely also had passengers from other cities, such as Constantinople (where the plague could also have spread to from Caffa; thus the 'Caffa event' could certainly be viewed as a 'super spreader' of the pest in the 14th century) [190].

From Italy plague spread to France and to the German regions in 1348, easily crossing the English Channel via ship to take its toll of lives in England. The plague also spread via ship and land to Scandinavia, Spain and North Africa [194].

After the experience of the pest epidemic, important trading centres developed strategies to protect themselves from epidemics. Lazaretto Nuovo is an island in the Venetian lagoon set up as a quarantine station for ships that were considered to be potential carriers of the plague. The ships (and their passengers) were put into quarantine on the island for forty days (quarantine = forty), and were only granted permission to continue their passage to Venice after being declared plague-free.

As part of my training as epidemiologist, I spent three weeks on the Isla de Lazaretto in the Bay of Mahon (Menorca), the Spanish Ministry of Health having placed the island at our disposal for our training. Originally, Lazaretto was established as a ship quarantine centre for the Spanish Mediterranean in the 18th century. Ships sailing for Barcelona but on which the plague had broken out were not even permitted to take anchor in Barcelona, and instead were decoyed directly to Menorca for quarantine in the Bay of Mahon.

Cholera had also reached London by ship by the mid-18th century: a sailor suffering from the disease and who had voyaged to London by the steamship *Elbe* transported it across the channel – from Hamburg in Germany. Subsequently, severe cholera epidemics were experienced in the city - year by year. Between 1859 and 1865, London solved the problem of cholera by building a water sewerage system whose infrastructure is the backbone of London's canalisation system to this very day.

The perceived significance of international seafaring for the spread of epidemics can clearly be seen in the architecture of the Hamburg Institute for Tropical Medicine, built in 1910, that rises above harbour and the *Landungsbrücken* ("Landing Bridges") of St. Pauli: the highest point of the venerable building is a small round tower providing a good overview of the harbour. If I were able to choose, I would set up my office there. But unfortunately, the tower has long since been out of use and is in correspondingly bad repair.

Should anyone want to know which European city experienced the last major cholera epidemic in the Western world, and you try to imagine the kind of unhygienic cesspool that this city must have been, the answer is: Hamburg! [195] In 1892, Hamburg was one of the most important harbours for emigrants from Europe to the USA. Probably, emigrants travelling from Russia brought the disease to the city. However, there were repeated instances of autochthonous cholera, i.e. of a disease originating in Hamburg, and not imported (such as cholera that was imported to London from Hamburg in 1848). Hamburg's drinking water was still drawn directly from the Elbe river at the time, since the Hamburg Senate was dominated by thrifty merchants who were not prepared to grant the funding of a sand-filter system. The result was that more than 8600 people died of cholera in Hamburg in the summer of 1892. Altona, west of Hamburg, a town which belonged to Prussia, (and is now an urban borough of the Federal State of Hamburg), was an independent harbour town and had such a sand filter system for water supply. Here, significantly fewer people died of the disease.

Pandemics

When a dangerous disease spreads across countries and continents, it is known as a pandemic (Greek *pan* = everything, *demos* = peoples). Diseases regularly become globalised. An example is the annual influenza virus strain that spreads throughout the world.

Could the outbreak of Ebola in West Africa in 2014 have reached catastrophic pandemic dimensions? Such an event is quite possible, of course, but is rather unlikely for Ebola, because of a number of characteristics specific to this disease. Ebola is an extremely dangerous disease for those who have been infected with the virus, but its spread is far less efficient than is the case for other microorganisms and viruses. Until 2014, I cited Ebola as an example of a virus that is unlikely to result in any large epidemics, since firstly, those infected become seriously ill so quickly that they retire to bed and withdraw from social life and secondly, the Ebola virus is transmitted by bodily contact and infectious body fluids and is not aerogenic. The new outbreaks of the infection in Guinea, Liberia and Sierra Leone in 2014 and 2015 were usually the result of such physical contact with close relatives who nursed the infected persons. However, because of funeral rites involving people taking farewell of the dead by touching them, some funerals caused a large number of people to be infected with the disease from the deceased infected person [196, 197].

Today I no longer tell my students that there are no major outbreaks of Ebola to be expected: the outbreak of the disease in West Africa was too great and too catastrophic. An Ebola epidemic is not inconceivable; that is something I have to concede after that epidemic of 2014/15.

It is nevertheless not directly the fear of an Ebola pandemic in itself that causes me concern. It is rather the fact that if Ebola can cause such a catastrophic epidemic despite its lacking efficiency to spread the disease, I shudder just to imagine the impact of a dangerous contagious organism that causes an infection already before the infected person is seriously ill, that is, before symptoms of the disease are evident. The disease SARS in 2002 and 2003 was extremely dangerous because of is efficient aerogenic spread. SARS caused symptoms very rapidly. The infected persons became seriously ill shortly after being infected. If the virus had been highly infectious long before the symptoms developed, the disease could have become a catastrophic pandemic [198].

SARS is the abbreviation for "Severe Acute Respiratory Syndrome". Incidentally, naming a new disease by its symptoms, i.e. according to the clinical indications, is typical. The term AIDS (Acquired Immune Deficiency Syndrome) was used before the HI (Human Immunodeficiency) virus was named. The clinical syndrome was noted and described, before the relative virus was identified.

Some symptoms increase the chances of contagion: for example, airborne viruses are released into the environment very efficiently through coughing and sneezing. So one could conclude that the start of infectiousness is functionally connected with the symptoms. This would be a soothing thought, since all dangerous new pathogens would become obvious in a short space of time.

But what if a "killer virus" were to cause a slight, harmless dry cough at first contact with the mucous membranes of the respiratory system, which was soon followed by a runny nose and frequent sneezing? If the cough soon became more bronchial, but the person with the infection still appeared healthy and mobile and of course went to work (of course, one cannot leave one's colleagues in the lurch). If the virus were to spread when the person sneezed and coughed, causing others in the environment to become infected? If, after a few days the infection were to spread to the lungs, permeate the thin alveolar wall and enter the bloodstream. After entering the bloodstream, the virus, which seemed to have been a typical respiratory infection, were to lead to an extremely serious, potentially fatal illness?

SARS has some of these characteristics. In 2003, an elderly Canadian couple was infected with the disease in Hong Kong and transported the SARS virus to Canada. The elderly woman became seriously ill and died. However, before she and her husband had appeared healthy enough despite being infected, and had been able to take the 15-hour flight back to Canada without anyone being aware of anything unusual. In Toronto, there was a grave outbreak of the disease in the hospital that was difficult to control. Cases of SARS were registered in other countries, too. However, no uncontrolled pandemic ensued. Perhaps we were just fortunate with that outbreak of SARS [199-201].

Let us summarise the facts: What characterises a high-risk pathogen?

- easily contagious and transmissible from human to human
- a grave disease with high fatality risk
- causes infection to young, mobile, otherwise healthy persons
- is difficult to treat
- no vaccination available
- allows the infected person to appear healthy long enough to infect others

What factors make our world of today vulnerable to pandemics?

- high population density, also in highly urbanised countries
- settlement in previously unpopulated regions, and fewer uninhabited areas, where epidemics could phase out in the past
- travelling and migration intensity
- insufficient water and sanitary infrastructure

Biological weapons

What lies behind 'Operation Vegetarian' is by no means a city initiative group propagating vegetarianism for everyone, but the British bioweapon programme in the second world war. The core concept was to deploy anthrax to harm the German population by dropping cattle cakes infected with linseed spores onto agricultural fields in Germany. With the resulting infection of farm animals, the Britons hoped to spread zoonotic mass infections throughout Germany, resulting in thousands, perhaps even millions of cattle, but also humans being infected. At the same time, the farm animals would have been decimated, while the wave of panic in the German population would have deterred the people from eating meat (thus the name of the programme 'Operation Vegetarian' [202]). The deployment of anthrax bacteria was tested on Gruinard Island, a small green island without vegetation lying in a bay about a kilometre off the northwest coast of Scotland. The test was extremely successful: the eighty sheep that were transported to the island were all infected and died of anthrax. The island became uninhabitable and was put under quarantine for over forty years.

Shortly after the test, there were attempts to decontaminate the island, but these were soon discontinued, since the anthrax spores proved to be extremely resilient and the bacteria and their spores had permanently populated the island. The particularly virulent anthrax stem had become endemic on the island, so to speak.

Only vehement, almost blackmail-like (and not absolutely legal) pressure from an activist group of anonymous university microbiologists and residents in the vicinity of the island in 1980, induced the government to decontaminate the island. The group 'Operation Dark Harvest' had threatened to deposit contaminated soil from Gruinard Island at "suitable spots", causing the government to take quick action. Decontamination was carried out in 1986 with 280 tons of formaldehyde solution and by removing the surface soil. The sheep that were settled on the island after the decontamination remained healthy. The decontamination was thus successful, but very elaborate.

Gruinard Island covers an area of 196 hectares. This is the area of a square with each side measuring 1400 metres. It does not bear considering how much effort and cost would be necessary to decontaminate a really large area with, a much more complex geography. Berlin covers an area of less than 90,000 hectares; this corresponds to a square with each side measuring 30 kilometres (30,000 metres).

Although the German army developed and deployed the first chemical and biological weapons in the first world war, there was no biological weapon programme worth mentioning in Nazi Germany in the second world war. The largest biological weapon programme was instituted in Japan, where it was known as Unit 731 and remains notorious to this day. Unit 731 long remained a taboo topic in Japan and even today, this dark chapter of Japanese history is clothed in secrecy whenever possible.

Yoshio Shinozuka joined the Japanese army in 1939 when he was 15 years old and was soon drafted to the Chinese province Manchuria, which was occupied by Japan. After arrival, he was instructed in the basics of hygiene and infectious diseases and was given the task of breeding pest fleas on live rats. The Japanese army operated research and development centres in Manchuria for both modern and weapons, but the special emphasis was on chemical and biological weapons. The test centres were mostly attached to prisons or prison camps, so that prisoners were available at any time to be abused for human experiments that were practically unrivalled in their cruelty. Most of the experiments were concluded with vivisections carried out on still conscious people, who died during the autopsies, their deaths resulting from the experiments.

Towards the end of the war, when Yoshio Shinozuka had just turned 20, he assisted at such live vivisections of people previously infected with typhoid fever. Similar to many other young people who have been involved in a war somewhere on earth, Yoshio was just a small cog in the mercilessly cruel machine. What is so special about him is that he went public in 1990 and reported about the horrors of Unit 731, partly to support Chinese victims' lawsuits [203]. Yoshio served in the Chinese army for an extended period after the war, but was also detained or interred in prison camps due to his previous potential involvement in war crimes. The leading figures, i.e. those who were mainly responsible for the programmes, could either successfully escape to Japan and go underground there, some of them even succeeding in pursing successful post-war careers in the USA, where they worked for programmes for the development of biological and chemical weapons, or remained in Japan after having disclosed the results of the experiments on humans to the Americans.

Although Unit 731 was originally disguised as a public health agency, its clearly defined goal was to develop weapons of mass destruction. Various aspects relevant to the ultimate task were dealt with in different sections: section 1 researched the effect of pathogens (mainly of the pest, typhoid fever, cholera and anthrax) on people who had been infected in prisons and prison camps; section 2 developed devices to deploy biological and chemical warfare agents, while section 3 developed bombs and explosive devices. Other sections dealt with non-biological warfare agents, training and personnel and also logistics and catering for the unit. There is documented evidence of several experimental contaminations conducted in cities and rural areas. In the Chinese port town Ningbo, for instance, planes airdropped wheat, corn, scraps of cotton cloth and sand infested with plague infected fleas, resulting in an epidemic with 99 fatalities. Unit 731 was not the only unit in the Japanese army that developed biological weapons.

Antibiotic resistance

The first antibiotics were not penicillin derivates, as is commonly assumed, but sulfonamides. There is no question that Alexander Fleming's discovery of the antibiotic effect of penicillin was a milestone in the control of infectious illnesses. Legend has it that in 1928 Fleming had by chance discovered and published the antibacterial effect in a mould that had developed on an accidentally contaminated staphylococcus culture plate. It was only ten years after Fleming's publishing the observation that Howard W. Florey, Ernst B. Chain and Norman Heatley continued and concluded Fleming's research. There was great military interest in a potent antibiotic in the second world war, which was why mass production of penicillin was a declared target for research, and was advanced by American laboratories.

As for the opponents, Germany and Japan, development was concentrated on sulfonamides, which had experienced a breakthrough in the medical treatment of infections in the early 20th century. The chemist Alfred Bertheim had synthesised hundreds of arsenic compounds in Paul Ehrlich's laboratory and had tested them on hundreds of animals for their bactericidal effect. Since these compounds were often in themselves very toxic, effort was mainly concentrated on finding compounds that had a significantly more toxic effect on bacterial cells than on eukaryote cells. As established by Paul Ehrlich and the Japanese bacteriologist Hata Sahachiro, who likewise worked in Paul Ehrlich's laboratory, one of the compounds, salvarsan, proved to be highly effective against spirochete bacteria. Salvarsan was then used successfully against syphilis and was thus the first medical substance to be used successfully against bacterial infections (today, syphilis is treated with penicillin G). Salvarsan was also found to be effective against other spirochete bacteria, such as yaws and recurrent fever caused by borrelia. The significance of syphilis in the 20th century can be seen in the fact that the Nobel prize for medicine was awarded to an Austrian psychiatrist, Julius Wagner-Jauregg, for the treatment of progressive paralysis, a form of late-stage syphilis, by intentionally infecting the patients with malaria parasites.

However, for the treatment of infected wounds, which were of particular relevance in war medicine, the efficacy spectrum of salvarsans was too restricted (to spirochetes).

The first available broad-spectrum antibiotic (even before penicillin) was prontosil, a sulfonomide that was synthesised by Fritz Mietsch and Josef Klarer, who worked in the chemical pigment division of the German pharmaceutical company Bayer in Wuppertal. The bacterial effectiveness of prontosil was discovered by Gerhard Domagk. He was awarded the Nobel prize for medicine in 1939 for this discovery, but could only accept the prize in 1947, since Adolf Hitler had prohibited German scientists from accepting Nobel prizes. (This prohibition was the consequence of awarding the Nobel peace prize to Carl von Ossietzky in 1936. Ossietzky was a pacifist who had made public the illegal rearmament programme of the German armed forces in the 1930s. This led to Ossietzky being sentenced to jail for spying, where he remained until his death in 1938.)

The Germans used prontosil widely for the treatment of wound infection during the second world war. So, if we regard 1935 as the beginning of the era of antibiotics, then this medication has been in use for a little over eighty years. There is no denying the advances in the medical field that have been made possible by treatment with antibiotics. But their effectiveness is endangered by the development of resistance to antibiotics.

When bacteria, viruses and parasites mutate and adapt so well that the drugs used to treat them are no longer effective, we talk of antibiotic resistance. Bacteria reproduce sexually by division and can thus achieve very high numbers in a short period of time. Enterobacteria such as *Escherichia coli* divide every 20 minutes on average, meaning that the number of cells doubles approximately every 20 minutes. Thus, when there were 100 bacteria to start with, the number of bacteria rises to one hundred thousand (10^5) in less than four hours, to 560 million in the eighth hour and 20 minutes later, explodes to over a billion (table 12).

Table 12: Example for the bacterial growth starting with 100 bacteria and a doubling time of 20 minutes (under ideal conditions in cultivation)

	1st hour			2nd hour			3rd hour		
time	20	40	60	80	100	120	140	160	180
bacteria	100	200	400	800	1,600	3,200	6,400	12,800	25,600

	4th hour			5th hour			6th hour		
time	200	220	240	260	280	300	320	340	360
bacteria	51,200	10^5	2×10^5	4×10^5	1.6 million		8.8 million		

	7th hour			8th hour			9th hour		
time	380	400	420	440	460	480	500	520	540
bacteria	72 million			560 million			4.48 billion		

If the patient is treated with antibiotics in the sixth hour of this thought experiment, most of the bacteria will be destroyed. Let us assume that, due to mutation, 25 of the just under 9 million bacteria have developed resistance to the antibiotic. The increase of these bacteria is unstoppable. After 40 minutes, the starting point of 100 bacteria will have already been reached, and after a further six hours, these will have developed into over 8 million bacteria, this time, however, all of them belonging to an antibiotic-resistant stem.

We have viewed the development of antibiotic resistance as a purely stochastic process. Meanwhile, the microbiological sciences are aware of numerous mechanisms of resistance. However, even without any knowledge of these mechanisms, the principle of selection appears to make the evolutionary development of antibiotic resistances under antibiotic therapy seem plausible and almost unavoidable. Of course this purely stochastic approach is a simplification, since, over a period of millions of years of co-evolution with the microorganisms that infect us, the human body has developed its own mechanisms of control and defence against infections, and therefore (fortunately) does not only depend on fighting bacteria with medication. This means that bacteria are combated by our immune defence system, e.g. through defence and scavenger cells and, at later stages of infection, also with specific antibodies. For this reason, bacteria cannot multiply as freely as shown in table 12.

However, antibiotics used for medication are by no means capable of targeting the infection precisely. Broad-spectrum antibiotics work something like blanket bombings: although the "enemy" bacteria are hit, so are the symbiotic microorganisms that continue to exist on and in us. We are only starting to develop a vague idea of the role of our microbiome [135, 204].

The house of diseases

The stochastic considerations described above give us a glimpse of where such antibiotic-resistant germs flourish, namely, where they are strongly exposed to antibiotics: in cattle sheds and hospitals. Let us consider hospital hygiene.

In the second half on the 1990s, I conducted my studies in Mannheim in south-west Germany, where Heidelberg University ran a medical faculty at the Mannheim Medical Centre for about a third of the medical students of one academic year. At the time, the Medical Centre was regarded as a model hospital throughout Germany, one that would demonstrate to the sluggish German health system how to run a major municipal hospital profitably. In 1997, the 'Klinikum Mannheim GmbH', the Mannheim University Clinic, was established as a limited liability company, with the Mannheim municipality being the sole associate. This partial privatisation turned the Mannheim Clinic into a trendsetter in Germany's largely state-funded healthcare system. And indeed, for years after the "assumption of power" by the economists, the hospital could be run at a profit.

The institution's glorious reputation was sorely tarnished in autumn 2014, when the regulatory authorities were tipped off anonymously regarding deficiencies in the hygiene of the Mannheim hospital, leading to an avalanche of investigations on the hygienic conditions there. Surgical instruments and supposedly sterilised devices were repeatedly found to be unhygienic, with contamination such as hairs, splintered bones or insects being visible to the naked eye [205].

A reconstruction of the hygiene scandal suggests that the hygienic conditions at the Mannheim Clinic had ranged between questionable and catastrophic for years. Grave deficiencies were documented for the previous ten years and proved that incidents had been systematically hushed up as early as in 2002 [206]. In June 2013, the entire central sterilisation section was flooded with sewage that rose from the canalisation via a floor drain that had been found to be deficient during a hygiene inspection as early as in 2007. This caused high bacteria levels in the section. Fungi, staphylococci, bacterial spores, multi-resistant pseudomonas germs, in a few words, everything from simple pus germs to hospital-specific multi-resistant 'Cuvées' were found in shelves and on counters, that means the places where operating instruments are serviced and stored after sterilisation [206, 207].

Furthermore, those people working in areas relevant to hygiene and sterilisation were not always sufficiently qualified for their tasks. Complaints from the staff that the savings on personnel had led to serious under-staffing in nursing and medical patient care are certainly not specific to the Mannheim Clinic, but prevalent in the entire health system.

Even with a functioning hygiene and sterilisation department, a hospital is a dangerous place. Firstly, there is a particularly large group of ailing, infection-prone people in a hospital, secondly, a large number of antibiotics are used, resulting in antibiotic-resistant bacteria being "bred", and thirdly, the protective outer skin layer of patients is regularly injured or tubes are inserted into body orifices, which facilitates germs entering the human body. And finally, the patients in a hospital are very frequently weak due to previous illnesses and are more prone to infection or disease-inducing courses of infections.

Lung germ approaching!

When talking about the defence system of the human body, the first thought that crosses the minds of many people is the body's most complicated and least visible component: the cellular immune system. This is where the scavenger cells are located, which swallow and digest the alien pathogens that have entered the body, immune cells, which dock on to pathogens and destroy them directly, surrender them to scavenger cells or form antibodies specifically for the intruding pathogens. After they have fought off a pathogen, these specific antibodies are archived so that if there is a repeated infection with the same pathogen, they can multiply to form a rapid and targeted response.

The simplified immune system as briefly explained here is in actual fact amazingly complex and complicated. When I attend specialist lectures focused on immunology, I mostly lose the thread of the issue after just a few minutes. The impressive complexity of the cellular immune system makes it easy to lose sight of the very important mechanical components in the human immune system. For a start, our skin prevents other organisms from easily penetrating our body. The equivalent of this mechanism inside our bodies are the mucous membranes, which, similar to the skin, act as a barrier against germs that could otherwise enter our body through the digestive system or the respiratory tract.

Lung infections are much-feared diseases and are often the cause of death. Pneumococci are the cause of serious lung infections that can be fatal. They can also often be found in the mucous membranes of the nose and throat, without the person hosting the pneumococci showing any symptoms of a disease. How do these pneumococci travel from person to person? When a person coughs, sneezes or talks, these germs find their way into the environment and are inhaled. Let us imagine we are a germ, say, a pneumococcus. Having lodged in the moist warm environment of a human lung, it is released from the lung to the bronchia and the upper respiratory tract together with other germs in a loose viscose compound of bacteria, slime, immune and epithelial cells by means of a few explosion-like bursts of air (coughing). During the next coughing spasm, glassy-green shiny mucous slime is coughed up which contains many pneumococci. One slimy mass ends up in an emesis dish, together with a few other smaller bits of slime. But our pneumococcus has been lucky. It finds itself together with a few other pneumococci in a tiny drop of spit that is so small that as a minute fluid-gaseous form, it is spun through the space with a few drifts of air and suddenly lands in a moving stream of air. This air comes from another person who happens to be in the room and who absorbs the minute drops of saliva with our pneumococcus through the nostrils during inhalation.

Inside the nose, hairs grow centripetally from the tip of the nose to the middle of the nostril. Larger dust particles and liquid drops are caught up in this barrier. But our little pneumococcus in its tiny drop-capsule moves elegantly past the nose hairs and reaches the moist humid inside of the nose, where the aggregate condition of the drop of moisture again becomes more stable, after it had almost evaporated.

In the nose, there are three diagonal plates covered with mucous membranes stretching from the inner lateral wall of the outer nose. These nasal conchae ('nose shells') warm the inhaled air. At the same time, they form areas covering the mucous membrane, where dust particles and drops of fluid are caught up. Some drops manage to pass between the nasal conchae and the inner wall of the nose and reach the top of the throat. Here, the air current changes course and turns downwards into the throat. At this point, many dust particles miss the downward turn and naturally get caught in the mucous membranes at the top and back of the throat. Possibly this is the reason why an immune centre for our cellular defence developed in an evolutionary process at this location: the tonsils.

When our pneumococcus has overcome this hurdle as well, it moves steeply downward towards the larynx. The epiglottis and the vocal cords lie at the entrance to the trachea (windpipe). This is attached to the bronchia, which branch out into the left and right lungs. These air funnels are clad with a very particular kind of mucous membrane: the ciliated epithelium. Tiny hairy filaments, the cilia, move at a high frequency (about 1000 times per minute) in the direction of the throat and transport impurities, dust, bacteria and phlegm upwards. The transport apparatus that disposes of the pneumococci is facilitated by mucous-producing goblet cells, which are distributed between the epithelial cells. It is interesting to note that the ciliated epithelium does not end at the main entrance to the lung, but continues its course in ever thinner layers into the tiniest of bronchioles deep inside the lungs, which open up in the alveoli.

The chance of our pneumococcus reaching the lung with a sufficiently high number of other pneumococci to trigger an infection directly in the lung is not very great, thanks to the described defence mechanisms. At the same time, it must become apparent how much more endangered our lungs are if the system is damaged. Heavy smoking damages the ciliated epithelia. This is no trivial malfunction: as described above, the cilia beat more than 1,000 times a minute, moving the mucus that lines the trachea upwards, thus transporting all possible kinds of impurities upwards that would otherwise remain in the lung and cause damage.

It is worth mentioning at this point that the cancer that is commonly known as "lung cancer" is actually not a malignant cell growth in the alveoli, but mostly originates in the bronchia or bronchioles. Smoking increases the risk of such bronchial carcinoma. (Tumours that actually do develop in the alveolar cells are rare.)

But let us return to our pneumococcus. The minute drop that transports our pneumococcus in a laminar central air stream was not thrown out of the curve, not even in the in the 90-degree curve that transitions from the nose to the throat. Other droplets and pneumococci have stuck to the mucosa of the oropharynx. We'll hear about them again later.

Our pneumococcus in its tiny drop of water has now also passed the larynx and is headed in the direction of the lung. Actually, we have two lungs: a right and a left lung. The main air passage branches into the right and left lung at the so-called bronchial bifurcation. Our little drop enters a small air vortex resulting from the branching of the main air stream and touches the mucosa, causing the drop to connect with the bronchial mucous.

Our pneumococcus and a few other pneumococci are now attached to the surface of the mucous membrane of the bronchial bifurcation. In a microscopic image, pneumococci often appear as diplococci. The layering of two pneumococci is typical. Just as with other streptococci (chain cocci), pneumococci also form chain- and cluster-like conglomerates. So, here at the bronchial bifurcation, a small pile of pneumococci has settled. These are immediately attacked by scavenger cells. A few pneumococci on the outer perimeter are successfully removed by the scavenger cells, but, because the mucous membrane is infected and the bifurcation can only be accessed directly by the scavenger cells coming from below, the colony of pneumococci can grow. Each pneumococcus subdivides every 20 minutes on average.

Other immune and inflammatory cells arrive at the spot where the pneumococci have accumulated, so that cell debris accumulates on the periphery. However, these cannot be transported away by the previously damaged ciliated epithelia (the person is apparently a heavy smoker). Suddenly a heavy coughing spasm catapults a significant part of the accumulated pneumococci away from the bifurcation and spreads smaller packages of pneumococci into the environment of the mucous membrane. Some also spread deeper down into the lower bronchi. The person's immune system seems to be overburdened even at this point already and the previously damaged ciliated epithelia is hardly able to cope with its task of removing the impurities. Due to such lack of resistance, it takes the number of settled pneumococci a little more than 20 minutes to double their numbers. Although the occasional coughing spasm catapults pneumococci packages upwards over and over again, new deposits are spread over all the mucous membranes and ultimately also to the lungs.

Further upwards, in the tonsils, another pneumococcus colony has formed from which nests of pneumococci spread downwards and infest the throat and the trachea. Here, too, the malfunction of ciliated epithelia is a real hindrance. The tonsils swell and the person with the infection has a very sore throat and difficulty in swallowing, which finally forces him to consult a doctor.

The doctor sees a massive infected tonsil and prescribes an antibiotic. At the same time, he makes a swab of the tonsil and sends it to a microbiological laboratory. At the laboratory, a culture is made of the swab – and the colony of pneumococci identified. The antibiogram provides information on the effectiveness of various antibiotics. The tonsillitis was a blessing in disguise because it produced symptoms at a spot in the body where it was possible to take a swab (it is not possible to take a swab at the lower respiratory tract from a conscious patient – at most, coughed up "sputum" can be examined). In our case, a specific therapy can be initiated before a severe lung infection could develop "further down" in the lung. However, the situation was only dangerous because the person with the infection had a weak immune system. If the person had been healthy, immune cells would have attacked the pneumococci systematically and ciliated epithelia cells would have removed the debris.

Hospitals often house patients with a weak immune defence due to previous illnesses. These patients' vulnerability towards infections is even increased by treatment that open a gateway into the body such as intravenous catheters, urinal catheters or intubation.

Let's use take the example of intubation, which is used for artificial respiration, where a tube made of silicon and rubber is inserted through the throat and between the glottis of the larynx into the trachea of the patient. If our previously described patient suffers another coughing spasm and catapults a few mucus particles and drops with pneumococci into the air, these could get into the silicon tube of another intubated patient in the ward and easily reach the lung of this patient, getting caught up by the mucous membranes in the nasopharynx.

When a winged infusion catheter is inserted, it causes an artificially opened wound to the skin surface. At the same time, bacteria can form on the plastic biofilms, which is why every infusion catheter can allow germs to gain entry into the bloodstream. A bladder catheter is a tube that is inserted into the bladder through the urethra. A bladder catheter can cause great relief to patients suffering from urinary retention. During my final year of study, I was instructed to insert a bladder catheter for a young man who was suffering from occasional post-operative urinary retention. This made urine flow possible and lead to great relief for the patient: I have rarely before or after encountered such gratitude in the face of a person.

This last example is important to me, so that I don't create the impression that doctors and nursing staff cause damage by applying invasive measures unnecessarily. No, persons working in the field of medicine are very much aware of the risks involved. And this is a good thing, since the risks are real. There is hardly any other place where so many antibiotic-resistant germs can be found as in hospitals. This makes a hospital a very dangerous place to be for a person with a weakened immune system. If economic and feasibility considerations were not such a central issue, the treatment of people requiring medical attention would decentralised, preferably to the homes of those seeking medical consultation. In such a system, however, the medical devices and instruments would have to delivered to the patient's home, which would be practically impossible to cope with organisationally. This is why we need hospitals. However, hospitals need to ensure that the increased environmental risks for the patients are kept to a minimum by careful adherence to the rules of hygiene. For years, this was not the case at the clinic in Mannheim.

There is high pressure to select antibiotics, which in turn increases the risk of dangerous antibiotic-resistant germs. It is also in hospitals where infectious and potentially existential risks are manifested. During epidemics in the past, a particularly high number of people were infected in hospitals by life-threatening germs such as the SARS virus in 2003 or the Ebola virus in 2014 in West.

The Spanish flu of 1918

In 2009, an influenza variant caused by the H1N1 virus, also known as the "swine flu", spread throughout the world and was declared a pandemic. Even if it did claim some victims, it must be conceded that this pandemic was not so threatening as to justify the degree of alarm raised by the epidemiologists. But one always knows better afterwards!

Where did the fear of this virus come from? A little less than 100 years previously, in 1918, an H1N1 influenza virus caused the most devastating epidemic of the 20th century: the Spanish flu. It is said to have cost more than 50 million people their lives in 1918, 3% of the world's population at the time. About 500 million people were infected with the virus, corresponding to a third of the then global population. This figure is considerably higher than the victims of the first world war, which ended in 1918 and is said to have killed about 20 million people [208, 209].

Today, 100 years later, in the anniversary year 2018, the story of the Spanish flu is again frequently being told [210]. The first cases were reported in March 1918 in an American army barracks in Kansas, and a month later, there were also cases of Spanish flu in Europe. Possibly, the virus originated on a pig farm in the American mid-west, could then easily spread to army barracks and was introduced into Europe by US soldiers who were posted to Europe [190].

Since Spain was not involved in the first world war, there was greater freedom of the press in the country: there were no restrictions on reporting and the variety of reports was much greater. This led to the impression that the influenza pandemic of 1918 must have originated in Spain. In contrast to the first world war, which was not waged throughout the world (this is where our Euro-centric perspective of history becomes obvious), the H1N1 virus actually did spread throughout the world. (The island Tristan da Cunha in the Southeast Pacific with a population of a little over 100 was possibly spared the Spanish flu of 1918 [211]). The war mobilisation with troops sent to foreign countries certainly contributed to the spread of the virus throughout the world. After the first wave of the epidemic, which ebbed off in July 1918, the second wave began in August (in Germany), a much worse wave [210], which remained in collective memory as the "autumn wave" and claimed the highest number of lives.

In contrast to normal seasonal flu epidemics, which mainly claim the lives of very young and very old people, a particularly high number of people between 20 and 40 years old died from the Spanish flu epidemic of 1918: about half of the flu victims came from this age group. The comparatively low mortality rate of people over 65 leads to the assumption that they had previously come into contact with a similar virus during their lifetime and accordingly had built up (partial) immunity to this virus. Or, the less intense immune response of the weaker immune systems of the old and young population groups had spared them the course of the disease, since symptoms can also be the expression of our immune systems battling the virus.

At the time, nobody spoke of H1N1 viruses. Viruses were basically unknown. It was only in the 1940s that viruses could be observed in electron microscopes. Previously, there was only indirect proof of non-bacterial or non-parasitic infectious agents. Infections of tobacco plants with bacteria-free extracts from infected tobacco leaves were indirect proof of infecting agents that were neither bacteria nor parasites, and for which the tobacco mosaic virus was made responsible. Intentional infections with cowpox by Edvard Jenner in the late 18th century was a procedure that led to the smallpox vaccine being developed, long before smallpox viruses were known. Richard Pfeiffer, a student of Robert Koch, who died in 1910, made a minor bacterium responsible for the Spanish flu. This bacterium is known by the name *Haemophilus influenzae.*

Apart from the usual mutation-conditioned changes, influenza viruses regularly exchange propensity for two subtypes that determine the main virus components, namely hemagglutinin (H) and neuraminidase (N). Eighteen various H-subtypes are known to exist and 11 various N-subtypes of the neuraminidase protein. A natural H1N1 virus is characterised by one H1 and one N1 antigen. Various HxNy virus types have different affinities to various host animals. H7N7 tends to attach itself to horses. Subtypes with H1, H2 and H3 antigens are the only subtypes (to date) that cause human influenza epidemics.

Why, then, do a few dead marine birds infected with H5N1 that are found on the Baltic Sea coast cause headlines throughout Germany, when the H5 antigen presents no great threat to humans? Well, occasionally, the antigen barriers might be overcome in humans that have a lot of contact with infected birds (for example chicken farmers). It then becomes dangerous for the individual infected person, since H5N1 usually does not tend to infect humans, but when this is the case, the infection can be very serious, often even fatal [212].

On the other hand, H5N1 thrives very well in marine birds, whose mobility causes the virus to be spread. Wild ducks serve as Trojan horses, since the host animals themselves do not become sick. Symptomatic H5N1 infections of birds tend to take a gastrointestinal course, spreading from bird to bird by way of a faecal-oral route. Hens and other domestic birds can be infected by the bird droppings even if mesh wiring prevents direct contact with wild birds. Persons who have frequent contact with domestic birds can then be infected, despite the species barriers. A

H5N1 virus that is contagious with efficient human-to-human transmission and that can cause grave illness is an epidemiological horror scenario [213].

But what do swine have to do with the swine flu of 2009 and the catastrophic Spanish flu of 1918?

In Egypt, the reaction to the threat of the swine flu in spring 2009 was to slaughter all the swine in the country. Pigs were held by Coptic Christian minority population in the mainly Muslim country. Experts throughout the world shook their heads at this blind activism, since there was practically no danger of infection from swine [214].

Why, then, was the swine flu in everybody's mouth? And why did the influenza epidemic of 1918 start on a pig farm? Indeed, pigs can play a role in the origin of an influenza epidemic, however, not so much with regard to the flu being spread, but with regard to the origins of the pandemic virus. Swine are more similar to humans than we would perhaps like to think when we eat the parts of their corpses as a tasty schnitzel in a creamy mushroom sauce. The H1N1 virus that caused the Spanish flu did not disappear after the pandemic. It continues to exist in swine and humans, albeit in a different form. The H1N1 offspring in humans are possibly less dangerous, since they have continued to exist in harmony, almost symbiotically, in humans. The virus in swine could become dangerous, however, when viruses manage to be transferred to the human population through persons who are highly exposed to swine (pig farmers, for example). Then they can be transferred from one (human) person to another.

Epidemiologists fear the function of swine as a 'mixing bowl' for viruses. As described above, H5N1 (bird flu virus) rarely infects humans, and when this is the case, the danger of the virus being transferred from one person to another is not great. For those who are infected however, the infection is extremely dangerous and is often fatal. In birds, the manifestation of the H5N1 virus is mostly gastrointestinal, and thus swine can become infected with the bird droppings. At the same time, because of the contact between swine and humans, swine can be infected with a human influenza virus (H antigen 1-3). The H-N antigen combination and the surface face of the virus can recombine in the pigs. It would be nightmare for epidemic control if a new virus were to develop that can be transferred from one person to another, and that could cause grave disease or even death.

Waking the sleeping influenza dragon

American scientists reconstructed the virus of the Spanish flu in 2005 and reported their results in the renowned medical journal *Science* [215]. In view of the pandemic of 1918 described previously, with millions of deaths worldwide, no detailed scientific knowledge is necessary to understand that doing so poses a great (if not existential) danger for humankind. Of course, the work of the scientists is justified by explaining that cultivating the virus allows vaccines to be created. However, these vaccines would be available to countries or firms that have the technology to produce them. In principle, the reconstructed virus can be turned into a biological weapon for those who "possess" the virus, since members of the own nation can be vaccinated, while the vaccination is withheld from the other (enemy)states.

If such a work had been carried out by Muslims in an enemy country, the western states are likely to have declared the involved scientists to be terrorists and would have attacked their laboratories with cruise missiles or bombs.

Interaction between microorganisms and macroorganisms

Every large animal is an ecosystem in its own right. When a large animal species becomes extinct, a habitat for numerous microorganisms is also lost [135]. How significant is the decline of species for the organisms that these species host? With our present level of knowledge, we cannot answer this question satisfactorily, not least because the well-researched microorganisms are only a fraction of all types of microorganisms, namely mostly human-pathogenic organisms of medical relevance. Even the human-pathogenic organisms reveal a host-spectrum that reaches far beyond the human spectrum, which is why new infectious diseases are mostly transferred from the animal kingdom to humans. Diseases that are transmitted from animals to humans are called zoonoses [212].

The transition from symbiotic coexistence to a harmless colonisation and ultimately to a disease-inducing infection is fluid. Pneumococci can thrive as harmless settlers in your nose and throat area, the nasopharyngeal region, or they can cause a fatal lung infection. Even pathogenic microorganisms can persist in humans without causing any symptoms for years. An everyday example is the herpes virus, which, after an initial infection, persists for a lifetime as a mostly silent and unnoticed subtenant in the ganglion cells (a type of nerve cell) and in the lymphocytes, but then cause unpleasant blisters around the mouth when we are suffering from stress and exactly at the moment when we could do without them.

The same applies to chicken pox virus, which, after the first infection in childhood, when it plagued us with itching red blisters, mostly continues to exist for a lifetime in the ganglion cells. Ganglion cells are nerve nodules that lie close to the spine. If, the chicken pox virus is revived in a ganglion of an adult, this results in a painful rash in the skin area that is innervated by nerves running together in the corresponding ganglion. This locally restricted skin infection is known as shingles. Fortunately, our immune system recognises the viruses from the first infection (chicken pox) and can quickly deploy antibodies to prevent the virus from being revived in other ganglions. Shingles thus usually remains in the restricted area of the ganglion-specific innervation area (the dermatome).

For the viruses themselves, such a dormant persistence with occasional eruptions, which then make it possible for the virus to infect non-immune individuals (by means of blisters filled with secretion, for instance), is an exceedingly successful strategy to enable the survival of the virus species. 'Strategy' is the wrong term, however, since viruses are not able to plan their actions. Viral replication cycles are simply the result of evolutionary selection. Chickenpox viruses of an earlier generation that had a pronounced ganglion cell tropism (the tendency to migrate to ganglion cells) could obviously survive well there, whereas other viruses of the same strain could not survive in other tissues. At the same time, viruses that have a pronounced dermatropic propensity (attraction to the skin) infect other individuals via oozing skin eruptions and in this way find a new habitat (new host organisms) for the virus. Thus the viruses do not decide to migrate in ganglion cells or skin cells; rather they are the offspring of viruses that happened to be attracted to these cells, and migrated to these cells, where they survived and were able to spread, or were given the opportunity to spread [216].

There are also many parasitic diseases that are caught between symbiotic coexistence and disease-causing infections. The pork tapeworm *Taenia solum* produces mature tapeworms in the human body, when a person has been infected by tapeworm larvae (bladder worms) through the intake of larvae harbouring in raw pork. When the person then discharges tapeworms, a faecal-oral self-infection with these eggs can occur. The larvae from the eggs can quickly hatch in the intestines and migrate into the body of the person, where they form cysts in various tissues, particularly in muscle flesh. The pathology manifested through these cysts is called cysticercosis. Cysts in the brain are particularly dangerous, since they can produce symptoms such as grave paralysis [217]. Cysticercosis infections are a common cause of epilepsy in endemic countries, and diagnosis can be very difficult [218].

Some microorganisms are not transferred directly, but by a vector organism from one infected being to another. Some of the most important infectious diseases worldwide (e.g. malaria and dengue fever) are transferred via vectors, mostly by insects. This can simply be a mechanical transfer, e.g. by a bluebottle flying from excrement to our picnic food. Biological vectors are part of complex transmission cycles and thus very pathogenic-specific.

This is how a plasmodium, the one-celled parasitical malaria pathogen, is transferred by *Anopheles* mosquitos. Viruses such as yellow fever, dengue, Chikungunya and the zika (ZIKV) viruses are transferred by the *Aedes* mosquito, and borrelia bacteria via ticks. Thus, such vectors do not only transport the pathogen, but are components in the cycle of development of the pathogen. Plasmodia, which cause malaria, must be ingested by mosquitos, in whose midgut they can further develop to become infectious, then migrate to the salivary gland of *Anopheles* to be transmitted to the next human whom the mosquito pricks for her next blood meal (only female mosquitos bite, as they require the blood for egg production). Plasmodium parasites can only develop in *Anopheles* mosquitos. In other mosquitos, e.g. *Aedes* mosquitos, plasmodium cannot develop to stages at which they are able to cause infections.

The distribution of the vector is decisive for vector-linked diseases to spread. In recent years, the Asian tiger mosquito, also known as the forest mosquito (*Aedes albopictus*), which transports the dengue and the Chikungunya virus, has also been sighted north of the Alps. The question whether incidents of dengue or the Chikungunya virus infections can be expected in countries such as Germany depends on other factors, especially the climate. Tropical viruses such as dengue, zika or the West-Nile virus require temperatures of above 25 degrees Celsius for several consecutive weeks to establish themselves in central Europe, according to Egbert Tannish, who heads the German National Reference Centre for Tropical Infection Agents in Hamburg [219]. The Chikungunya virus seems to be capable of multiplying itself in the tiger mosquito at temperatures of about 18 degrees Celsius [220]. In warmer regions of Germany, such as in the south-west, such temperatures can be found to persist for several weeks in the summer months.

A new world

At the close of the 15th century, the Italian seafarer Christopher Columbus, who served the Castilian royalty, discovered a large continent far west of Europe. He thought he was in India, however, which is why the Caribbean islands, which he first reached during the expedition, are called the "West Indian Islands" to this day. The cartographer from Freiburg in Germany, Martin Waldseemüller, called the new continent "America" after the seafarer Amerigo Vespucci, who first established and subsequently recorded the fact that the mass of land was not India, as first thought, but a previously unknown continent.

When I was a child, cowboys and Indians were the very epitome of America for me. The term "Indian" reflects and preserves the glaring misconception on the part of Columbus. In traditional stories of the Wild West, the function of Indians was to make it difficult for the brave pioneers to open the frontiers to the west. At best, the American native population were highly stylised into noble wild people, their lower status compared to the civilised settlers always being implied in the description.

When viewed with all due honesty, the settlers in America acted with extreme brutality towards the indigenous population. There is no doubt that the native Americans were driven back with weapons and were massacred. Nevertheless, it is practically inconceivable that the small group of white settlers brought an entire culture to its knees and exterminated entire peoples.

At present it is surmised that the original settlement of America took place when peoples migrated from Asia 20,000 to 35,000 years ago via the Bering Straits, and that, when Columbus discovered America for the Europeans in around 1500, there were about 40 to 60 million people living on the continent. Estimating the pre-Columbian population figures in America is difficult, certainly unreliable and is regularly revised, mostly upwards. But what is certain is that the continent was not unpopulated, and it must be assumed that the native Americans made their mark on the countryside and environment [221].

Tenochtitlan, the main city of the Aztecs, may well have had more than 120,000 inhabitants, and thus could have been larger than the European metropolises of the time, such as Venice. In South America, (more so than in North America), a significant proportion of the population lived in cities, which implies a considerable measure of division of labour in a society. But there were also pre-Columbian cities in North America, such as Cahokia, situated north of modern-day St. Louis in Missouri, which was a centre of the Mississippi culture with several ten thousand inhabitants [221].

How could European settlers have subjugated and overthrown all these peoples? By means of epidemics! We have to assume today that the Europeans brought infectious diseases with them that were completely new for the indigenous population of America, meaning that they had no immunity against the causative pathogen at all [222]. Other diseases were imported into the county with the trans-Atlantic slaves from Africa. Generations of Eurasians had had no exposure to malaria and yellow fever. They were thus just as susceptible to other diseases from the old world as the natives of America were. The first attempt to build the Panama Canal had to be abolished because of the mass deaths of the European construction workers and engineers. So it is obvious that the Europeans later also suffered diseases for which their immune systems were not prepared; however, these were mainly diseases from Africa [223].

But why were the Europeans, who brought disease to the native Americans from the very beginning, not in turn wiped out by American epidemics? The most plausible explanation seems to lie in the comparison of domesticated animals on the Eurasian and the American land masses (table 13):

Table 13: Pre-Columbian domesticated animals in Eurasia and America

America	Eurasia
New-World camels (lamas, alpaca)	
	reindeer
	swine
	goats
	sheep
	horses
	donkeys
	domestic cattle
	water buffalo
	yak
	Old-World camels (dromedary, Bactrian camels)
dogs	dogs
guinea pigs	
turkeys	
Muscovy ducks	
	hens
	ducks
	geese

The American natives had ample contact with wild animals, due to their hunting and eating habits, and use of animals' bones, hide, skin and intestines. But there were no close ties with tame farm and domesticated animals and pets in America, as was the case in Eurasia. Also, there were only very few regions in America with the domestic animals listed in the table above. Dogs were probably eaten in central and south America and used as pack animals in north America, while alpaca and lamas were domesticated only in certain regions in the Andes in South America. Only the Indians living in forests in South America had Muscovy ducks, and turkeys were only kept in Mexico.

The Eurasians coexisted with domestic animals, so to speak, and it must be assumed that this led to an exchange of microorganisms through the generations, with the corresponding adaptation of microbiomes. The people living in Eurasia were the offspring of people who had not fallen victim to an infectious disease, at least not before reproduction. Pathogens which, while they still caused diseases among Europeans, but which were not always fatal, caused widespread deaths among the native Americans. In the old world, some of the worst epidemic diseases have adapted themselves to the *Homo sapiens* to such an extent that they are no longer considered zoonoses, but are always transferred from human to human, among these smallpox and measles, and also the bacterial disease typhoid fever. Whereas the Europeans transported a whole range of infectious diseases to the New World, syphilis was the only infectious disease previously unknown to the Europeans (Table 14).

Table 14: Infectious diseases carried from Eurasia to America, and infectious diseases originating in America and transported to Eurasia

America => Eurasia	Eurasia => America
syphilis	
	smallpox
	typhoid fever
	tuberculosis
	Influenza
	plague
	cholera
	mumps
	measles

Smallpox was completely new to the natives of America and to their immune system, which is why masses of native Americans became infected and died of the disease. The same applies for measles.

In the field of epidemiology, the so-called basic reproduction figure is a measure of degree of the contagiousness of an agent. Assuming a completely receptive (non-immune) population, the basic reproduction figure lists the number of individual new infections. Influenza viruses, such as that of the Spanish flu caused by the H1N1 virus, have a basic reproduction figure of 2 to 3. If one considers the devastating effect of the Spanish influenza pandemic of 1918, the effect of diseases with a still higher reproduction figure is not difficult to imagine. An infection with the smallpox virus (basic reproduction figure 6) in a non-immune population causes an average of about 6 secondary infections (each of which trigger 6 further infections, etc.) Measles has the basic reproduction figure of about 15 [224]!

In a few words: the original American population had no chance to escape these biological weapons of mass destruction. It is estimated that 90% to 95% of the original inhabitants fell victim to epidemics and displacement.

Are epidemics an existential threat to humankind?

In order for there to be an existential risk for the continued survival of humankind, an epidemic must infect humankind completely and either kill the infected population or hinder reproduction in those who are infected, making it impossible for a new population to be established to again multiply and reproduce. The agent to trigger such an event would probably have to be from another world or another time, such as the pathogens which were brought to America in 1493 with the Eurasians and Africans and caused mass mortality among the American native population. In a globalised world, the phrase "from another world" makes one imagine agents from another planet. But I don't want to start speculating here about how probable it is that extra-terrestrial creatures might want to visit the earth one day. It is considered possible that frozen microorganisms can be found on the planet Mars, which lies very close to the earth [225]. Since importing extra-terrestrial microorganisms could have inconceivable results, the Soviet Union and the USA agreed to a prohibition of the release of extra-terrestrial microorganisms in 1967, right in the middle of the Cold War [226]. In practical terms, a high pathogenesis of extra-terrestrial microorganisms seems unlikely, since they can hardly be adapted to humans and accordingly are unlikely to be capable of causing infections. Microorganisms from a former time can be released when permafrost soil thaws, and uncovers cadavers of mammals, for instance. These microorganisms could conceivably adjust well to the human host organism, while, due to a lack of exposure, the human body would no longer be suitably equipped to cope with an infection from such a microbe from the ice. Well-known agents as tularaemia or anthrax already induce epidemics in areas of melting permafrost soil [227].

Routes towards (self-) destruction

The American linguist, pacifist scientist and regime critic Noam Chomsky considers it a miracle that humankind has managed not to destroy itself with weapons of mass destruction (yet). Chomsky believes that the two greatest threats to civilisation or at least to more or less dignified survival are a nuclear war and destruction of the environment. In contrast to the threat of epidemics, these two threats have been caused by humans themselves. Thus, it also lies in the hands of humans to (not) take the decisive steps towards (self-) destruction. I myself would add the extermination of humankind by infectious organisms. One might like to counter that this has not occurred in the past and that even the worst epidemics were far removed from becoming existential threats. So, what has changed meanwhile to make epidemics an existential threat? I believe that there are essentially two circumstances that appear to make this a possible scenario:

1) The world has become globalised: for the first time in the history of humankind, there are no isolated groups or peoples that could easily be spared an infectious disease transferred from person to person.

2) Biotechnology has developed methods to make it increasingly more possibly to produce "designer organisms". This makes it conceivable for someone to intentionally construct a perfect "killer virus".

In principle, an epidemic capable of the (self-)destruction of humankind does not require steps taken by humankind. However – as this book explains – human action influences the prerequisites and conditions for epidemics to spread, and thanks to advances made in the molecular and biotechnologies, humankind will soon also have the opportunity for (self-) destruction by creating a biological weapon in a laboratory.

At some stage, humankind will be destroyed or will destroy itself. However, most people want to live. If we want to guarantee the right to live for future generations, decisions and actions must also be based on the intention to extend the time of survival of humankind. However, our prospects of long-term survival could appear gloomy precisely because of the very intelligence that is the basis of human decisions and actions: perhaps the German-born American biologist Ernst Mayr was right in stating that long-term survival of a species tends to be inversely proportional to its intelligence. It might be the case that species, such as bacteria, that are not only capable of withstanding environmental influences, but also rapidly adapt at a population level by means of mutation-based selection mechanisms (and therefore without cognitive intervention), have considerably higher prospects of long-term survival compared to humankind.

12 The Pandora principle

Greek mythology tells of Pandora's box, which contains all that is evil in the world, but also hope. When Pandora opens the box (in the original Greek stories, it was a jar), evils previously unknown to humankind, labour, disease and death escape, while hope remains in the box, since Pandora hastens to close it quickly. The idiom 'Pandora's box' used in modern contexts is often used to portray a situation in which a political, societal or technological development has taken a bad turn and this seems to be irreversible. For example, the book by the German author Jörg Leonard on the first world war bears the title *Pandora's Box* [228]. The nuclear bomb that was dropped over Hiroshima is also sometimes referred to as Pandora's box being opened [229].

So it can be said the Pandora's box is an image for something that has come into the world (or has been brought into the world) that cannot be reversed again. It is an interesting fact that many efforts of humankind in the field of science were intended to eradicate the mythological contents of the Pandora's box, namely labour, disease and death, and meanwhile there are serious voices demanding that the eradication of these three scourges of humankind should be regarded as an attainable goal [170].

At the same time, the sciences have opened innumerable Pandora's boxes, the consequences of which consequences humankind now has to cope with. Things can be invented, but nothing can be "dis-invented". Once an item of knowledge has entered the world, it cannot be removed from the world, this being much more the case today in our networked world than ever in the past. Theoretically, we can eliminate all the nuclear bombs, but in principle we cannot undo the ability of humans to construct nuclear weapons. I can walk backwards, I can walk back to something, I can think back to something. But thinking backwards (in the sense of 'de-think') is something I cannot do.

The Pandora box opener Thomas Midgley

Developments, events and decisions that appear harmless can have long-term consequences for all humankind. In his book *A Short History of Nearly Everything*, Bill Bryson tells the story of an American engineer who is probably completely unknown to most people [230]. Thomas Midgley developed the petrol additive tetraethyl lead to suppress hammering in car engines, although it soon became obvious that lead was a potential nerve poison that enters the food chain. For people growing up in the era after Midgley's invention, this resulted in levels of lead concentration in the blood that was several hundred times higher than that in people before petrol was leaded. Midgley was given the dubious honour of slowly poisoning all life on earth with lead.

One of my childhood memories is the debate on lead-free petrol and the necessity to equip motor cars with catalytic converters ("cats"). Leaded petrol was banned in the EU in 2000. In view of the powerful car lobby and the oil lobby it can be assumed that this decision was not easily made. In 2017, leaded petrol was forbidden worldwide, except in three countries (Algeria, Yemen and Iraq) [231]. The lead concentration in human blood samples has been on the decrease since the reduction of lead emissions [232, 233]. This raises hope that sensible decisions for the wellbeing of humankind are possible, despite the dominant economic imperative of plutocratic power structures [234].

Midgley, who, as shareholder in the manufacturing company, made a profit from leaded petrol, denied the harmful effects of lead throughout his entire life. One headline-grabbing example of this is when he set out to prove this by pouring tetraethyl lead over his hand to show that it was harmless. Thomas Midgley was a very talented inventor and chemist, who held more than 170 patents, and also contributed to improvements in the manufacture of rubber, for instance.

Unfortunately, Midgley left the world another lasting legacy apart from the lead contamination. Early fridges or cooling systems were run on methyl chloride, ammonia or sulphur dioxide, substances that were not only poisonous, but were also prone to combustion. Midgley developed the non-toxic non-flammable supplement chlorofluorocarbon (CFC), which was used as a cooling agent in refrigeration systems and refrigerators. CFCs are very long-lived and decompose very slowly in the atmosphere. They form free halogenic radicals (chlorine, bromine) in the stratosphere, which act as catalysts to decompose the ozone layer. This is what depleted the hole in the ozone layer that was discovered in the 1980s.

Midgley died in a tragic accident in 1944. Since he became ever less physically mobile as a result of having contracted polio late in life, he devised an elaborate system of ropes and pulleys to lift himself out of bed. One morning, he became entangled in the device and died of strangulation. Perhaps he had a premonition that after all the lead was not as harmless as he had always claimed it to be. However, it must be said in his favour that he could not have known about the destructive effect of CFCs on the atmosphere of the earth. The ozone layer protects the earth from rays, mainly from the UVB rays from the sun, which, due to the dwindling ozone layer, particularly in Australia and New Zealand, has caused an increase in cases of skin cancer.

Since the Montreal Protocol (1989) determined a ban on CFCs, the ozone layer seems to have regenerated somewhat and the hole in the ozone layer appears to be closing. The successful implementation of the Montreal Protocol was facilitated by replacing CFCs in cooling systems with propane and butane, which was developed in a cooperation of the environmental organisation Greenpeace with the Hygiene Institute in Dortmund, Germany [235]. The Montreal Protocol is a signal of hope that common sense is possible in the political arena, too. However, this hope has been dampened slightly by a publication that proves that somewhere in the world, illegal CFC emission are threatening the success of the Montreal Protocol [95].

Thomas Midgley had ideas that led to immediate improvement, but wrought much damage in the long-term. Although his praise of leaded petrol may to a certain extent also have been financially motivated, his basic intentions were certainly good.

The plastic age

Gabon is located on the equator and lies on the West African Atlantic coast. It is almost completely covered with tropical rainforests. Gabon covers an area of 267,667 km², somewhat larger than the United Kingdom (245,590 km²) and roughly the size of Colorado in the USA. Since Gabon has a population of only about 2 million, of which 700,000 live in the capital Libreville, the population density with the exclusion of those living in Libreville is lower than 5 persons per km² (1.3 million / 267,667 km²). Thus, large areas of Gabon are uninhabited.

What is still more remarkable is that long stretches of the Gabon coastline are also uninhabited. I lived in Lambaréné, a small town in Gabon from late 2002 until autumn 2005, working as a doctor to conduct epidemiological research. Towards the end of my stay, I travelled to the south-western coast of Gabon in order to visit the Petit Loango National Park, which I had read about in either a *Geo* or a *National Geographic* magazine that I had come across in our research centre. There were reports about large animals such as elephants and hippopotami bathing in the surf of the Atlantic on magical beaches.

Apart from the fantastic landscape and the fascinating animal world, what I remembered about this visit was also the sobering sight of huge masses of plastic waste lying on the (deserted) beach. I had previously already noticed the huge piles of rubbish and torn plastic bags hanging in bushes and trees in other African countries. Water currents and the wind carry our waste material everywhere, also to areas that should remain largely free of human habitation.

Meanwhile, there are hundreds of kilometres of "trash packs" swirling in the oceans, and in some places entire "trash rafts" floating on the surface of the water cover its surface [236]. An initiative to collect and remove the waste from the oceans has sprung up meanwhile [237].

The swimming trash is caused to drift together for collection with tubular u-formed swimming booms, which are stabilised with weights floating hundreds of metres below the water. Unfortunately, the project is not profitable, which is why capitalist incentives and reward systems do not function. At present (2018), the project is funded by donations (crowdfunded) and still at a technical test stage on the Dutch North-Sea coast. But the more well-known the project becomes, the greater are the realistic chances of its being implemented.

However, at the same time, huge masses of waste material continue to be washed into the oceans. If the effort to remove the trash is ultimately to be more than the proverbial drop in the ocean, the technologies must be made compatible with mass production and be as inexpensive as possible – perhaps by using suitable plastic products. If the technology were then used by coastal regions throughout the world and the coastal states were to assume responsibility for their own marine waters, this project could become a genuine contribution to improving the situation. The people in those coastal regions who are actively involved in removing waste from their waters will probably also make an effort to avoid accumulating new waste. The waste collection initiative would thus also contribute to an increasing awareness of the problem among responsible local authorities and the general population.

Taking the planet as a whole, modern *Homo sapiens* also distinguishes itself from all other species on earth and from its own forefathers by its human remains, which are not only restricted to the humans' own excrements and remains of physical decomposition (such as bones), but also includes numerous artefacts and shards of artefacts. The adjective "modern" used in connection with *Homo sapiens* needs particular emphasis in this connection, since, in comparison with present times, *Homo sapiens* managed to cope with daily life with very few artefacts in for a large part of its approximately 300,000-year-old history. Mostly only objects made of stone have remained intact from pre-historical times, although we have to assume that the people of the "stone age" probably used and possessed artefacts made from wood or animal material (bones, skins, hides), which, however, did not stand the test of time.

For archaeologists, the discovery of a glacier mummy by hikers in the Ötztal Alps in 1991 presented a unique opportunity to gain insight into the artefacts that a human carried with him in Central Europe in the New Stone Age about 5225 years ago [13, 238]. The type, number and purpose of the artefacts probably changed little during the centuries afterward. The distinction in the utensils used by a hiker 500 years ago probably lay in the way the material was worked 5,000 years before, but the source material (wooden objects and artefacts from animal material) remained the same. This cannot be said for the artefacts (clothing, personal objects) that can be found on a hiker in the past 50 years. Synthetic material has become part of modern lifestyle. On examining a dead mountaineer or hiker on Mount Everest, the clothing, tent and sleeping bag would be made from modern synthetic material, the mountaineering lamp and the glacier glasses from plastic, and it would be difficult to find pure natural material in the other artefacts.

Unfortunately, traces of synthetics are not only found on human corpses but increasingly in land and marine animals. The cadavers of dead albatrosses full of plastic artefacts on the Midway Islands have become the very epitome of global environmental pollution by plastic waste [239].

However, we oversimplify things for ourselves when we demonise the polymer chemists to whom we owe the development of modern synthetic materials. If we try to imagine a modern world without synthetics, this might appear to be an aesthetic one in our nostalgic view. But it would mean that we would have to do without many of the objects that we use in everyday life. If all the objects that we use today were to be made of natural materials such as wood or metals, our planet would probably have to pay a price of a different kind. Just imagine how much wood seafaring nations (e.g. the Greeks, Romans, Phoenicians) in the Mediterranean region needed and the effect it had on the vegetation. In the remaining parts of Europe, too, humans contributed to a massive decline in forests [240].

Plastic bags are so much part of our daily lives that it is difficult to think that synthetic materials did not exist only a few generations ago. Even for the generation of my great-grandparents, who lived in the late 19th and early 20th century, synthetic materials were practically unknown. The first one-piece plastic bag was patented by the Swedish company Celloplast in 1965 and quickly spread throughout Europe. By 1979, plastic bags were being used in 80% of the European market [241]. In Germany, the chain store Horten first introduced clothing in plastic wrapping as early as 1961 [242]. Meanwhile, plastic bags and other plastic materials are omnipresent: in the bushes and trees of Africa, on the beaches of Gabon and also in the cadavers of dead albatrosses on the Midway Islands.

Not only have visible plastic objects spread, but so has microplastic, i.e. small plastic particles from disintegrating plastic objects or that are produced more or less intentionally (in peeling ingredients, for instance). Plastic is thus increasingly entering the (formerly) natural cycle of life and food chains [243].

Toxins as an existential threat to humankind

In December 1984, in the Indian town Bhopal, more than 27 tons of methyl isocyanate (MIC) for the production of chemical pesticides leaked from a chemical factory belonging to the American company Union Carbide India Limited (UCIL). More than 2000 people died from the direct exposure to methyl isocyanate (MIC). The total number of deaths is considerably higher, however, with many people becoming seriously ill and dying of the consequences of the poisoning in the following months, years and decades. The organisation "International Campaign for Justice in Bhopal" estimates the total death toll was 22,000 (as of 2014), and the number of injured or handicapped people to be 157,000 [244].

The impact on the environment and water in the area surrounding Bhopal are serious and long-lasting. The Bhopal disaster was thus one of the worst human-induced (non-war) industrial catastrophes. However, it did not pose an existential threat to humankind, since the damage remained restricted to the surrounding region of Bhopal.

Is it conceivable that humankind can be destroyed as a result of a local leakage of a toxic substance? Yes, in principle it is. However, I find it difficult to think of a poison that is so toxic that it can still be lethal after the enormous dilution that takes place while it spreads.

Rather, I tend to consider potential for existential threats to lie in noxious substances that are released continuously and gradually, and remain unnoticed at first. Such noxious substances can destroy the living conditions that are essential for human survival. The extent to which climate change constitutes an existential threat to humankind as result of greenhouse gases such a carbon dioxide and methane being released constantly throughout the world, as already been discussed in some detail in the chapter "climate change".

But can the direct effect of a poison on the human organism become a hazard for humankind? The long unnoticed absorption in the human organism of the lead released from petrol in cars with internal combustion engines has shown that harmful substances can reach every *Homo sapiens* living on earth and accumulate in human organisms [230]. Lead was first mixed into petrol in 1921 to suppress hammering in the engines of motor cars. It has been banned in most countries since 2000. So much lead was emitted during the course of eight decades that the increase in lead concentration could be recorded in every human organism.

A toxic substance with faster action would probably result in rapid countermeasures. But let us imagine a substance that is released into the atmosphere by a technological mass product, and which does not seem to be toxic initially, but is absorbed in the bloodstream of the human body and affects the human foetus. A lethal toxic effect on the developing human organism is likely to be noticed soon and lead to countermeasures.

Let us imagine a harmful effect on the later fertility of the developing foetus of a substance that is absorbed in all humans. Let us imagine that the impairment to fertility cannot be detected microscopically and becomes obvious only later, say, after a period of about two decades, when a substantial number of people have not been able to fulfil their wish to have children. The imagined substance would by now have reached high concentrations in the atmosphere, in the food chain and in every human organism, so that the generation we have imagined with their unfulfilled wish for children might be the last generation of humans.

Designer organisms and their unforeseeable consequences

In principle, target-specific genome modification allows humans to alter living beings, be they plants, microorganisms or animals.

One direct (and potentially existential) threat for humans lies in the targeted production or modification of pathogens, such as the reconstruction of the influenza virus of 1918 by American scientists several years ago.

In order to protect the species, biotechnologies make it possible for species to be archived in genome databases and long extinct species to be revived. A mammoth or even a dinosaur would be a huge attraction for zoos and theme parks (at least initially). However, "reawakening" species from the distant past leads to unforeseeable consequences. When globalisation began in the late 15th century with international seafaring, plants and animal species were transported to unfamiliar and new continents where they could previously not be found. Together with the "First Fleet" in Australia, i.e. former prisoners who were shipped to the continent as settlers, hares and rabbits also entered Australia. At first they were kept in cages, until a passionate hobby huntsman released 24 wild rabbits and a house rabbit on his farm in Barwon Park, Victoria, for hunting purposes. The rabbits duly multiplied "like rabbits" and soon became a pest in the country, driving off and threatening other species, such as species the Australian marisipial species, with extinction.

Since the 1950s, rabbits have been controlled using "biological weapons". A flea- or mosquito-carried virus called myxomatosis was used to reduce the rabbit population of an estimated 600 million in 1950 to about 100 million. However, some of the rabbits that survived were resistant to the myxomatosis. These rabbits multiplied despite the virus, which resulted in the rabbit population again increasing to about 200 – 300 million.

At present attempts are being made to control the rabbit population by deploying the rabbit calicivirus, which causes fatal haemorrhagic fever. We assume that this virus is not dangerous for humans [245].

For Australia, the rabbits were an invasive species "from another world". Invasive species "from another time" could be revived by biotechnological means. What could the likely consequences for the marine ecological system be if the trilobites that were so successful over millions of years in primeval times were to be revived, and then reproduce in the oceans of the world, not unlike the rabbits in Australia?

Every large animal hosts innumerable microorganisms, forming its microbiome. The *Tyrannosaurus rex* kept in the „Jurassic Zoo" would surely also have its very own microbiome colony (which, however, would stem from our modern environment). Most of the newly emerging diseases infecting humans originate from infections transported from animals to humans (called 'spill over'). This seems to entail the particularly grave danger of generating a new fatal epidemic, particularly in human populations that have not had a long and close history of interaction with the other species. The European settlers in America had lived for centuries with farm animals and brought with them to the New World bacteria that had originated from interaction between the species. These bacteria and viruses had the effect of acting as devastating biological weapons among the indigenous peoples of

America. Could revived species perhaps select micro-organisms that are similarly alien to today's human population as the European settlers' pathogens were for the indigenous population?

Finally, let us briefly consider biotechnology on humans. What would the consequences be if species in the direct line of descendants to our forefathers were resurrected? Or to do so with Neanderthals, a species with which our forefathers also coupled, but which became extinct 40,000 years ago (possibly with the involvement of *Homo* sapiens)?

Intervention with modification of the human genome will lead to a new wave of eugenics (this time at least not a selective mass-murdering eugenics approach, but an approach in which privileged people optimise their genes or the genes of their offspring). The degree to which genetic changes will take place in *Homo sapiens* (individual cases, groups, the entire human population) cannot be foreseen. The consequences for human cohabitation are likely to be immense and will not leave the societal and social structures untouched. Decisions regarding the regulation of the access to genetic optimisation will certainly determine the entire future of humankind.

There is no doubt that biotechnology can be implemented for purposes that are directly beneficial to the individual, such as in healing diseases or counteracting the process of aging. However, this is also a double-edged sword. If we consider the extreme consequences of suppressing disease and aging, this will reveal a *Homo sapiens* that can live extremely long, except in cases of death by external violence [170]. At the same time, the living space and the resources on earth are finite. Even today, the growth of the global population has taken on threatening dimensions. If we were able to abolish disease and aging, who would have the right to the privilege of a long life? Who would be the people that were allowed to procreate and who would be forced make their exit from this world in order to make way for the future generations?

In the 20th century, atomic energy was regarded as the source of energy of the future, but also as a potential source of total extinction. The International Atomic Energy Agency as a UN organisation was founded to maintain an overview of the consequences and to regulate them. Perhaps it is time to establish an international UN biotechnological organisation.

Immediate and long-term consequences of technological innovations

Possibly this has been the recurring melody to be heard throughout the span of human civilisation: beneficial advances whose side effects only manifest themselves long-term. We struggle to find solutions to problems that escaped from Pandora's box when it was opened a long time ago – and we are still opening new boxes. We already have nuclear weapons, biological weapons and chemical weapons in our world. But their further development could increase their potential threat, which even now is great, and ultimately become an existential threat to humankind.

Weapons of mass destruction such as nuclear bombs could be developed to become "clean" mass weapons that only cause death to the people in certain regions, leaving the infrastructure and resources intact. The thoughts and ideas have already escaped the box and the technological developments are already underway. Decreasing the size of weapons of mass destruction and delivery systems and constructing smaller nuclear weapons will not increase security globally.

Toxic substances such as Midgley's additive to petrol, lead, but also chemical weapons could be absorbed into the food chain and gradually poison humans or impede their fertility.

The idea to modify organisms or to create new organisms has long since escaped Pandora's box and, with regard to the modification of the human genome or that of micro-bacteria that could cause harm to humans, has been the subject matter of ominous dystopian films and literature. CRISPR /Cas methods have paved the road to the technological development of genome modification. The knowledge required for this is out there in the world.

What all these new technological advances have in common is that they also constitute a threat to humans. This can only be countered by cautious action and by further innovations that serve to control these advances. But they cannot be reversed.

The insight that insight is not reversible seems to be deeply anchored in the collective memory of humankind. After Adam and Eve had eaten of the fruit of knowledge, they could not reverse their knowledge – and this brought their comfortable life in paradise to an end.

13   Reference list

1.   Chomsky N. Priorities and Prospects. https://chomsky.info/hegemony01/. Excerpted from Hegemony or Survival, Metropolitan Books, 2003. Zuletzt eingesehen am 29.3.2018. **2003.**

2.   Daase C, Kessler O. Knowns and Unknowns in the `War on Terror': Uncertainty and the Political Construction of Danger. *Security Dialogue* **2007**,38:411-434.

3.   Zizek S. Philosophy, the "unknown knowns," and the public use of reason. *Topoi* **2006**,25:137-142.

4.   Zizek S. What Rumsfeld Doesn't Know That He Knows About Abu Ghraib. http://www.lacan.com/zizekrumsfeld.htm. Zuletzt eingesehen am 25.12.2018. *Lacan Dot Com* **2004.**

5.   Taleb NN. *The Black Swan. The Impact of the highly improbable.* London: Allen Lane; 2007.

6.   Cobb K. Albert Bartlett: On message about exponential growth to the end. http://www.resilience.org/stories/2013-09-15/albert-bartlett-on-message-about-exponential-growth-to-the-end/. Zuletzt eingesehen am 21.2.2018. *Resilience* **2013.**

7.   Roser M. Our World in Data. https://ourworldindata.org/wp-content/uploads/2013/05/updated-World-Population-Growth-1750-2100.png. Zuletzt eingesehen am 27.2.2018.

8.   Factfish. Landwirtschaftliche Nutzfläche (Quadratkilometer) - für alle Länder. http://www.factfish.com/de/statistik/landwirtschaftliche nutzfl%C3%A4che. Zuletzt eingesehen am 19.12.2018.

9.   Signer D. Weniger Kinder, mehr Wachstum. https://www.nzz.ch/international/demografie-in-afrika-weniger-kinder-mehr-wachstum-ld.1308410. Zuletzt eingesehen am 16.5.2018. *Neue Züricher Zeitung* **2017.**

10.   Niehus J, Schaefer T, Schröder C. Arm und Reich in Deutschland: Wo bleibt die Mitte? Forschungsberichte aus dem Institut der deutschen Wirtschaft Köln. **2013**,89.

11.   Niejahr E. "Uns fehlt das dritte Kind". *Die Zeit* **2016**,42.

12.   Varoufakis Y. Time for Change. Wie ich meiner Tochter die Wirtschaft erkläre. Bastei Lübbe Verlag. **2016.**

13.   Bryson B. At Home. *Black Swan Books* **2010.**

14.   Hager S. H. L. Hunt is a key to the JFK assassination. https://stevenhager420.wordpress.com/2013/11/27/h-l-hunt-is-a-key-to-the-jfk-assassination/. Zuletzt eingesehen am 31.03.2018. **2013.**

15.   Porterfield B. H. L. Hunt's Long Goodbye. https://www.texasmonthly.com/articles/h-l-hunts-long-goodbye/. Zuletzt eingesehen am 31.3.2018. *Texas Monthly* **1975.**

16.   Phillips K. American Dynasty: Aristocracy, Fortune, and the Politics of Deceit in the House of Bush. Penguin Books. **2004.**

17.   Lüders M. Armageddon im Orient. Wie die Saudi Connection den Iran ins Visier nimmt. Beck Verlag. **2018.**

18.   Bröckers M. Der falsche Schwager. https://www.heise.de/tp/features/Der-falsche-Schwager-3435939.html. Zuletzt eingesehen am 19.12.2018. *TELEPOLIS* **2004.**

19. Preston P. Observer Books. A love affair that survived even 9/11. House of Bush, House of Saud by Craig Unger. https://www.theguardian.com/theobserver/2004/jul/25/politics Zuletzt eingesehen am 19.12.2018. *The Guardian* **2004.**

20. Lobosco K. Tracking Trump's changing claims on jobs from Saudi arms deal. https://edition.cnn.com/2018/10/22/politics/trump-jobs-saudi-arms-deal/index.html. Zuletzt eingesehen am 19.12.2018. *CNN* **2018.**

21. eia. U.S. Energy Information Adminsitration https://www.eia.gov/todayinenergy/detail.php?id=28672. Zuletzt eingesehen am 31.7.2018.

22. eia. U.S. Energy Information Adminsitration https://www.eia.gov/dnav/pet/hist/LeafHandler.ashx?n=PET&s=WCRF PUS2&f=W. Zuletzt eingesehen am 31.7.2018.

23. Clemente J. Global Oil Demand Can Only Increase. https://www.forbes.com/sites/judeclemente/2016/08/28/global-oil-demand-can-only-increase/ - 52641c2931a0. Zuletzt eingesehen am 25.2.2018.

24. esa. United Nations Department of Economic and Social Affairs [https://esa.un.org/]. Dataset: WPP2017_POP_F01_1_TOTAL_POPULATION_BOTH_SEXES.xlsx. Zuletzt eingesehen am 31.3.2018. **2017.**

25. Ländervergleich. Erdölverbrauch in Barrel pro Jahr je Einwohner. https://www.welt-in-zahlen.de/laendervergleich.phtml?indicator=94. Zuletzt eingesehen am 25.2.2018.

26. Lüders M. Wer den Wind sät: Was westliche Politik im Orient anrichtet. Beck Verlag. **2015.**

27. Mansfield P. A History of the Middle East. Fourth Edition revised and updated by Nicolas Pelham. . **2013.**

28. Pötzl N. Treibstoff der Feindschaft. *Spiegel Geschichte Persien* **2010,**2:104-109.

29. Brzezinski Z. The Grand Chessboard: American Primacy And Its Geostrategic Imperatives. *Basic Books* **1997.**

30. Krone-Schmalz G. Eiszeit. Wie Russland dämonisiert wird und warum das so gefährlich ist. C.H.Beck Verlag. **2017.**

31. Vikan H. The 1991 Gulf Crisis and US Policy Means. An Analysis of the Transition from 'Soft Line' to 'Hard Line' in US Foreign Policy Toward Iraq. Master-Level Thesis in Political Science The University of Oslo. Institute of Political Science.https://www.duo.uio.no/bitstream/handle/10852/14614/vikan.pdf?sequence=6. Zuletzt eingesehen am 19.12.2018. **1998.**

32. Ali MM, Shah IH. Sanctions and childhood mortality in Iraq. *Lancet* **2000,**355:1851-1857.

33. Zaidi S. Child mortality in Iraq. *Lancet* **1997,**350:1105.

34. UNICEF. (United Nations Children's Fund) Iraq surveys show 'humanitarian emergency' https://www.unicef.org/newsline/99pr29.htm, Zuletzt eingesehen am 6.3.2018. **1999.**

35. Dyson T, Cetorelli V. Changing views on child mortality and economic sanctions in Iraq: a history of lies, damned lies and statistics. *BMJ Glob Health* **2017,**2:e000311.

36. Abdulrazaq T. How the West whitewashes killing children in Iraq. https://www.trtworld.com/opinion/how-western-nations-whitewash-the-killing-of-children-in-iraq-9845. Zuletzt eingesehen am 6.3.2018. **2017.**

37. Ganser D. Illegale Kriege. Wie die NATO Länder die UNO sabotieren. Eine Chronik von Kuba bis Syrien. *Orell Füssli Verlag* **2016.**

38. Stieglitz J. The Great Divide: Unequal Societies and What We Can Do About Them. **2015**.

39. Wolf E. Finanz-Tsunami: Wie das globale Finanzsystem uns alle bedroht. **2017**.

40. Dowell W. Foreign Exchange: Saddam Turns His Back on Greenbacks. *TIME* **2000**,156.

41. Swanson D. Libya: another neocon war. Liberal supporters of this 'humanitarian intervention' have merely become useful idiots of the same old nefarious purposes. https://www.theguardian.com/commentisfree/cifamerica/2011/apr/21/libya-muammar-gaddafi, Zuletzt eingesehen am 6.3.2018. *The Guardian* **2011**.

42. Hoff B. Hillary Emails Reveal True Motive for Libya Intervention https://www.foreignpolicyjournal.com/2016/01/06/new-hillary-emails-reveal-true-motive-for-libya-intervention/ . Zuletzt eingesehen am 23.3.2018. *Foreign Policy Journal* **2016**.

43. Blume G, Sydow C. Gaddafis langer Schatten. http://www.spiegel.de/politik/ausland/nicolas-sarkozy-in-polizeigewahrsam-muammar-al-gaddafis-langer-schatten-a-1198999.html. Zuletzt eingesehen am 31.3.2018. *Spiegel Online* **2018**.

44. Tilouine J, Piel S. Financement libyen de la campagne de 2007 : Nicolas Sarkozy en garde à vue. http://www.lemonde.fr/police-justice/article/2018/03/20/financement-libyen-de-la-campagne-de-2007-nicolas-sarkozy-en-garde-a-vue_5273446_1653578.html. Zuletzt eingesehen am 31.3.2018. *Le Monde* **2018**.

45. Schwarz J. Jimmy Carter: The U.S. is an "Oligarchy with unlimited political bribery". https://theintercept.com/2015/07/30/jimmy-carter-u-s-oligarchy-unlimited-political-bribery/. Zuletzt eingesehen am 20.12.2018. *The Intercept* **2015**.

46. Chomsky N. Profit over people. War against people. Neoliberalismus und globale Weltordnung, Menschenrechte und Schurkenstaaten. 8. Auflage 2016. Piper Verlag. **2016**.

47. Longwell HJ. Out Of Gas: The future of the oil and gas industry: past approaches, new challenges. https://web.archive.org/web/20081003081853/http://www.worldenergysource.com/articles/pdf/longwell_WE_v5n3.pdf . Zuletzt eingesehen am 26.2.2018. *World Energy* **2002**.

48. 20 Largest Natural Gas Fields in the World. https://www.worldlistmania.com/20-largest-natural-gas-fields-in-the-world/. Zuletzt eingesehen am 1.4.2018. *Worldlistmania*.

49. Bentley RW. Global oil & gas depletion: an overview. *Energy Policy* **2002**,30:189-205.

50. Lüders M. Die den Sturm ernten. Wie der Westen Syrien ins Chaos stürzte. Beck Verlag. **2017**.

51. Marshall T. Die Macht der Geographie. Wie sich Weltpolitik anhand von 10 Karten erklären lässt. dtv Verlag. **2015**.

52. Agenturmeldung. USA ziehen Truppen aus Syrien ab. https://www.zeit.de/politik/ausland/2018-12/us-militaereinsatz-usa-syrien-truppenabzug. Zuletzt eingesehen am 20.12.2018. *Zeit Online* **2018**.

53. Güsten S. Türkei plant neue Invasion in Nordsyrien. https://www.tagesspiegel.de/politik/kurdenkonflikt-tuerkei-plant-neue-invasion-in-nordsyrien/23766970.html. Zuletzt eingesehen am 20.12.2018. *Der Tagesspiegel* **2018**.

54. Robbins J. What Ever Happened to Public Transportation? Zuletzt eingeshen am 20.12.2018. *The Huffington Post* **2010**.

55. Dimroth F, Grave M, Beutel P, Fiedeler U, Karcher C, Thomas ND, Oliva TE, Siefer G, Schachtner M, Wekkeli A, Bett AW, Krause R, Piccin M, Blanc M, Drazek C, Guiot E, Ghyselen B, Salvetat T, Tauzin A, Signamarcheix T, Dobrich A, Hannappel T, Schwarzburg K. Wafer bonded four-junction GaInP/GaAs//GaInAsP/GaInAs concentrator solar cells with 44.7% efficiency. *Progress in Photovoltaics: Research and Applications* **2014**,22.

56. Mihm A. SOLAR-SUBVENTIONEN : Ein sonniges Geschäft. http://www.faz.net/aktuell/wirtschaft/solar-subventionen-ein-sonniges-geschaeft-1950239.html. Zuletzt eingesehen am 5.4.2018. *Frankfurter Allgemeine Zeitung* **2010**.

57. dpa. SOLARMODUL-HERSTELLER: Solarworld ist schon wieder pleite. http://www.handelsblatt.com/unternehmen/energie/solarmodul-hersteller-solarworld-ist-schon-wieder-pleite/21122208.html. Zuletzt eingesehen am 5.4.2018. *Handelsbaltt* **2018**.

58. energieinfo. Energielexikon → Batterie. http://www.energieinfo.de/eglossar/batterie.html. Zuletzt eingesehen am 5.4.2018. **2018**.

59. Paschotta R. Energetische Amortisationszeit. https://www.energie-lexikon.info/energetische_amortisationszeit.html. Zuletzt eingesehen am 5.4.2018. **2018**.

60. Sorge NV, Eckl-Dorna W. Deutschland ohne Diesel und Benzin - kann das funktionieren? http://www.manager-magazin.de/unternehmen/autoindustrie/elektroautos-wie-wuerde-ein-verbrenner-verbot-funktionieren-a-1116158-7.html. Zuletzt eingesehen am 20.12.2018. *Manager Magazin* **2016**.

61. Ulrich S. Kaum Rohstoffengpässe für Photovoltaikherstellung. *Photovoltaik.* https://www.photovoltaik.eu/Archiv/Meldungsarchiv/article-594978-110949/kaum-rohstoffengpaesse-fuer-photovoltaikherstellung-.html. *Zuletzt eingesehen am 5.4.2018.* **2014**.

62. Helmers E, Hilgenberg J, Müller-Görnert M. Versprochen – Gebrochen. Wie die deutsche Autoindustrie den Klimaschutz ignoriert. Eine Analyse von BUND und VCD auf Grundlage der Studie „Die Modellentwicklung in der deutschen Autoindustrie: Gewicht contra Effizienz". . **2015**.

63. Worldometers. Northern Africa Population. http://www.worldometers.info/world-population/northern-africa-population/. Zuletzt eingesehen am 25.3.2018. **2018**.

64. Sackmann C. Hat der Nestlé-Chef wirklich einmal gesagt, Wasser sei kein Menschenrecht? https://www.finanzen100.de/finanznachrichten/wirtschaft/debatte-um-schweizer-konzern-hat-der-nestle-chef-wirklich-einmal-gesagt-wasser-sei-kein-menschenrecht_H2029013325_546809/. Zuletzt eingesehen am 20.12.2018. *Finanzen100* **2018**.

65. CAWATERinfo. Database of the Aral Sea. http://cawater-info.net/aral/data/tabs_e.htm. Zuletzt eingesehen am 25.3.2018. **2018**.

66. Akimbayev AM. The Biological Safety in Kazakhstan. Edited by Sandra S. Essbauer, Ernst-Jürgen Finke, Stefan O. Frey and Bryan R. Thoma. Bundeswehr Institute of Microbiology, Munich, Germany. **2016**.

67. Pabst V. Eine Stadt sitzt auf dem Trockenen. https://www.nzz.ch/international/eine-stadt-sitzt-auf-dem-trockenen-ld.1347581. Zuletzt eingesehen am 25.3.2018. *Neue Züricher Zeitung* **2018**.

68. Kolonko G. Pakistan: Ist der Wassermangel gefährlicher als das Talibanproblem? https://www.heise.de/tp/features/Pakistan-Ist-der-Wassermangel-gefaehrlicher-als-das-Talibanproblem-3814010.html. Zuletzt eingesehen am 25.3.2018. *TELEPOLIS* **2017**.

69. Banach O. Atommächte auf Konfrontationskurs: Droht ein Wasserkrieg zwischen Indien und Pakistan?https://deutsch.rt.com/asien/41392-atommachte-auf-konfrontationskurs-droht-wasserkrieg/. Zuletzt eingesehen am 25.3.2018. *RT Deutsch* **2016**.

70. Muhammad J. Grand Ethiopian Renaissance Dam nears completion, but not without controversy. https://www.finalcall.com/artman/publish/World_News_3/Grand-Ethiopian-Renaissance-Dam-nears-completion-but-not-without-controversy.shtml. Zuletzt eingesehen am 20.12.2018. *The Final Call* **2018**.

71. Gawhary KE. Am Nil braut sich etwas zusammen. *Die Rheinpfalz* **2018**,Jahrgang 74:3.

72. Behrens C. Wie Dubai dem Meer Trinkwasser abringt. https://www.sueddeutsche.de/wissen/meerwasserentsalzung-wie-dubai-dem-meer-trinkwasser-abringt-1.3630919. Zuletzt eingesehen am 20.12.2018. *Süddeutsche Zeitung* **2017**.

73. Lattemann S. Meerwasserentsalzung .In: WARNSIGNAL KLIMA: Genug Wasser für alle? 3.Auflage (2011) - Hrsg. Lozán, J. L. H., Graßl, P. Hupfer, L. Karbe & C.-D. Schönwiese. http://www.climate-service-center.de/imperia/md/content/csc/warnsignalklima/warnsignal_klima_kap4_4.2_latemann.pdf. Zuletzt eingesehen am 26.3.2018. **2011**:452-458.

74. Fischer L. Eisberge sollen Kapstadt vor Dürre retten. https://www.spektrum.de/news/eisberge-sollen-kapstadt-vor-duerre-retten/1562774. Zuletzt eingesehen am 3.5.2018. *Spektrum*.

75. Schönherr M. Eisberge aus Antarktis sollen Wasserkrise in Kapstadt lösen. https://www.tagesspiegel.de/weltspiegel/plan-eines-suedafrikanischen-experten-eisberge-aus-antarktis-sollen-wasserkrise-in-kapstadt-loesen/21249314.html. Zuletzt eingesehen am 20.12.2018. *Der Tagesspiegel* **2018**.

76. Kern J. Trinkwasser aus Eisbergen. http://www.quellonline.de/trinkwasser-aus-eisbergen/. Zuletzt eingesehen am 4.5.2018. *Quell* **2009**.

77. Schönherr M. Kapstadt freut sich über regenreichen Winter. https://www.tagesspiegel.de/weltspiegel/nach-wasserkrise-in-suedafrika-kapstadt-freut-sich-ueber-regenreichen-winter/22999938.html. Zuletzt eingesehen am 20.12.2018. *Der Tagesspiegel* **2018**.

78. Lobe A. Wenn den Wüstenländern der Sand ausgeht. https://www.welt.de/vermischtes/article136519785/Wenn-den-Wuestenlaendern-der-Sand-ausgeht.html. Zuletzt eingesehen am 24.3.2018. *Welt* **2015**.

79. Menon N. Illegal Sand Mining: India's Biggest Environmental Challenge? https://weather.com/en-IN/india/news/news/2018-10-26-illegal-sand-mining-indias-biggest-environmental-challenge. Zuletzt eingesehen am 20.12.2018. *India News* **2018**.

80. Sträter A, Matzarakis A. Biowetter: Ideale Wohlfühl-Temperaturen liegen bei 25 Grad. https://www1.wdr.de/wissen/mensch/biowetter-interview-100.html. Zuletzt eingesehen am 20.12.2018. *WDR* **2018**.

81. Kohnert K, Serafimovich A, Metzger S, Hartmann J, Sachs T. Strong geologic methane emissions from discontinuous terrestrial permafrost in the Mackenzie Delta, Canada. *Scientific Reports* **2017**,7:5828.

82. Etheridge DM, Steele LP, Langenfelds RL, Francey RJ, Barnola J-M, Morgan VI. Natural and anthropogenic changes in atmospheric CO2 over the last 1000 years from air in Antarctic ice and firn. Online Data repository: http://cdiac.ess-dive.lbl.gov/trends/co2/lawdome.html. Zuletzt eingesehen am 5.3.2018. *Journal of Geophysical Research* **1996**,101:4115-4128.

83. CDIAC. Carbon Dioxide Information Analysis Center. Historical Records from the Law Dome DE08, DE08-2, and DSS Ice Cores. Prepared by Monica Martinez and Tom Boden on the 26.06.1998. http://cdiac.ess-dive.lbl.gov/trends/co2/lawdome-graphics.html. Zuletzt eingesehen am 31.07.2018.

84. Watts J. Global atmospheric CO2 levels hit record high. https://www.theguardian.com/environment/2017/oct/30/global-atmospheric-co2-levels-hit-record-high. Zuletzt eingesehen am 6.3.2018. *The Guardian* **2017**.

85. Reuters. CO2-Konzentration steigt so schnell wie nie. http://www.spiegel.de/wissenschaft/mensch/co2-konzentration-steigt-so-schnell-wie-nie-a-1175568.html. Zuletzt eingesehen am 28.7.2018. *Spiegel Online* **2017**.

86. Allen JG, MacNaughton P, Satish U, Santanam S, Vallarino J, Spengler JD. Associations of Cognitive Function Scores with Carbon Dioxide, Ventilation, and Volatile Organic Compound Exposures in Office Workers: A Controlled Exposure Study of Green and Conventional Office Environments. *Environ Health Perspect* **2016**,124:805-812.

87. Satish U, Mendell MJ, Shekhar K, Hotchi T, Sullivan D, Streufert S, Fisk WJ. Is CO2 an indoor pollutant? Direct effects of low-to-moderate CO2 concentrations on human decision-making performance. *Environ Health Perspect* **2012**,120:1671-1677.

88. Umweltbundesamt. Gesundheitliche Bewertung von Kohlendioxid in der Innenraumluft. Mitteilungen der Ad-hoc-Arbeitsgruppe Innenraumrichtwerte der Innenraumlufthygiene-Kommission des Umweltbundesamtes und der Obersten Landesgesundheitsbehörden. *Bundesgesundheitsblatt* **2008**,51:1358-1369.

89. IPCC. Climate Change 2013. The Physical Science Basis. WG1. Intergovermental Panel on Climate Change. **2014**.

90. Caesar L, Rahmstorf S, Robinson A, Feulner G, Saba V. Observed fingerprint of a weakening Atlantic Ocean overturning circulation. https://www.nature.com/articles/s41586-018-0006-5. Zuletzt eingesehen am 12.4.2018. *Nature* **2018**.

91. Wöhrbach O. Extremwetter und Klimawandel. Über den Wolken aus der Puste. https://www.tagesspiegel.de/wissen/extremwetter-und-klimawandel-ueber-den-wolken-aus-der-puste/22893494.html. Zuletzt eingesehen am 28.10.2018. *Der Tagesspiegel* **2018**.

92. 7,000 underground gas bubbles poised to 'explode' in Arctic. *The Siberian Times*. http://siberiantimes.com/science/casestudy/news/n0905-7000-underground-gas-bubbles-poised-to-explode-in-arctic/. *Zuletzt eingesehen am 1.4.2018.* **2017**,20 March 2017.

93. Rosenthal E, Lehren A. Relief in Every Window, but Global Worry Too. http://www.nytimes.com/2012/06/21/world/asia/global-demand-for-air-conditioning-forces-tough-environmental-choices.html. Zuletzt eingesehen am 13.3.2018. *New York Times* **2012**.

94. Fischer L, Groos JU. Wird die Ozonschicht wieder dünner? https://www.zeit.de/wissen/umwelt/2018-05/ozonloch-fckw-

fluorchlorkohlenwasserstoffe-atmosphaere-ozonschicht. Zuletzt eingesehen am 18.5.2018. *Zeit Online* **2018**.

95. Montzka SA, Dutton GS, Yu P, Ray E, Portmann RW, Daniel JS, Kuijpers L, Hall BD, Mondeel D, Siso C, Nance JD, Rigby M, Manning AJ, Hu L, Moore F, Miller BR, Elkins JW. An unexpected and persistent increase in global emissions of ozone-depleting CFC-11. *Nature* **2018**,557:413-417.

96. Taleb NN. *Antifragile. Things that gain from disorder*. London: Penguin Books; 2012.

97. WWF. World Wildlife Found. Klimawandel und Auswirkung auf die Meere.Stellungnahme. https://www.wwf.de/fileadmin/fm-wwf/Publikationen-PDF/Klimawandel-Auswirkung-auf-die-Meere.pdf. Zuletzt eingesehen am 21.12.2018.

98. Gittings JA, Raitsos DE, Krokos G, Hoteit I. Impacts of warming on phytoplankton abundance and phenology in a typical tropical marine ecosystem. *Sci Rep* **2018**,8:2240.

99. R. L, M. S, Simmon R. What are Phytoplankton? https://earthobservatory.nasa.gov/features/Phytoplankton. Zuletzt eingesehen am 21.12.2018. *NASA Earth Observatory* **2010**.

100. NSIDC. Average Monthly Arctic Sea Ice Extent. February 1979-2018. National Snow and Ice Data Centre. http://nsidc.org/arcticseaicenews/category/analysis/. Zuletzt eingesehen am 31.07.2018. . **2018**.

101. Pomrehn W. Arktis: Nordost-Passage offen. https://www.heise.de/tp/news/Arktis-Nordost-Passage-offen-3812985.html. Zuletzt eingesehen am 18.3.2018. *TELEPOLIS* **2017**.

102. Lindinger M, Primus Y. NEGATIVREKORD AM SÜDPOL : Forscher warnen vor massiver Eisschmelze. http://www.faz.net/aktuell/wissen/erde-klima/negativrekord-am-suedpol-das-antarktis-eis-schmilzt-schneller-als-erwartet-14153639.html. Zuletzt eingesehen am 2.4.2018. *Frankfurter Allgemeine Zeitung* **2016**.

103. Mooney C. Antarctic ice loss has tripled in a decade. If that continues, we are in serious trouble. https://www.washingtonpost.com/news/energy-environment/wp/2018/06/13/antarctic-ice-loss-has-tripled-in-a-decade-if-that-continues-we-are-in-serious-trouble/?noredirect=on&utm_term=.8580a7557a1f. Zuletzt eingesehen am 21.12.2018. *Washington Post.* **2018**.

104. Borunda A. We Know West Antarctica Is Melting. Is the East In Danger, Too? https://www.nationalgeographic.com/environment/2018/08/east-antarctic-ice-sheet-melting/. Zuletzt eingesehen am 21.12.2018. *National Geographic* **2018**.

105. IPCC. Climate Change 2013, Working Group I: The Science of Climate Change, 13.2. **2013**.

106. Yi S, Sun W, Heki K, Qian A. An increase in the rate of global mean sea level rise since 2010. *Geophysical Research Letters* **2015**,42.

107. Church JA, White NJ. A 20th century acceleration in global sea-level rise. *Geophysical Research Letters* **2006**,33.

108. Schätzing F. Nachrichten aus einem unbekannten Universum. . *Kiepenheuer & Witsch* **2006**.

109. Lingenhöhl D. Küstenschutz. Flussdeltas auf dem Rückzug. http://www.zeit.de/wissen/umwelt/2009-09/Erde-SD-Flussdeltas. Zuletzt eingesehen am 3.4.2018. *Zeit Online* **2009**.

110. Bojanowski A. Tsunami-Katastrophe im Steinzeitparadies. http://www.spiegel.de/wissenschaft/natur/tsunami-in-nordsee-storegga-

rutschung-traf-menschen-in-steinzeit-a-1011946.html. Zuletzt eingesehen am 21.12.2018. *Spiegel Online* **2015.**

111. Pomrehn W. Grönland: Eis weniger stabil als gedacht. https://www.heise.de/tp/news/Groenland-Eis-weniger-stabil-als-gedacht-2504836.html. Zuletzt eingesehen am 28.10.2018. *TELEPOLIS* **2014.**

112. Trotier K. Sturmflut 1962. Chronologie der Katastrophe. https://www.zeit.de/2018/30/sturmflut-1962-hamburg-katastrophe-chronologie .Zuletzt eingesehen am 21.12.2018. *Zeit Online* **2018.**

113. Oyedele D. Der schwindende See. https://www.dandc.eu/de/article/der-klimawandel-der-tschadsee-region-wirkt-sich-auf-mehrere-laender-negativ-aus. Zuletzt eingesehen am 3.4.2018. *E+Z, Entwicklung und Zusammenarbeit* **2017,**e-paper 6:19.

114. Oyedele D. Kühe im Maniok-Feld. https://www.dandc.eu/de/article/verzweifelte-hirten-bedraengen-nigerianische-farmer. Zuletzt eingesehen am 3.4.2018. *E+Z, Entwicklung und Zusammenarbeit* **2017,**e-paper 6:20.

115. LCBC. Lake Chad Basin Commission. History of the Lake Chad Basin. http://www.cblt.org/en/climate. Zuletzt eingesehen am 3.4.2018. **2018.**

116. LCBC. Lake Chad Basin Commission. History of the Lake Chad Basin. http://www.cblt.org/en/history-lake-chad-basin. Zuletzt eingesehen am 3.4.2018. **2018.**

117. Firscher L. Warum der Hunger zurück nach Afrika kommt. https://www.spektrum.de/news/warum-der-hunger-zurueck-nach-afrika-kommt/1441612. Zuletzt eingesehen am 3.4.2017. *Spektrum* **2017.**

118. Chomsky N, Polychroniou CJ. Optimism over Despair. Penguin Books. **2017.**

119. Goldenberg S, Bengtsson H. Oil and gas industry has pumped millions into Republican campaigns. *The Guardian* **2016.**

120. Soffen K, Lu D. What Trump cut in his agency budgets. https://www.washingtonpost.com/graphics/politics/trump-presidential-budget-2018-proposal/?utm_term=.be535c259ae5. Zuletzt eingesehen am 21.12.2018. *Washington Post.* **2017.**

121. OMB. (Office of Management and Budget). An American Budget. Fiscal year 2019. https://www.whitehouse.gov/wp-content/uploads/2018/02/budget-fy2019.pdf. Zuletzt eingesehen am 21.12.2018. *U.S. Government Publishing Office* **2018.**

122. Mausfeld R. Warum schweigen die Lämmer? Wie Elitendemokratie und Neoliberalismus unsere Gesellschaft und unsere Lebensgrundlagen zerstören. Westend Verlag. **2018.**

123. Turvey ST, Pitman RL, Taylor BL, Barlow J, Akamatsu T, Barrett LA, Zhao X, Reeves RR, Stewart BS, Wang K, Wei Z, Zhang X, Pusser LT, Richlen M, Brandon JR, Wang D. First human-caused extinction of a cetacean species? *Biol Lett* **2007,**3:537-540.

124. IUCN. International Union for Conservation of Nature. Red List http://www.iucnredlist.org. Balaena mysticetus. Zuletzt eingesehen am 18.05.2018. **2018.**

125. Taylor BL, Chivers SJ, Larese J, Perrin WF. Generation length and percent mature estimates for IUCN assessments of cetaceans. National Marine Fisheries Service, Southwest Fisheries Science Center. **2007.**

126. IUCN. International Union for Conservation of Nature. Red List http://www.iucnredlist.org. Physeter macrocephalus. Zuletzt eingesehen am 18.05.2018. **2018.**

127. IUCN. International Union for Conservation of Nature. Red List http://www.iucnredlist.org. Balaenoptera musculus. Zuletzt eingesehen am 18.05.2018. **2018.**

128. DESTATIS. Statistisches Bundesamt. Tiere und tierische Erzeugung. Haltungen mit Rindern und Rinderbestand für Mai 2017 und November 2017. **2017.**

129. IUCN. International Union for Conservation of Nature. Red List http://www.iucnredlist.org. Bison bonasus. Zuletzt eingesehen am 18.05.2018. **2018.**

130. Hilbert F. Amt Lebus lässt Wisent erschießen. https://www.lr-online.de/nachrichten/brandenburg/amt-lebus-laesst-wisent-erschiessen_aid-4840006. Zuletzt eingesehen am 15.2.2018. *Lausitz Nachrichten* **2017.**

131. Andrews E. Were Humans Responsible for Killing Off the Wooly Mammoth. https://www.history.com/news/were-humans-responsible-for-killing-off-the-wooly-mammoth. Zuletzt eingesehen am 21.12.2018. *History* **2015.**

132. Kalashnikoff A. Why did mammoths go extinct? Scientists are close to solving an Ice Age mystery. https://www.rbth.com/science-and-tech/328469-why-did-mammoths-go-extinct. Zuletzt eingesehen am 21.12.2018. *Russia Beyond* **2018.**

133. Leander L. Wie funktioniert die C-14-Methode? https://www.weltderphysik.de/thema/hinter-den-dingen/c-14-methode/. Zuletzt eingesehen am 21.12.2018. *Welt der Physik* **2010.**

134. Dodd MS, Papineau D, Grenne T, Slack JF, Rittner M, Pirajno F, O'Neil J, Little CT. Evidence for early life in Earth's oldest hydrothermal vent precipitates. *Nature* **2017,**543:60-64.

135. Yong E. I contain multitudes. The Microbes within us and a grander view of life. Vintage Penguin Random House, London. **2017.**

136. Dawkins R. The Gene Machine. In The Selfish Gene. 30th anniversary edition 2006. Oxford University Press. **1976.**

137. Rauchhaupt Uv. Fünfmal ging die Welt schon unter. http://www.faz.net/aktuell/wissen/massenaussterben-fuenfmal-ging-die-welt-schon-unter-14424429.html. Zuletzt eingesehen am 13.3.2018. *FAZ* **2016.**

138. Reduktion des Sauerstoffgehaltes der Atemluft am Arbeitsplatz. https://www.komnet.nrw.de/_sitetools/dialog/3922. Zuletzt eingesehen am 10.3.2018. . *KOMNET-WISSENSDATENBANK* **2006.**

139. Jablonski D, Chaloner WG. Extinctions in the Fossil Record [and Discussion]. In: Philosophical Transactions of the Royal Society of London B: Biological Sciences. . **1994,**344:11-17.

140. De Vleeschouwer D, Da Silva AC, Sinnesael M, Chen D, Day JE, Whalen MT, Guo Z, Claeys P. Timing and pacing of the Late Devonian mass extinction event regulated by eccentricity and obliquity. *Nat Commun* **2017,**8:2268.

141. Kazlev MA. Gorgonopsia. http://www.kheper.net/evolution/therapsida/Gorgonopsia.htm. Zuletzt eingesehen am 21.12.2018. **2005.**

142. Burgess SD, Bowring S, Shen SZ. High-precision timeline for Earth's most severe extinction. *Proc Natl Acad Sci U S A* **2014,**111:3316-3321.

143. Gorder PF. Big Bang In Antarctica -- Killer Crater Found Under Ice. https://news.osu.edu/news/2006/06/01/erthboom/. Zuletzt eingesehen am 19.5.2018. **2006.**

144. Sobolev SV, Sobolev AV, Kuzmin DV, Krivolutskaya NA, Petrunin AG, Arndt NT, Radko VA, Vasiliev YR. Linking mantle plumes, large igneous provinces and environmental catastrophes. *Nature* **2011**,477:312-316.

145. Rothman DH, Fournier GP, French KL, Alm EJ, Boyle EA, Cao C, Summons RE. Methanogenic burst in the end-Permian carbon cycle. *Proc Natl Acad Sci U S A* **2014**,111:5462-5467.

146. Puiu T. During the greatest mass extinction in Earth's history the world's oceans reached 40°C – lethally hot. https://www.zmescience.com/research/studies/great-pre-permian-mass-extinction-temperature-too-hot-941432/. Zuletzt eingesehen am 12.3.2018. **2012**.

147. Whiteside JH, Olsen PE, Eglinton T, Brookfield ME, Sambrotto RN. Compound-specific carbon isotopes from Earth's largest flood basalt eruptions directly linked to the end-Triassic mass extinction. *Proc Natl Acad Sci U S A* **2010**,107:6721-6725.

148. Lesch H, Kamphausen K. Die Menschheit schafft sich ab. Die Erde im Griff des Anthropozäns. . *KNAUR* **2016**.

149. Smil V. Harvesting the biosphere: the human impact. *Population and Development Review* **2011**,37:613-636.

150. Dennett DC. From Bacteria to Bach and Back. The Evolution of Minds. Norton Verlag. New York. **2018**.

151. Amos W, Hoffman JI. Evidence that two main bottleneck events shaped modern human genetic diversity. *Proc Biol Sci* **2010**,277:131-137.

152. Kane S. The human race once came dangerously close to dying out — here's how it changed us. http://www.businessinsider.com/genetic-bottleneck-almost-killed-humans-2016-3?IR=T. Zuletzt eingesehen am 5.4.2018. *Business Insider* **2016**.

153. Behringer W. Kulturgeschichte des Klimas. Von der Eiszeit bis zur globalen Erwärmung. *C.H. Beck Verlag* **2011**.

154. Petraglia M, Korisettar R, Boivin N, Clarkson C, Ditchfield P, Jones S, Koshy J, Lahr MM, Oppenheimer C, Pyle D, Roberts R, Schwenninger JL, Arnold L, White K. Middle Paleolithic assemblages from the Indian subcontinent before and after the Toba super-eruption. *Science* **2007**,317:114-116.

155. Hublin JJ, Ben-Ncer A, Bailey SE, Freidline SE, Neubauer S, Skinner MM, Bergmann I, Le Cabec A, Benazzi S, Harvati K, Gunz P. New fossils from Jebel Irhoud, Morocco and the pan-African origin of Homo sapiens. *Nature* **2017**,546:289-292.

156. Richter D, Grun R, Joannes-Boyau R, Steele TE, Amani F, Rue M, Fernandes P, Raynal JP, Geraads D, Ben-Ncer A, Hublin JJ, McPherron SP. The age of the hominin fossils from Jebel Irhoud, Morocco, and the origins of the Middle Stone Age. *Nature* **2017**,546:293-296.

157. Ambrose SH. Late Pleistocene human population bottlenecks, volcanic winter, and differentiation of modern humans. *J Hum Evol* **1998**,34:623-651.

158. Huff CD, Xing J, Rogers AR, Witherspoon D, Jorde LB. Mobile elements reveal small population size in the ancient ancestors of Homo sapiens. *Proc Natl Acad Sci U S A* **2010**,107:2147-2152.

159. Thomas E. Biogeography of the Late Paleocene Benthic Foraminiferal Extinction. Division III Faculty Publications. 300. https://wesscholar.wesleyan.edu/div3facpubs/300 . Zuletzt eingesehen am 1.4.2018. **1998**.

160. Gutjahr M, Ridgwell A, Sexton PF, Anagnostou E, Pearson PN, Palike H, Norris RD, Thomas E, Foster GL. Very large release of mostly volcanic

carbon during the Palaeocene-Eocene Thermal Maximum. *Nature* **2017**,548:573-577.

161. Bidder B. Vergessener Held. Der Mann, der den dritten Weltkrieg verhinderte. http://www.spiegel.de/einestages/vergessener-held-a-948852.html. Zuletzt eingesehen am 1.3.2018. *Spiegel Online* **2014**.

162. Oliver J. Nuclear Weapons: Last Week Tonight with John Oliver (HBO) https://www.youtube.com/watch?v=1Y1ya-yF35g. Zuletzt eingesehen am 1.3.2018. **2014**.

163. ICAN. International Campaign to abolish nuclear weapons. How many nuclear weapons are there in the world? http://www.icanw.org/the-facts/nuclear-arsenals/. Zuletzt eingesehen am 2.3.2018. **2018**.

164. Dillon MB. Determining optimal fallout shelter times following a nuclear detonation. *Proceedigs of the Royal Society* **2013**.

165. FEMA. (Federal Emergency Management Agency). Planning Guidance for Response to a Nuclear Detonation. Second Edition, June 2010. National Service Center for Environmental Publications (NSCEP). **2010**.

166. Mills MJ, Toon OB, Turco RP, Kinnison DE, Garcia RR. Massive global ozone loss predicted following regional nuclear conflict. *Proc Natl Acad Sci U S A* **2008**,105:5307-5312.

167. Briseno C. So heimtückisch tötet Polonium-210. http://www.spiegel.de/gesundheit/diagnose/gutachten-zu-arafat-so-toetet-polonium-210-a-932246.html. Zuletzt eingesehen am 3.3.2018. *Spiegel Online* **2014**.

168. Higuchi T. 'Clean' bombs: Nuclear technology and nuclear strategy in the 1950s. *Journal of Strategic Studies* **2006**,29:83-116.

169. Harari YN. Sapiens. A Brief History of Humankind. **2014**.

170. Harari YN. Homo Deus. A Brief History of Tommorrow. Vintage, Penguin Random House. **2018**.

171. Bickel M. Die Profiteure der Macht. Wie Deutschland an Kriegen verdient und arabische Diktaturen stärkt. Westend Verlag. Frankfurt. **2017**.

172. Ganser D. Europa im Erdölrausch. Die Folgen einer gefährlichen Abhängigkeit. *Orell Füssli Verlag* **2014**.

173. BMAS. Bundesministerium für Arbeit und Soziales. Fünfter Armuts- und Reichtumsbericht beschlossen http://www.armuts-und-reichtumsbericht.de/DE/Service/Aktuelles/Meldungen/fuenfter-armuts-und-reichtumsbericht-beschlossen.html. Zuletzt eingesehen am 10.04.2018. **2018**.

174. Butterwegge C. Zensiert und geschönt. https://www.zeit.de/politik/deutschland/2017-04/armutsbericht-grosse-koalition-schoenung-kritik. Zuletzt eingesehen am 22.12.2018. *Zeit Online* **2017**.

175. WFP. World Food Programme. https://www.wfp.org/content/hunger-map-2015. Zuletzt eingesehen am 21.3.2018. **2015**.

176. WFP. World Food Programme. Hunger weltweit – Zahlen und Fakten. http://de.wfp.org/hunger/hunger-statistik. Zuletzt eingesehen am 21.3.2018. **2018**.

177. Zank W. Chinas "Großer Sprung": Maos blutige Ernte. http://www.zeit.de/2012/17/Riesenreich-China. Zuletzt eingesehen am 10.04.2018. *Zeit Online* **2012**.

178. Mishra P. Staying Power. Mao and the Maoists. https://www.newyorker.com/magazine/2010/12/20/staying-power-3. Zuletzt eingesehen am 23.3.2018. *The New Yorker* **2010**.

179. Müller-Haeseler W. Indien - Land ohne Hoffnung.
http://www.zeit.de/1969/01/indien-land-ohne-hoffnung. Zuletzt
eingesehen am 23.3.2018. *Die Zeit* **1969**,01/1969.

180. Nagarajan R. Nein, es gibt keine Bevölkerungsexplosion in Indien.
http://www.spiegel.de/gesundheit/schwangerschaft/indien-die-
entschaerfte-bevoelkerungsbombe-a-1098022.html. Zuletzt eingesehen am
23.3.2018. *Spiegel Online* **2016**.

181. WFP. World Food Programme. 10 Facts About Nutrition in China
https://www.wfp.org/stories/10-facts-about-nutrition-china. Zuletzt
eingesehen am 21.3.2018. **2018**.

182. Landwirtschaftsverlag. Globaler Landkauf im sehr großen Stil?
https://www.wochenblatt.com/landwirtschaft/nachrichten/globaler-
landkauf-im-sehr-grossen-stil-8880857.html. Zuletzt eingesehen am
10.04.2018. *Wochenblatt für Landwirtschaft und Landleben* **2016**.

183. Scholl-Latour P. Die Welt aus den Fugen. Betrachtungen zu den Wirren der
Gegenwart. 7. Auflage. Ullstein Buchverlage. **2014**.

184. Masala C. Weltunordnung. Die globalen Krisen und das Versagen des
Westens. Beck Verlag. **2016**.

185. Bergen P, Sterman D, Salyk-Virk M, Sims A, Ford A. U.S. Drone Strikes in
Pakistan. https://www.newamerica.org/in-depth/americas-
counterterrorism-wars/pakistan/. Zuletzt eingesehen am 22.12.2018. *New
America* **2018**.

186. AP. (Associated Press) US, South Korea to stage war game exercises despite
North Korea. https://nypost.com/2017/08/11/us-south-korea-to-stage-
war-game-exercises/ Zuletzt eingesehen am 22.12.2018. *New York Post* **2017**.

187. Rupp R. Aufmarsch gegen Nordkorea: Wem nützt das Zündeln im Fernen
Osten? https://kenfm.de/aufmarsch-gegen-nordkorea-zuendeln-im-
fernen-osten-i/. Zuletzt eingesehen am 22.12.2018. *KenFM* **2017**.

188. WFP. Hungersnot. http://de.wfp.org/hungersnot. Zuletzt eingesehen am
21.3.2018. **2018**.

189. Telgenbüscher J. Der Triumph des Todes. *Geo Epoche* **2015**,75.

190. Ehlkes L, May J. Seuchen – gestern, heute, morgen.
http://www.bpb.de/apuz/206105/seuchen-gestern-heute-morgen?p=all.
Zuletzt eingesehen am 23.12.2018. *Aus Politik und Zeitgeschichte* **2015**.

191. LIS. (Landesinstitut für Schulentwicklung Baden Württemberg).
Ausbreitung der Pest von Asien nach Europa. http://www.schule-
bw.de/faecher-und-schularten/gesellschaftswissenschaftliche-und-
philosophische-faecher/geschichte/unterrichtsmaterialien/fenster-zur-
welt-globalgeschichte/mongolen/11-pest.pdf Zuletzt eingesehen am
23.12.2018. *Landesbildungsserver Baden Württemberg*.

192. Stackl E. Die Pestschleudern vor Kaffa. https://derstandard.at/839585/Die-
Pestschleudern-vor-Kaffa. Zuletzt eingesehen am 7.4.2018. *Der Standard*.

193. Wittmann J. Der schwarze Planet. Skurrile Reiseziele, Morbides, Düsteres &
Schräges.https://der-schwarze-planet.de/der-schwarze-tod-1/. Zuletzt
eingesehen am 14.4.2018. **2012**.

194. Irmscher A. Das Tor zur Neuzeit: Italien und die große Pest.
http://www.sempre-italia.de/service/feuilleton/das-tor-zur-neuzeit-
italien-und-die-gro%C3%9Fe-pest-2009-3.xhtml. Zuletzt eingesehen am
7.4.2018. *Sempre Italia* **2018**.

195. Evans JE, Klewer KA. Tod in Hamburg. Stadt, Gesellschaft und Politik in
den Cholera-Jahren 1830 - 1910. **1996**.

196. Ehlkes L, Kreuels B, Schwarz NG, May J. [Epidemiology of Ebola virus
disease and of other highly contagious, life-threatening diseases with low

incidence in Germany]. *Bundesgesundheitsblatt Gesundheitsforschung Gesundheitsschutz* **2015**,58:705-713.

197. Carroll MW, Matthews DA, Hiscox JA, Elmore MJ, Pollakis G, Rambaut A, Hewson R, Garcia-Dorival I, Bore JA, Koundouno R, Abdellati S, Afrough B, Aiyepada J, Akhilomen P, Asogun D, Atkinson B, Badusche M, Bah A, Bate S, Baumann J, Becker D, Becker-Ziaja B, Bocquin A, Borremans B, Bosworth A, Boettcher JP, Cannas A, Carletti F, Castilletti C, Clark S, Colavita F, Diederich S, Donatus A, Duraffour S, Ehichioya D, Ellerbrok H, Fernandez-Garcia MD, Fizet A, Fleischmann E, Gryseels S, Hermelink A, Hinzmann J, Hopf-Guevara U, Ighodalo Y, Jameson L, Kelterbaum A, Kis Z, Kloth S, Kohl C, Korva M, Kraus A, Kuisma E, Kurth A, Liedigk B, Logue CH, Ludtke A, Maes P, McCowen J, Mely S, Mertens M, Meschi S, Meyer B, Michel J, Molkenthin P, Munoz-Fontela C, Muth D, Newman EN, Ngabo D, Oestereich L, Okosun J, Olokor T, Omiunu R, Omomoh E, Pallasch E, Palyi B, Portmann J, Pottage T, Pratt C, Priesnitz S, Quartu S, Rappe J, Repits J, Richter M, Rudolf M, Sachse A, Schmidt KM, Schudt G, Strecker T, Thom R, Thomas S, Tobin E, Tolley H, Trautner J, Vermoesen T, Vitoriano I, Wagner M, Wolff S, Yue C, Capobianchi MR, Kretschmer B, Hall Y, Kenny JG, Rickett NY, Dudas G, Coltart CE, Kerber R, Steer D, Wright C, Senyah F, Keita S, Drury P, Diallo B, de Clerck H, Van Herp M, Sprecher A, Traore A, Diakite M, Konde MK, Koivogui L, Magassouba N, Avsic-Zupanc T, Nitsche A, Strasser M, Ippolito G, Becker S, Stoecker K, Gabriel M, Raoul H, Di Caro A, Wolfel R, Formenty P, Gunther S. Temporal and spatial analysis of the 2014-2015 Ebola virus outbreak in West Africa. *Nature* **2015**,524:97-101.

198. Drosten C, Gunther S, Preiser W, van der Werf S, Brodt HR, Becker S, Rabenau H, Panning M, Kolesnikova L, Fouchier RA, Berger A, Burguiere AM, Cinatl J, Eickmann M, Escriou N, Grywna K, Kramme S, Manuguerra JC, Muller S, Rickerts V, Sturmer M, Vieth S, Klenk HD, Osterhaus AD, Schmitz H, Doerr HW. Identification of a novel coronavirus in patients with severe acute respiratory syndrome. *N Engl J Med* **2003**,348:1967-1976.

199. Borgundvaag B, Ovens H, Goldman B, Schull M, Rutledge T, Boutis K, Walmsley S, McGeer A, Rachlis A, Farquarson C. SARS outbreak in the Greater Toronto Area: the emergency department experience. *CMAJ* **2004**,171:1342-1344.

200. Hung LS. The SARS epidemic in Hong Kong: what lessons have we learned? *J R Soc Med* **2003**,96:374-378.

201. Kahn LH. Who is in charge. Leadership during Epidemics, Bioterror Attacks, and Other Public Health Crises. Santa Barbara, CA: Praeger Security International, 2009. **2009**:41.

202. THE BRITISH PLAN TO COVER GERMANY WITH ANTHRAX-OPERATION VEGETARIAN. http://www.todayifoundout.com/index.php/2017/12/world-war-ii-secret-operation-vegetarian/. Taken from Uncle John's Bathroom Reader, December 26, 2017. Zuletzt eingesehen am 18.3.2018. . **2017**.

203. Kunz A. Tötungsfabrik „Einheit 731". http://www.taz.de/!1092345/. Zuletzt eingesehen am 23.12.2018. *TAZ* **2002**.

204. Blaser M. Missing Microbes. *Oneworld Publications* **2014**.

205. Frank HG, Hofman M. Südwestpresse (swp.de). https://www.swp.de/politik/inland/hygieneskandal_-insider-spricht-von-_oekonomischem-diktat_-21566287.html. Zuletzt eingesehen am 15.3.2018. **2014**.

206. Brandt K. Verschmutztes OP-Besteck vor Schädelöffnung. http://www.zeit.de/wissen/gesundheit/2015-09/hygiene-uniklinik-mannheim-op-besteck-koerperverletzung. Zuletzt eingesehen am 15.3.2018. *Zeit Online* **2015.**

207. Brandt K. Verschweigen statt aufklären. http://www.zeit.de/wissen/gesundheit/2015-03/uniklinik-mannheim-hygiene-skandal. Zuletzt eingesehen am 15.3.2018. *Zeit Online* **2015.**

208. Centre européen Robert Schuman. Partenariat Educatif. Grund TVIG 2009-2011. Bilanz in Ziffern des Ersten Weltkrieges. http://www.centre-robert-schuman.org/userfiles/files/REPERES - Modul 1-1-1 - Notiz - Bilanz in Ziffern des Ersten Weltkrieges - DE.pdf. Zuletzt eingesehen am 12.4.2018. **2011.**

209. Kloth M. Grippe-Katastrophe von 1918/19: "Nehmen Sie alle Tischler und lassen Sie Särge herstellen". http://www.spiegel.de/einestages/grippe-katastrophe-von-1918-19-a-948269.html. Zuletzt eingesehen am 13.4.2018. *Spiegel Online* **2008.**

210. Winkelheide M. Vor 100 Jahren: Erste Fälle der Spanischen Grippe gemeldet. http://www.deutschlandfunk.de/vor-100-jahren-erste-faelle-der-spanischen-grippe-gemeldet.871.de.html?dram:article_id=412706. Zuletzt eingesehen am13.4.2018. *Deutschlandfunk.*

211. Belyea A. The Infamous Spanish Influenza. Museum of Health Care at Kingston, Canada. https://museumofhealthcare.wordpress.com/2017/05/19/the-infamous-spanish-influenza/. Zuletzt eingesehen am 13.4.2018. *Museum of Health Care Blog* **2017.**

212. Quammen D. Spillover. Animal Infections and the next human pandemic. W.W. Norton & Company, New York, USA. **2012.**

213. Kaufmann SHE. Wächst die Seuchengefahr. Globale Epidemien und Armut: Strategien zur Seucheneindämmung in einer vernetzten Welt. Fischer Taschenbuch Verlag. **2008.**

214. Gehlen M. Schweinegrippe: Kairos eigentümlicher Kampf gegen Schweine. http://www.zeit.de/online/2009/22/schweinegrippe-aegypten-schweine. Zuletzt eingesehen am 14.4.2018. *Zeit Online* **2009.**

215. Tumpey TM, Basler CF, Aguilar PV, Zeng H, Solorzano A, Swayne DE, Cox NJ, Katz JM, Taubenberger JK, Palese P, Garcia-Sastre A. Characterization of the reconstructed 1918 Spanish influenza pandemic virus. *Science* **2005,**310:77-80.

216. Ryan F. Virolution. . *Harper Collins London* **2009.**

217. Winkler AS, Da Costa CP. Täniose/Zystizerkose (Schweinebandwurm). In: Eine Einschätzung des Beitrags deutscher Institutionen bei der Forschung zu vernachlässigten Tropenkrankheiten. Herausgeber Jürgen May, Achim Hoerauf, Markus Engstler, Carsten Köhler. Redaktion Johanna Brinkel. Bernhard-Nocht-Institut für Tropenmedizin, Hamburg. https://www.bnitm.de/index.php?id=736. Zuletzt eingesehen am 23.12.2018. **2018.**

218. Schwarz NG, Loderstaedt U, Hahn A, Hinz R, Zautner AE, Eibach D, Fischer M, Hagen RM, Frickmann H. Microbiological laboratory diagnostics of neglected zoonotic diseases (NZDs). *Acta Trop* **2017,**165:40-65.

219. BNITM. (Bernhard-Nocht-Institut für Tropenmedizin). Erwiesen: Mücken können tropisches Chikungunya-Virus auch bei niedrigen Temperaturen verbreiten. https://www.bnitm.de/en/news/communications/7436-erwiesen-muecken-koennen-tropisches-chikungunya-virus-auch-bei-

niedrigen-temperaturen-verbreiten/. Zuletzt eingesehen am 23.12.2018. **2018.**

220. Heitmann A, Jansen S, Luhken R, Helms M, Pluskota B, Becker N, Kuhn C, Schmidt-Chanasit J, Tannich E. Experimental risk assessment for chikungunya virus transmission based on vector competence, distribution and temperature suitability in Europe, 2018. *Euro Surveill* **2018,**23.

221. Mann CC. 1493. How Europe's Discovery of the Americas Revolutionized Trade, Ecology and Life on Earth. Granta Publications, London. . **2011.**

222. Diamond J. Guns, Germs, and Steel. . *W.W. Norton* **1997.**

223. Reid LM. The Panama Canal Death Tolls. https://thesilverpeopleheritage.wordpress.com/2008/12/17/the-panama-canal-death-tolls/. Zuletzt eingesehen am 23.12.2018. *The Silver People Heritage Foundation* **2008.**

224. Aragon TJ, Reingold A. Epidemiologic Concepts for the Prevention and Control of Infectious Diseases. UC Berkeley. https://escholarship.org/uc/item/7687z08g. Zuletzt eingesehen am 31.8.2018. **2011.**

225. Klesman A. Is there (frozen) life on Mars? http://www.astronomy.com/news/2017/11/is-there-frozen-life-on-mars. Zuletzt eingesehen am 14.7.2018. *Astronomy* **2017.**

226. Smith-Strickland K. Why Scientists Have Been Scared of Space Germs for Almost 50 Years. https://gizmodo.com/why-scientists-have-been-scared-of-space-germs-for-almo-1712562498. Zuletzt eingesehen am 14.7.2018. *GIZMODOD* **2015.**

227. Revich B, Tokarevich N, Parkinson AJ. Climate change and zoonotic infections in the Russian Arctic. *Int J Circumpolar Health* **2012,**71:18792.

228. Leonhard J. Die Büchse der Pandora. Geschichte des Ersten Weltkriegs. C.H. Beck Verlag. **2014.**

229. Gupta OD. Angst vor der Bombe. Serie: Albtraum Atombombe (1). http://www.sueddeutsche.de/politik/serie-albtraum-atom-leben-mit-der-angst-vor-der-bombe-1.983703. Zuletzt eingesehen am 8.3.2018. *Süddeutsche Zeitung* **2010.**

230. Bryson B. A Short History of Nearly Everything. *Black Swan Books* **2003.**

231. UNEP. United Nations Environmental Programme. Leaded Petrol Phase-out: Global Status as at March 2017. Nairobi: United Nations Environment Programme; 2017. http://www.who.int/mediacentre/factsheets/fs379/en/. Zuletzt eingesehen am 14.4.2018. **2017.**

232. Alarcon WA, State Adult Blood Lead E, Surveillance Program I, State Adult Blood Lead E, Surveillance API. Summary of Notifiable Noninfectious Conditions and Disease Outbreaks: Elevated Blood Lead Levels Among Employed Adults - United States, 1994-2012. *MMWR Morb Mortal Wkly Rep* **2015,**62:52-75.

233. EHATLAS. Canadian Environmental Health Atlas. Biomonitoring Lead Levels. http://www.ehatlas.ca/lead/public-health/biomonitoring-lead-levels. Zuletzt eingesehen am 14.4.2018. **2018.**

234. Mies U, Wernicke J. Fassadendemokratie und tiefer Staat. Promedia Verlag. **2017.**

235. Vorholz F. Eiskalt abgeblockt. https://www.zeit.de/1992/32/eiskalt-abgeblockt. Zuletzt eingesehen am 23.12.2018. *Die Zeit* **1992,**32.

236. Christoph. Die 5 großen Müllstrudel im Meer. https://www.careelite.de/muellstrudel-im-meer/. Zuletzt eingesehen am 10.05.2018. **2017.**

237. OCEANCLEANUP. The Largest Cleanup in History. https://www.theoceancleanup.com/. Zuletzt eingesehen am 29.12.2018. **2018.**

238. Romey K. Here's What the Iceman Was Wearing When He Died 5,300 Years Ago. https://news.nationalgeographic.com/2016/08/otzi-iceman-european-alps-mummy-clothing-dna-leather-fur-archaeology/. Zuletzt eingesehen am 10.5.2018. *National Geographic* **2016.**

239. Glazner E. Midway Albatross an Icon of the Plastic Pollution Problem. http://www.plasticpollutioncoalition.org/pft/2015/9/5/midway-albatross-an-icon-of-the-plastic-pollution-problem. Photographs by Chris Jordan. Zuletzt eingesehen am 10.5.2018. **2015.**

240. Kaplan JO, Krumhardt KM, Zimmermann N. The prehistoric and preindustrial deforestation of Europe. *Quaternary Science Reviews* **2009**,28:3016-3034.

241. UNENVIRONMENT. (United Nations Environment Programme). From birth to ban: A history of the plastic shopping bag. https://www.unenvironment.org/news-and-stories/story/birth-ban-history-plastic-shopping-bag. Last accessed 11.7.2019. **2018.**

242. Wichert F. Plastiktüten - praktisch, aber umweltbelastend. https://reset.org/knowledge/plastiktueten-praktisch-aber-umweltbelastend. Zuletzt eingesehen am 10.5.2018. **2013.**

243. Jungblut S-I. Mikroplastik – Klein, fies und überall. https://reset.org/knowledge/mikroplastik-%E2%80%93-klein-fies-und-ueberall-04192018. Zuletzt eingesehen am 10.5.2018. **2018.**

244. ICJB. International Campaign for Justice in Bhopal .WHAT HAPPENED IN BHOPAL? https://www.bhopal.net/what-happened-in-bhopal/. Zuletzt eingesehen am 5.5.2018. **2014.**

245. Lenz M. Kaninchenkrieg in Australien. https://www.spektrum.de/news/kaninchenkrieg-in-australien/1340509. Zuletzt eingesehen am 6.5.2018. *Spektrum* **2015.**

14 Index

Index

Index

Index